£1.20

A NOTE BOOK IN
PURE MATHEMATICS

By the same author

MATHEMATICS TWO
MATHEMATICS THREE
MATHEMATICS FOUR FORMAL SYLLABUS
MATHEMATICS FOUR ALTERNATIVE SYLLABUS
ORDINARY LEVEL MATHEMATICS
TRIGONOMETRY AT ORDINARY LEVEL
A GENERAL CERTIFICATE CALCULUS
A NOTE BOOK IN PURE MATHEMATICS
A NOTE BOOK IN APPLIED MATHEMATICS
FUN WITH FIGURES
HINTS FOR ORDINARY LEVEL MATHEMATICS
FOUR-FIGURE MATHEMATICAL TABLES
MODERN MATHEMATICS AT ORDINARY LEVEL
HINTS FOR 'A' LEVEL MATHEMATICS
PURE MATHEMATICS AT ADVANCED LEVEL
ADDITIONAL PURE MATHEMATICS
EXERCISES AND EXAMPLES AT ORDINARY LEVEL

Also by L. Harwood Clarke and F. G. J. Norton
OBJECTIVE TESTS IN ORDINARY LEVEL MATHEMATICS
OBJECTIVE TESTS IN C.S.E. MATHEMATICS
ADDITIONAL APPLIED MATHEMATICS

All published by Heinemann Educational Books Ltd

A NOTE BOOK
IN
PURE MATHEMATICS

By
L. HARWOOD CLARKE, M.A.
Vice-Master, Bedford School

METRIC EDITION

A companion to
" A Notebook in Applied Mathematics "
by the same author

HEINEMANN EDUCATIONAL BOOKS
LONDON

Heinemann Educational Books Ltd

LONDON EDINBURGH MELBOURNE AUCKLAND TORONTO
SINGAPORE HONG KONG KUALA LUMPUR
NAIROBI IBADAN JOHANNESBURG
LUSAKA NEW DELHI

ISBN 0 435 51178 5

First Published 1953
Reprinted
1954, 1956, 1958, 1960, 1961, 1963, 1964
Second Edition 1966
Reprinted 1968
Third (metric) Edition 1970
Reprinted 1974

Published by
Heinemann Educational Books Ltd
48 Charles Street, London W1X 8AH

Printed in Great Britain by
Butler & Tanner Ltd, Frome and London

FOREWORD

THIS book is written to give, in condensed form, all the work necessary for Advanced level (but not Scholarship level) in Pure Mathematics for the various Boards. It is intended for use chiefly in revision and so some of the methods used early on will not appeal to the beginner but are chosen as the best for Certificate purposes. It is hoped that the book with its selection of the important topics will save the reader much time in that he will be spared the task of extracting from larger books those sections of particular importance, and because he may have confidence that the book-work required is at his fingers' ends. I also hope that the student who is working on his own or who has little tuition will find the book helpful. It should save him, too, much labour and time and he has now at his disposal a selection of the subject matter most important to him for examination purposes.

If this savours too much of cheating the examiners or of giving the impression that the only importance of knowledge is for examination purposes, I would regret it. Knowledge and understanding are vital but there are many reference books in which the student may find the padding ; here, I hope, he will find the essentials and before an examination the essentials are very important.

I should like to place on record my grateful thanks to Mr. Alan Hill of Messrs. Heinemann for his unfailing help and courtesy. I also acknowledge with thanks permission to reprint questions set in past examinations by the following Examining Boards :

Cambridge Local Examinations Syndicate (*C*)
London Universities School Examination Council (*L*)
Northern Universities Joint Matriculation Board (*NU*)
Oxford and Cambridge Joint Board (*O & C*)

L. H. C.

Bedford, 1953.

NOTE TO SECOND EDITION

IN this edition an appendix is added mainly in order to include a section on Complex Numbers which are now part of the A Level syllabus for all Boards. The opportunity is taken to add a note on Recurring Series which have also been included by some Boards.

1966   L. H. C.

NOTE TO THIRD EDITION

THE need for yet another reprint of this book gave us the opportunity to change all references to imperial units to metric units.

1970   F. G. J. N.

CONTENTS

I. ALGEBRA

II. CALCULUS

CONTENTS

CONTENTS

APPENDIX

ALGEBRA

PERMUTATIONS AND COMBINATIONS

THE number of combinations of n things taken r at a time $(_nC_r)$ means the number of ways of choosing r things from n. Order does not affect the choice; the same r things, whatever the order in which they are chosen, can count as one combination only.

The number of permutations of n things taken r at a time $(_nP_r)$ means the number of ways of choosing r things from n, different orders of selection counting as different permutations. So any one combination will give many permutations.

The value of $_nP_r$

Let us imagine we are choosing r things from n. For our first choice, we may choose any one of n things; having made this choice, we may choose any one of $(n-1)$ things and so on, until for our rth choice, we may choose any one of $(n - r + 1)$ things. The total number of ways in which we can choose r things, giving due consideration to the order in which they are chosen, is

$$n(n-1)(n-2)\ldots.(n-r+1).$$

Therefore
$$_nP_r = n(n-1)\ldots.(n-r+1)$$
$$= \frac{n(n-1)\ldots.(n-r+1)(n-r)\ldots.1}{(n-r)\ldots.1}$$
$$= \frac{n!}{(n-r)!}.$$

The number of ways of arranging n things in line

Putting $r = n$ in the preceding formula, we see the number of ways of arranging n things in line is $n!$.

The number of ways of seating n people at a circular table

The chain of people has no end and no beginning and so the vital factor is the arrangement relative to one given person. So we may fix one person and arrange the other $(n-1)$ people about him. The number of ways is therefore $(n-1)!$.

The number of ways of threading n beads on a wire

Here we have the further complication that the beads may be

1

viewed from both sides so that there will be no difference between corresponding clockwise and anti-clockwise arrangements.

The number then is $\frac{1}{2}[(n-1)!]$.

The value of $_nC_r$

Different orders of selection for the same r things count as one combination. Each combination will therefore give $r!$ permutations and so

$$_nC_r \times r! = {}_nP_r$$

and
$$_nC_r = \frac{n!}{(n-r)!\, r!}.$$

The number of ways of arranging n things in line if p are alike of one kind and q are alike of another kind

Any one arrangement could be made into $p!$ arrangements if the p alike things were replaced by p things all different; similarly, any one arrangement could be made into $q!$ arrangements by replacing the q alike things by different things. If the number of arrangements required is x, then $x.p!\, q!$ must equal the total number of arrangements if all the things were different, i.e. $n!$.

Therefore
$$x = \frac{n!}{p!\, q!}.$$

The number of ways of dividing $(p + q + r)$ things into three unequal groups, the first to contain p, the second q and the third r

The number of ways of choosing p from $(p + q + r)$ is $_{p+q+r}C_p$. The number of ways of choosing q from the remaining $(q + r)$ is $_{q+r}C_q$ and we shall automatically be left with the r group. The number of ways is therefore

$$_{p+q+r}C_p \cdot {}_{q+r}C_q = \frac{(p+q+r)!}{p!\,(q+r)!} \cdot \frac{(q+r)!}{q!\, r!}$$
$$= (p + q + r)!/p!\, q!\, r!.$$

The number of ways of dividing $3p$ things into three equal groups each containing p things

Here we must allow for the fact that if we make the choice of groups in the order A, B, C say, we may also make later the choices B, C, A and C, A, B, etc. Since the groups are now of equal size, these must not all be counted as different. So we have counted $3!$ ways which are apparently different but which are essentially the same. By the last formula, the number of ways without taking into account the equality of the groups is $\dfrac{(3p)!}{(p!)^3}$. Therefore the number of different ways is $\dfrac{(3p)!}{(p!)^3 . 3!}$.

The number of different selections from n things if any number may be taken

Each thing may be taken or left, i.e. we have two choices for each. This applies to all the things and so the total number of selections is $2 \times 2 \times 2 \ldots.$ to n factors, i.e. 2^n. But this includes the case in which no thing is taken and so the number of different selections is

$$2^n - 1.$$

$N.B.$—The number of ways of choosing one thing is $_nC_1$. The number of ways of choosing two things is $_nC_2$ and so on until finally the number of ways of choosing n things is $_nC_n$.

Therefore $\quad _nC_1 + _nC_2 + _nC_3 + \ldots. + _nC_n = 2^n - 1$

(we shall meet this again later).

The number of selections from n different things, p similar things of one kind and q similar things of another kind, if any number may be taken

For each of the different things we have two choices. From the p similar things, we may take $0, 1, 2, \ldots.p$, i.e. we have $(p + 1)$ choices. For the q similar things, we have $(q + 1)$ choices. So remembering that we must take at least one thing, the number of selections is

$$2^n . (p + 1)(q + 1) - 1.$$

Two important relations

There are two relations connecting combinations which are important and which are often needed.

(1) $_nC_r = _nC_{n-r}$. This follows immediately from the formula for $_nC_r$. It may also be proved by reasoning that if we choose r things from n, we must leave $(n - r)$ and so we are automatically making the choice of $(n - r)$ at the same time. This is used in writing down the numerical values of combinations. For example, to evaluate $_{11}C_8$, we say first it must equal $_{11}C_3$ and this is $\dfrac{11.10.9}{1.2.3}$, the number of factors in both numerator and denominator being 3.

(2) $_nC_r + _nC_{r+1} = _{n+1}C_{r+1}$. This is used in the proofs of the Binomial Theorem and of Leibnitz' Theorem.

In choosing $(r + 1)$ things from $(n + 1)$, consider one particular thing. The number of choices which include this particular thing is $_nC_r$ and the number of choices which exclude it is $_nC_{r+1}$. But the sum of these must be the total number of choices altogether, i.e. $_{n+1}C_{r+1}$.

An alternative proof by the formula for $_nC_r$ is given.

$$_nC_r + {_nC_{r+1}} = \frac{n!}{r!\,(n-r)!} + \frac{n!}{(r+1)!\,(n-r-1)!}$$

$$= n!\frac{r+1+n-r}{(r+1)!\,(n-r)!}$$

$$= \frac{(n+1)!}{(r+1)!\,(n-r)!}$$

$$= {_{n+1}C_{r+1}}.$$

EXERCISES I

1. Find the number of ways of seating 8 people at a circular table.

2. How many different arrangements are there of the letters in the word *added* ?

3. In how many ways can 6 people be divided into 3 pairs ?

4. In how many ways can a team of 6 be chosen from 8 people ?

5. How many numbers greater than 200 can be formed from the digits 1, 2, 3, 4 ?

6. How many even numbers can be formed using all the digits 1, 2, 3, 4 ?

7. A party of 10 people is to be divided into three groups, the first containing 5 people, the second 3 and the last 2. In how many ways can this be done ?

8. How many different selections are there from 4 oranges, 3 bananas and 2 apples, if any number may be taken ?

9. There are 6 different flowers in a vase. If any number may be taken, how many different selections are possible ?

10. What is the number of ways of forecasting the results of 6 football matches ?

THE METHOD OF INDUCTION

The method of induction is a powerful weapon which has many uses. There are two restrictions on its use—first, the answer must be known or guessed, and second, the proof will apply for integral values only. The following examples illustrate the versatility of the method.

Example 1. Prove that
$$1^2 + 2^2 + 3^2 + \ldots + n^2 = \tfrac{1}{6}n(n + 1)(2n + 1).$$

Assume that the series holds for one particular value of n, say $n = k$. Then
$$1^2 + 2^2 + 3^2 + \ldots + k^2 = \tfrac{1}{6}k(k + 1)(2k + 1).$$

Add to each side $(k + 1)^2$ and we get
$$\begin{aligned}1^2 + 2^2 + 3^2 + \ldots + k^2 + (k + 1)^2 &= \tfrac{1}{6}k(k + 1)(2k + 1) + (k + 1)^2 \\ &= \tfrac{1}{6}(k + 1)(2k^2 + k + 6k + 6) \\ &= \tfrac{1}{6}(k + 1)(k + 2)(2k + 3).\end{aligned}$$

But this is the sum for the value $n = (k + 1)$. So if the statement is true for the value k, it is also true for the value $(k + 1)$. The value of $\tfrac{1}{6}n(n + 1)(2n + 1)$ when $n = 1$ is 1 and the sum of the first term on the left-hand side is also 1. The formula for the sum is therefore true for $n = 1$; so for $n = 2$; and so, by the same argument, it is true for all positive integral values of n.

Example 2. Prove that $9^{2n} - 1$ is a multiple of 80 for all integral values of n.

Assume that for one value of n, say k, the expression is a multiple of 80, i.e. that $9^{2k} - 1 = 80p$, say.

Rearranged, this gives $\qquad 9^{2k} = 80p + 1.$
Now, $\qquad 9^{2(k+1)} - 1 = 9^2 \cdot 9^{2k} - 1 = 81(80p + 1) - 1$
$$= 81(80p) + 80,$$

which is obviously a multiple of 80. Thus the statement is also true for the value $(k + 1)$. But $9^{2(1)} - 1 = 80$ and so the statement is true for the value $n = 1$; therefore it is true for all integral values of n.

Example 3. If n is a positive integer, prove that
$$(a + x)^n = a^n + {}_nC_1a^{n-1}x + {}_nC_2a^{n-2}x^2 + \ldots + {}_nC_ra^{n-r}x^r + \ldots + {}_nC_nx^n.$$

Assume that this expansion is true for the value $n = k$. Then
$$(a + x)^k = a^k + {}_kC_1a^{k-1}x + \ldots$$
$$+ {}_kC_ra^{k-r}x^r + {}_kC_{r+1}a^{k-r-1}x^{r+1} + \ldots + {}_kC_kx^k.$$

Multiplying both sides of this equation by $(a + x)$,
$$(a + x)^{k+1} = a^{k+1} + \ldots + a^{k-r}x^{r+1}({}_kC_r + {}_kC_{r+1}) + \ldots + {}_{k+1}C_{k+1}x^{k+1}$$
since $\qquad {}_kC_k = {}_{k+1}C_{k+1} = 1.$

But $\qquad {}_kC_r + {}_kC_{r+1} = {}_{k+1}C_{r+1}$ (see Combinations), and the series becomes the original series with $(k + 1)$ replacing n.

But $\qquad (a + x)^2 = a^2 + {}_2C_1ax + {}_2C_2x^2$

and so the expansion is true for the value $n = 2$. It is therefore true for all integral values of n.

EXERCISES II

Prove by induction :

1. $1^3 + 2^3 + \ldots + n^3 = \dfrac{n^2(n + 1)^2}{4}$;

2. $1.2 + 2.3 + \ldots + n(n + 1) = \dfrac{n(n + 1)(n + 2)}{3}$

3. $\displaystyle\sum_1^n r(r + 2) = \dfrac{n(n + 1)(2n + 7)}{6}$;

4. $1^2 - 2^2 + 3^2 - 4^2 \ldots + (2n - 1)^2 - (2n)^2 = -n(2n + 1)$;

5. $\displaystyle\sum_1^n r(r + 1)(r + 2) = \dfrac{n(n + 1)(n + 2)(n + 3)}{4}$;

6. That $(8^{2n} - 1)$ is a multiple of 63 ;

7. That $(7^n - 1)$ is a multiple of 6 ;

8. That $n(n + 1)(n + 2)$ is a multiple of 6.

THE BINOMIAL THEOREM

We have proved in the last example the Binomial Theorem, that for all positive integral values of n and for all x

$$(a + x)^n = a^n + {}_nC_1a^{n-1}x + \ldots + {}_nC_ra^{n-r}x^r + \ldots + {}_nC_nx^n.$$

Relations between coefficients

Writing the coefficients as C_0, C_1, C_2, etc. (i.e. $C_0 = 1$ and $C_r = {}_nC_r$) and putting $a = 1$, we have

$$(1 + x)^n = C_0 + C_1x + C_2x^2 + C_3x^3 + \ldots + C_nx^n \quad . \quad . \quad (1)$$

Now put $x = 1$,

$$C_0 + C_1 + C_2 + \ldots + C_n = 2^n \text{ (see Combinations).}$$

Putting $x = -1$ in equation (1),

$$0 = C_0 - C_1 + C_2 - C_3 + \ldots + (-1)^nC^n.$$

Therefore

$$C_0 + C_2 + C_4 + C_6 + \ldots = C_1 + C_3 + C_5 + \ldots = \tfrac{1}{2}(2^n) = 2^{n-1}.$$

Differentiating equation (1) with respect to x,

$$n(1 + x)^{n-1} = C_1 + 2C_2x + 3C_3x^2 + \ldots + nC_nx^{n-1}.$$

Now putting $x = 1$,
$$C_1 + 2C_2 + 3C_3 + \ldots nC_n = n \cdot 2^{n-1}.$$

To obtain the sum of a series in which the squares of C_r occur, always use the following method.

Since $C_r = C_{n-r}$ (Combinations), the coefficients in equation (1) read the same from both ends and the equation may be written in the following two ways:

$$(1 + x)^n = C_0 + C_1 x + C_2 x^2 + \ldots + C_{n-1} x^{n-1} + C_n x^n$$

and $(1 + x)^n = C_n + C_{n-1} x + C_{n-2} x^2 + \ldots + C_1 x^{n-1} + C_0 x^n$.

The coefficient of x^n in the product of these two expansions is $C_0{}^2 + C_1{}^2 + C_2{}^2 + \ldots + C_n{}^2$ which therefore equals the coefficient of x^n in $(1 + x)^n \cdot (1 + x)^n$ or in $(1 + x)^{2n}$.

This coefficient is $_{2n}C_n$ or $\dfrac{(2n)!}{(n!)^2}$.

Therefore $C_0{}^2 + C_1{}^2 + C_2{}^2 + \ldots + C_n{}^2 = \dfrac{(2n)!}{(n!)^2}$.

Negative and fractional indices

The Binomial Theorem also holds in some cases for negative and fractional indices but the proof in these cases is not expected. The expansion becomes

$$(1 + x)^n = 1 + nx + \frac{n(n-1)}{1 \cdot 2} x^2 + \frac{n(n-1)(n-2)}{1 \cdot 2 \cdot 3} x^3 + \ldots$$

N.B.—The expansion holds only for $(1 + x)^n$ and not for $(a + x)^n$ and x must lie between the limits -1 and $+1$.

Since, if n is fractional or negative, the continued product $n(n-1)(n-2)(n-3) \ldots$ will never become zero, the expansion is now in the form of an infinite series. Important special cases are the following expansions:

$$(1 + x)^{-1} = 1 - x + x^2 - x^3 + x^4 - \ldots$$
$$(1 - x)^{-1} = 1 + x + x^2 + x^3 + x^4 + \ldots$$
$$(1 - x)^{-2} = 1 + 2x + 3x^2 + 4x^3 + \ldots$$

provided, in each case, $-1 < x < 1$.

Approximations

The Binomial Theorem for fractional and negative indices is especially useful when x is small and may be used to evaluate square and cube roots to any desired accuracy.

If x is so small that x^2 may be neglected then
$$(1 + x)^n \doteqdot 1 + nx$$

and the error is of the order $\dfrac{n(n-1)}{1 \cdot 2} x^2$.

A better approximation is

$$1 + nx + \frac{n(n-1)}{1.2}x^2$$

and the error is now of the order $\dfrac{n(n-1)(n-2)}{1.2.3}x^3$.

Example 1. Evaluate $(1\cdot06)^{1/3}$ to six places of decimals.

$$(1 + x)^n = 1 + nx + \frac{n(n-1)}{1.2}x^2$$
$$+ \frac{n(n-1)(n-2)}{1.2.3}x^3 + \frac{n(n-1)(n-2)(n-3)}{1.2.3.4}x^4 + \dots.$$

Putting $x = \cdot06$ and $n = \frac{1}{3}$,

$$(1\cdot06)^{1/3} = 1 + \tfrac{1}{3}(\cdot06) + \frac{(\frac{1}{3})(-\frac{2}{3})}{1.2}(\cdot06)^2 + \frac{(\frac{1}{3})(-\frac{2}{3})(-\frac{5}{3})}{1.2.3}(\cdot06)^3$$
$$+ \frac{(\frac{1}{3})(-\frac{2}{3})(-\frac{5}{3})(-\frac{8}{3})}{1.2.3.4}(\cdot06)^4 + \dots.$$

$$= 1 + \cdot02 - \cdot0004 + \cdot0000133 - \cdot00000053$$

(other terms may obviously be neglected)

$$= 1\cdot0196128$$
$$\doteqdot 1\cdot019613.$$

Example 2. Evaluate, to four decimal places, $\sqrt{25\cdot1}$.

$$25\cdot1 = 25(1 + \cdot004)$$

Therefore $\sqrt{25\cdot1} = 5(1 + \cdot004)^{1/2}$

$$= 5\left\{1 + \tfrac{1}{2}(\cdot004) + \frac{\frac{1}{2}(-\frac{1}{2})}{1.2}(\cdot004)^2 + \dots.\right\}$$
$$= 5\{1 + \cdot002 - \cdot000002\dots.\}$$
$$= 5(1\cdot001998)$$
$$= 5\cdot00999$$
$$\doteqdot 5\cdot0100.$$

The greatest term

We are sometimes asked to find the greatest term in an expansion. Each problem should be considered on its own merits as in the following example.

Example. Find the greatest term (numerically) in the expansion of $(1 + 2x)^{10\frac{1}{2}}$ when $x = \frac{3}{7}$.

$$(1 + 2x)^{21/2} = 1 + \tfrac{2\cdot1}{2}(2x) + \frac{(\frac{21}{2})(\frac{19}{2})}{1.2}(2x)^2 + \frac{(\frac{21}{2})(\frac{19}{2})(\frac{17}{2})}{1.2.3}(2x)^3 + \dots.$$

The $(r + 1)$th term,

$$u_{r+1} = \frac{(\frac{21}{2})(\frac{19}{2})\ldots(\frac{23}{2} - r)}{1.2\ldots r}(2x)^r.$$

$\therefore u_{r+1} > u_r$

if $\dfrac{(\frac{21}{2})(\frac{19}{2})\ldots(\frac{23}{2} - r)}{1.2\ldots r}(2x)^r > \dfrac{(\frac{21}{2})(\frac{19}{2})\ldots(\frac{25}{2} - r)}{1.2\ldots(r - 1)}(2x)^{r-1},$

i.e.   if $\dfrac{(\frac{23}{2} - r)}{r}(2x) > 1,$

or   if $(\frac{23}{2} - r)(\frac{6}{7}) > r$ or   if $69 - 6r > 7r,$

i.e.   if $13r < 69$ or $r < 5\frac{4}{13}.$

Therefore if $r < 5\frac{4}{13}, u_{r+1} > u_r$ but conversely if $r > 5\frac{4}{13}, u_{r+1} < u_r.$
The greatest value of r for which $u_{r+1} > u_r$ is 5 and then $u_6 > u_5$ but $u_7 < u_6.$ The sixth term is therefore the greatest and its value is

$$\frac{(\frac{21}{2})(\frac{19}{2})(\frac{17}{2})(\frac{15}{2})(\frac{13}{2})}{1.2.3.4.5}(2x)^5 = \frac{21.19.17.15.13}{2^5.5!}\left(\frac{6}{7}\right)^5 = \frac{21.19.17.15.13}{5!}\left(\frac{3}{7}\right)^5.$$

N.B.—If instead of $5\frac{4}{13}$ we had arrived at an integer, two terms would have been equal and greater than all the rest.

EXERCISES III

1. Write down the first four terms in the expansions of

(a) $(1 - x)^{-3}$, (b) $(1 + 2x)^{-\frac{3}{2}}$, (c) $(1 + 5x)^{\frac{1}{5}}$, (d) $(1 - 4x)^{\frac{1}{2}}$.

2. If the coefficient of x^r in the expansion of $(1 + x)^n$ is denoted by C_r, evaluate

$$C_1{}^2 + 2C_2{}^2 + 3C_3{}^2 + \ldots + nC_n{}^2.$$

3. Using the binomial theorem, evaluate correct to 4 places of decimals (a) $\sqrt{36\cdot1}$, (b) $\sqrt[3]{1\cdot09}$, (c) $\dfrac{1}{\sqrt{1\cdot04}}$, (d) $\sqrt[3]{125\cdot4}$.

4. Find the greatest term in the expansion of $(1 - 3x)^{-\frac{7}{3}}$ when $x = \frac{1}{4}$.

5. Find the coefficient of x^3 in the expansion of $(1 + x + x^2)^{12}$.

6. Find the coefficient of x in the expansion of $(1 + x)^2(1 - x)^6$.

7. Find the term independent of x in the expansion of $\left(3x - \dfrac{4}{x^2}\right)^9$.

8. Find the coefficient of x^2 in the expansion of $\dfrac{1 + x}{(1 - 2x)^3}$.

9. Find the coefficient of x^4 in the expansion of $(1 - x^2 + x^3)^5$.

10. What is the 8th term in the expansion of $(2x + 3y)^{12}$?

PARTIAL FRACTIONS

In more elementary Algebra, we have often been asked to add together fractions of the type $\dfrac{3}{x-1}$ and $\dfrac{2.}{x-2}$. The result is $\dfrac{5x-8}{(x-1)(x-2)}$, but the sum of the two fractions is often a more convenient way of expressing the result. Splitting a fraction into the sum of two or more simpler fractions is called expressing it in its *partial fractions* and is useful in many ways, e.g. integration.

Fractions with numerator of smaller degree than denominator

In finding the Partial Fractions, assume the numerator of each fraction to be the most general polynomial of degree one lower than the denominator. The following examples will illustrate this point.

(1) $$\frac{5x-8}{(x-1)(x-2)} = \frac{A}{x-1} + \frac{B}{x-2}.$$

(2) $$\frac{x^2}{(x-1)(x^2+1)} = \frac{A}{x-1} + \frac{Bx+C}{x^2+1}.$$

(3) $$\frac{x^4-1}{(x^2+1)(x^3+x+1)} = \frac{Ax+B}{x^2+1} + \frac{Cx^2+Dx+E}{x^3+x+1}.$$

There is only one apparent exception to this rule which occurs in the case of a repeated factor in the denominator. As a numerator corresponding to $(x-1)^2$ we should expect to find $Ax+B$ and this leads to a perfectly correct result. Supposing the result were $\dfrac{3x-4}{(x-1)^2}$, this can be expressed as $\dfrac{3(x-1)-1}{(x-1)^2}$ or $\dfrac{3}{x-1} - \dfrac{1}{(x-1)^2}$ and this latter form is the form required when Partial Fractions are asked for.

So for a denominator $(x-1)^2$ we make immediately the assumption $\dfrac{A}{x-1} + \dfrac{B}{(x-1)^2}$; similarly for $(x-1)^3$ we should assume $\dfrac{A}{x-1} + \dfrac{B}{(x-1)^2} + \dfrac{C}{(x-1)^3}$. The following examples will help to clarify the idea.

(1) $$\frac{3x-1}{(x-1)(x+1)^2} = \frac{A}{x-1} + \frac{B}{x+1} + \frac{C}{(x+1)^2}.$$

(2) $$\frac{x^3-x}{(x^2+1)(x-2)^3} = \frac{Ax+B}{x^2+1} + \frac{C}{x-2} + \frac{D}{(x-2)^2} + \frac{E}{(x-2)^3}.$$

Numerator with degree at least equal to that of denominator

In this case, it is necessary first to divide to find the quotient.
N.B.—It is not necessary to find the remainder.

Having found this quotient, we assume the Partial Fractions to be the sum of it and fractions of exactly the same type as in the previous work. A few examples will make this clearer.

(1) $\dfrac{x^2}{(x-1)(x-2)}$. The quotient in this division is obviously 1 and we assume that the fraction is equal to

$$1 + \frac{A}{x-1} + \frac{B}{x-2}.$$

(2) $\dfrac{x^4}{(x-1)(x^2+1)}$.

$$x^3 - x^2 + x - 1 \overline{)x^4} \quad \left(x + 1\right.$$
$$\underline{x^4 - x^3}$$
$$x^3$$

The division shows that the quotient is $(x+1)$ and we need go no further. The assumption is therefore

$$x + 1 + \frac{A}{x-1} + \frac{Bx+C}{x^2+1}.$$

Methods of finding the coefficients

Once the correct assumption has been made, it is a simple matter to evaluate the coefficients. It is most essential to make the correct assumption otherwise, of course, the rest of the working will be completely fruitless. There are various methods which may be used to find the coefficients and the following examples will illustrate their uses.

Example 1. $\dfrac{5x-8}{(x-1)(x-2)}$.

Assume $\dfrac{5x-8}{(x-1)(x-2)} \equiv \dfrac{A}{x-1} + \dfrac{B}{x-2}$.

Then $5x - 8 \equiv A(x-2) + B(x-1)$.

This is an identity, true for all values of x. Give x in turn the values 1 and 2 and we get immediately $-3 = A(-1)$ and $2 = B$, i.e. $A = 3$, $B = 2$ (see beginning of section).

It will always pay to give values to x, if possible, which make terms of the right-hand side zero.

Notice that A is the value of the fraction $\dfrac{5x-8}{x-2}$ when $x = 1$ and this is a particular case of the following general rule.

If the factors of the denominator are linear, the coefficient corresponding to any denominator may be found by blotting out this denominator in the original fraction and, in the remainder, putting x equal to the value which makes the term blotted out zero.

For example, in $\dfrac{5x - 8}{(x - 1)(x - 2)}$, the coefficient of $\dfrac{1}{x - 1}$ is got by putting $x = 1$ in $\dfrac{5x - 8}{x - 2}$; the coefficient of $\dfrac{1}{x - 2}$ is got by putting $x = 2$ in $\dfrac{5x - 8}{x - 1}$.

Example 2. $\dfrac{x^2}{(x - 1)(x^2 + 1)}$.

Assume $\dfrac{x^2}{(x - 1)(x^2 + 1)} \equiv \dfrac{A}{x - 1} + \dfrac{Bx + C}{x^2 + 1}$.

Then $x^2 \equiv A(x^2 + 1) + (Bx + C)(x - 1)$.

Putting $x = 1$,
$$1 = 2A \quad \text{and therefore} \quad A = \tfrac{1}{2}.$$
We complete the example by the method of equating coefficients.
Equating coefficients of x^2,
$$1 = A + B \text{ and so } B = \tfrac{1}{2}.$$
Equating coefficients of x,
$$0 = C - B \text{ and so } C = \tfrac{1}{2}.$$
The Partial Fractions are
$$\frac{1}{2(x - 1)} + \frac{1}{2} \cdot \frac{x + 1}{x^2 + 1}.$$

Example 3. $\dfrac{x^3 - x}{(x^2 + 1)(x - 2)^3}$.

Assume
$$\frac{x^3 - x}{(x^2 + 1)(x - 2)^3} \equiv \frac{Ax + B}{x^2 + 1} + \frac{C}{x - 2} + \frac{D}{(x - 2)^2} + \frac{E}{(x - 2)^3}.$$
Therefore
$$x^3 - x \equiv (Ax + B)(x - 2)^3 + C(x^2 + 1)(x - 2)^2$$
$$+ D(x^2 + 1)(x - 2) + E(x^2 + 1).$$
Putting $x = 2$, $6 = E(5)$ and so $E = \tfrac{6}{5}$.

We can proceed by the method of equating coefficients but the manipulation becomes rather laborious. The following method shortens the work somewhat.

Putting $E = \tfrac{6}{5}$,
$$x^3 - x - \tfrac{6}{5}(x^2 + 1)$$
$$\equiv (Ax + B)(x - 2)^3 + C(x^2 + 1)(x - 2)^2 + D(x^2 + 1)(x - 2).$$

Since $(x - 2)$ is a factor of the right-hand side, it must also be a factor of the left-hand side, which equals

$$(x - 2)(x^2 + \tfrac{4}{5}x + \tfrac{3}{5}).$$

Therefore

$(x - 2)(x^2 + \tfrac{4}{5}x + \tfrac{3}{5})$
$$\equiv (Ax + B)(x - 2)^3 + C(x^2 + 1)(x - 2)^2 + D(x^2 + 1)(x - 2)$$

or

$x^2 + \tfrac{4}{5}x + \tfrac{3}{5} \equiv (Ax + B)(x - 2)^2 + C(x^2 + 1)(x - 2) + D(x^2 + 1).$

Putting $x = 2$ again,

$$4 + \tfrac{8}{5} + \tfrac{3}{5} = D(5). \quad \therefore \ D = \tfrac{31}{25}.$$

Giving D this value,

$x^2 + \tfrac{4}{5}x + \tfrac{3}{5} - \tfrac{31}{25}(x^2 + 1) \equiv (Ax + B)(x - 2)^2 + C(x^2 + 1)(x - 2).$

The left-hand side equals

$$-\tfrac{6}{25}x^2 + \tfrac{4}{5}x - \tfrac{16}{25} = -\tfrac{2}{25}(3x^2 - 10x + 8)$$
$$= -\tfrac{2}{25}(x - 2)(3x - 4).$$

Therefore

$-\tfrac{2}{25}(x - 2)(3x - 4) \equiv (Ax + B)(x - 2)^2 + C(x^2 + 1)(x - 2)$

and so

$$-\tfrac{2}{25}(3x - 4) \equiv (Ax + B)(x - 2) + C(x^2 + 1).$$

Putting $x = 2$ again,
$$-\tfrac{2}{25}(2) = C(5) \quad \therefore \ C = -\tfrac{4}{125}.$$

Giving C this value,
$$-\tfrac{2}{25}(3x - 4) + \tfrac{4}{125}(x^2 + 1) \equiv (Ax + B)(x - 2).$$

The left-hand side equals
$$\tfrac{4}{125}x^2 - \tfrac{6}{25}x + \tfrac{44}{125} = \tfrac{2}{125}(2x^2 - 15x + 22)$$
$$= \tfrac{2}{125}(x - 2)(2x - 11).$$

Therefore $\qquad \tfrac{2}{125}(x - 2)(2x - 11) \equiv (Ax + B)(x - 2)$

and so $\qquad\qquad \tfrac{2}{125}(2x - 11) \equiv Ax + B.$

The Partial Fractions are

$$\frac{2}{125} \cdot \frac{2x - 11}{x^2 + 1} - \frac{4}{125(x - 2)} + \frac{31}{25(x - 2)^2} + \frac{6}{5(x - 2)^3}.$$

This method has the added advantage that an error in the working will probably be shown up in the subsequent factorizing.

EXERCISES IV

Put into partial fractions :

1. $\dfrac{x}{(x - 1)(x - 2)}$;   2. $\dfrac{x^2}{(x - 1)(x - 2)}$;   3. $\dfrac{x^2}{(x - 1)(x - 2)(x - 3)}$;

4. $\dfrac{x+1}{x(x-2)}$;   **5.** $\dfrac{x}{(x^2+1)(x-1)}$; **6.** $\dfrac{x}{(x-1)(x+1)^2}$;

7. $\dfrac{1}{x(x+1)^2}$;   **8.** $\dfrac{x^3}{(x-1)(x+1)}$.

SUMMATION OF SERIES

Consider the series

$$1.2.3. + 2.3.4. + 3.4.5. \dots + n(n+1)(n+2).$$

The rth term is $r(r+1)(r+2)$ and the sum of the series S may be written

$$S = \sum_1^n r(r+1)(r+2).$$

Let u_r stand for $r(r+1)(r+2)$ and v_r for $r(r+1)(r+2)(r+3)$. Then

$$
\begin{aligned}
v_r - v_{r-1} &= r(r+1)(r+2)(r+3) - (r-1)(r)(r+1)(r+2) \\
&= r(r+1)(r+2)\{(r+3) - (r-1)\} \\
&= r(r+1)(r+2)\,(4) \\
&= 4u_r.
\end{aligned}
$$

Writing down repeated applications of this formula,

$$
\begin{aligned}
v_n - v_{n-1} &= 4u_n \\
v_{n-1} - v_{n-2} &= 4u_{n-1} \\
\cdot \quad \cdot \quad &\cdot \quad \cdot \quad \cdot \quad \cdot \quad \cdot \\
\cdot \quad \cdot \quad &\cdot \quad \cdot \quad \cdot \quad \cdot \quad \cdot \\
\cdot \quad \cdot \quad &\cdot \quad \cdot \quad \cdot \quad \cdot \quad \cdot \\
v_1 - v_0 &= 4u_1.
\end{aligned}
$$

Adding these equations,

$$v_n - v_0 = 4S.$$

Therefore $S = \tfrac{1}{4}(v_n - v_0)$.

This formula applies for the sum of any series in which the general term is the product of consecutive factors of the type $(r+k)$. To find the sum, multiply the nth term by the next highest integer, subtract the zero value and divide by the new number of factors.

N.B.—The zero value is so often zero that it is easily forgotten.

Two examples of this use of this rule are given.

$$1 + 2 + 3 + \dots + n = \frac{n(n+1) - 0}{2} = \tfrac{1}{2}n(n+1).$$

$$
\begin{aligned}
2.3 + 3.4 + 4.5 &+ \dots + (n+1)(n+2) \\
&= \frac{(n+1)(n+2)(n+3) - 1.2.3.}{3}
\end{aligned}
$$

[The zero value is obtained by putting $n = 0$ in
$$(n + 1)(n + 2)(n + 3).]$$

This method may be adapted to sum series in which the factors are not consecutive by suitably arranging the general term.

The sum of the squares of the first n integers

$$S_n = 1^2 + 2^2 + 3^2 + \ldots + n^2.$$

The general term is $r^2 = r(r + 1) - r.$

Therefore

$$\sum_1^n r^2 = \sum_1^n r(r + 1) - \sum_1^n r$$

$$= \frac{n(n + 1)(n + 2) - 0}{3} - \frac{n(n + 1) - 0}{2}$$

$$= \frac{n(n + 1)}{6}(2n + 4 - 3)$$

$$= \tfrac{1}{6}n(n + 1)(2n + 1).$$

The sum of the cubes of the first n integers

$$S_n = 1^3 + 2^3 + 3^3 + \ldots + n^3.$$

The general term is $r^3 = (r - 1)r(r + 1) + r.$

Therefore

$$\sum_1^n r^3 = \sum_1^n (r - 1)r(r + 1) + \sum_1^n r$$

$$= \frac{(n - 1)n(n + 1)(n + 2) - 0}{4} + \frac{n(n + 1) - 0}{2}$$

$$= \frac{n(n + 1)}{4}(n^2 + n - 2 + 2)$$

$$= \left[\frac{n(n + 1)}{2}\right]^2.$$

This last formula is easily remembered as it is the square of the sum of the first n integers.

The formulae for the sum of the squares and the sum of the cubes should be learnt by heart as they give another method of summing series. We shall now do an example by the two alternative methods. Sometimes one is preferable, sometimes the other, but both are easy of application and should give no difficulty.

Example. Sum $1.3.5 + 2.4.7. + 3.5.9. + \ldots$ to n terms.

First Method. The rth term is $r(r + 2)(2r + 3)$ which equals

$$r(r + 2)[(2r + 2) + 1]$$
$$= 2r(r + 1)(r + 2) + r(r + 2)$$
$$= 2r(r + 1)(r + 2) + r(r + 1) + r$$

(arranging so that each term is the product of consecutive factors).

$$\therefore \sum_1^n r(r + 2)(2r + 3)$$

$$= 2\sum_1^n r(r + 1)(r + 2) + \sum_1^n r(r + 1) + \sum_1^n r$$

$$= \frac{2n(n + 1)(n + 2)(n + 3)}{4} + \frac{n(n + 1)(n + 2)}{3} + \frac{n(n + 1)}{2}$$

$$= \frac{n(n + 1)}{6}\{3(n + 2)(n + 3) + 2n + 4 + 3\}$$

$$= \frac{n(n + 1)}{6}(3n^2 + 17n + 25).$$

Second Method.

$$\sum_1^n r(r + 2)(2r + 3) = \sum_1^n (2r^3 + 7r^2 + 6r)$$

$$= 2\sum_1^n r^3 + 7\sum_1^n r^2 + 6\sum_1^n r$$

$$= \frac{2n^2(n + 1)^2}{4} + \frac{7n(n + 1)(2n + 1)}{6} + \frac{6n(n + 1)}{2}$$

$$= \frac{n(n + 1)}{6}\{3n(n + 1) + 7(2n + 1) + 18\}$$

$$= \frac{n(n + 1)}{6}(3n^2 + 17n + 25).$$

N.B.—In an example of this sort, we may come across $\sum_1^n 1$. This, remember, is n and not 1.

The method of induction must be constantly in mind when dealing with series. It can always be used if the sum is given or known and is often the quickest and best method.

Method of Partial Fractions

When the rth term has a denominator which is the product of factors containing r, *use Partial Fractions*. This is best illustrated by a few examples.

Example 1. Sum to n terms $\dfrac{1}{1.2} + \dfrac{1}{2.3} + \dfrac{1}{3.4} + \ldots$.

The rth term $\quad (u_r) = \dfrac{1}{r(r+1)} = \dfrac{1}{r} - \dfrac{1}{r+1}$.

Expressing each term in this way,

$$u_1 = \tfrac{1}{1} - \tfrac{1}{2}$$
$$u_2 = \tfrac{1}{2} - \tfrac{1}{3}$$
$$u_3 = \tfrac{1}{3} - \tfrac{1}{4}$$
$$\cdots \cdots \cdots$$
$$\cdots \cdots \cdots$$
$$u_n = \dfrac{1}{n} - \dfrac{1}{n+1}.$$

Adding, we see that $S_n = 1 - \dfrac{1}{n+1} = \dfrac{n}{n+1}$.

If S_n is the sum of n terms of a series, and S_n tends to a finite limit S as n tends to infinity, S is called the sum to infinity of the series. In this case $S_n \to 1$ as $n \to \infty$.

So the sum to infinity is 1.

Example 2. Sum to n terms

$$\frac{1}{1.2.4} + \frac{1}{2.3.5} + \frac{1}{3.4.6} + \ldots.$$

$$u_r = \frac{1}{r(r+1)(r+3)} = \frac{1}{3r} - \frac{1}{2(r+1)} + \frac{1}{6(r+3)}.$$

Expressing each term in this way,

$$u_1 = \tfrac{1}{3}(\tfrac{1}{1}) - \tfrac{1}{2}(\tfrac{1}{2}) + \tfrac{1}{6}(\tfrac{1}{4})$$
$$u_2 = \tfrac{1}{3}(\tfrac{1}{2}) - \tfrac{1}{2}(\tfrac{1}{3}) + \tfrac{1}{6}(\tfrac{1}{5})$$
$$u_3 = \tfrac{1}{3}(\tfrac{1}{3}) - \tfrac{1}{2}(\tfrac{1}{4}) + \tfrac{1}{6}(\tfrac{1}{6})$$
$$u_4 = \tfrac{1}{3}(\tfrac{1}{4}) - \tfrac{1}{2}(\tfrac{1}{5}) + \tfrac{1}{6}(\tfrac{1}{7})$$
$$\cdots \cdots \cdots \cdots \cdots \cdots \cdots$$
$$\cdots \cdots \cdots \cdots \cdots \cdots \cdots$$
$$u_{n-3} = \tfrac{1}{3}\left(\frac{1}{n-3}\right) - \tfrac{1}{2}\left(\frac{1}{n-2}\right) + \tfrac{1}{6}\left(\frac{1}{n}\right)$$
$$u_{n-2} = \tfrac{1}{3}\left(\frac{1}{n-2}\right) - \tfrac{1}{2}\left(\frac{1}{n-1}\right) + \tfrac{1}{6}\left(\frac{1}{n+1}\right)$$

$$u_{n-1} = \tfrac{1}{3}\left(\frac{1}{n-1}\right) - \tfrac{1}{2}\left(\frac{1}{n}\right) + \tfrac{1}{6}\left(\frac{1}{n+2}\right)$$

$$u_n = \tfrac{1}{3}\left(\frac{1}{n}\right) - \tfrac{1}{2}\left(\frac{1}{n+1}\right) + \tfrac{1}{6}\left(\frac{1}{n+3}\right).$$

On addition, since $\tfrac{1}{6} + \tfrac{1}{3} = \tfrac{1}{2}$, the terms in $\dfrac{1}{n}$ cancel.

This means that all the terms except five at the beginning and four at the end cancel.

Therefore

$$S_n = \tfrac{1}{3} - \tfrac{1}{2}(\tfrac{1}{2}) + \tfrac{1}{3}(\tfrac{1}{2}) - \tfrac{1}{2}(\tfrac{1}{3}) + \tfrac{1}{3}(\tfrac{1}{3}) + \tfrac{1}{6}\left(\frac{1}{n+1}\right) + \tfrac{1}{6}\left(\frac{1}{n+2}\right)$$

$$- \tfrac{1}{2}\left(\frac{1}{n+1}\right) + \tfrac{1}{6}\left(\frac{1}{n+3}\right)$$

$$= \tfrac{1}{3} - \tfrac{1}{4} + \tfrac{1}{6} - \tfrac{1}{6} + \tfrac{1}{9} + \tfrac{1}{6}\left(\frac{1}{n+2}\right) + \tfrac{1}{6}\left(\frac{1}{n+3}\right) - \tfrac{1}{3}\left(\frac{1}{n+1}\right)$$

$$= \tfrac{7}{36} + \tfrac{1}{6}\left(\frac{1}{n+2}\right) + \tfrac{1}{6}\left(\frac{1}{n+3}\right) - \tfrac{1}{3}\left(\frac{1}{n+1}\right).$$

The sum to infinity is $\tfrac{7}{36}$.

Power series

Power series are series in which each term is a multiple of a power of r or x. The simplest example is the Geometric Series,

$$S_n = a + ar + ar^2 + ar^3 + ar^4 + \ldots + ar^{n-1}.$$

Here we multiply by r, getting

$$r.S_n = ar + ar^2 + ar^3 + \ldots + ar^{n-1} + ar^n.$$

On subtraction, $\qquad S_n(1 - r) = a - ar^n,$

and therefore $\qquad\qquad S_n = a\dfrac{1 - r^n}{1 - r}.$

If $-1 < r < +1$, r^n tends to 0 as n tends to infinity and therefore the sum to infinity is $\dfrac{a}{1-r}$.

This method is applied to all power series.

Example. Sum to n terms

$$1 + 2x + 3x^2 + 4x^3 + \ldots.$$

$$S_n = 1 + 2x + 3x^2 + \ldots + nx^{n-1}.$$

$$\therefore\ xS_n = x + 2x^2 + \ldots + (n-1)x^{n-1} + nx^n.$$

$$\therefore\ S_n(1 - x) = (1 + x + x^2 + \ldots + x^{n-1}) - nx^n.$$

$$= \frac{1 - x^n}{1 - x} - nx^n \text{ (using G.P. formula)}$$

$$\therefore S_n = \frac{1 - x^n}{(1 - x)^2} - \frac{nx^n}{1 - x}.$$

If $-1 < x < +1$, the sum to infinity is $\dfrac{1}{(1 - x)^2}$ (see Binomial

Theorem).

EXERCISES V

Find the sum to n terms of the following series :

1. $1.4 + 2.5 + 3.6 + \ldots$;   **2.** $1.2.4 + 2.3.5 + 3.4.6 + \ldots$;

3. $1^2 + 3^2 + 5^2 + \ldots$;   **4.** $1^3 + 3^3 + 5^3 + \ldots$;

5. $\dfrac{1}{1.2.3} + \dfrac{1}{2.3.4} + \dfrac{1}{3.4.5} + \ldots$;

6. $x + 3x^2 + 5x^3 + 7x^4 + \ldots$;   **7.** $1^4 + 2^4 + 3^4 + \ldots$

8. $\dfrac{3}{1.2} - \dfrac{5}{2.3} + \dfrac{7}{3.4} - \dfrac{9}{4.5} + \ldots$

THE EXPONENTIAL AND LOGARITHMIC SERIES

Let us consider $f(x) = \underset{n \to \infty}{\text{Lt}} \left(1 + \dfrac{x}{n}\right)^n.$

Expanded by the Binomial,

$$\left(1 + \frac{x}{n}\right)^n = 1 + n\left(\frac{x}{n}\right) + \frac{n(n - 1)}{1.2}\left(\frac{x}{n}\right)^2$$
$$+ \frac{n(n - 1)(n - 2)}{1.2.3}\left(\frac{x}{n}\right)^3 + \ldots$$

$$= 1 + x + \frac{\left(1 - \dfrac{1}{n}\right)}{1.2}x^2 + \frac{\left(1 - \dfrac{1}{n}\right)\left(1 - \dfrac{2}{n}\right)}{1.2.3.}x^3 + \ldots$$

So, as n tends to infinity,

$$f(x) = 1 + x + \frac{x^2}{2!} + \frac{x^3}{3!} + \frac{x^4}{4!} + \ldots$$

In $\left(1 + \dfrac{x}{n}\right)^n$ put $x/n = 1/m$, so that $n = mx$.

Then $$\left(1 + \frac{x}{n}\right)^n = \left(1 + \frac{1}{m}\right)^{mx} = \left\{\left(1 + \frac{1}{m}\right)^m\right\}^x.$$

As $n \to \infty$, $m \to \infty$ and so

$$\operatorname*{Lt}_{m \to \infty} \left(1 + \frac{1}{m}\right)^m = \operatorname*{Lt}_{n \to \infty} \left(1 + \frac{1}{n}\right)^n = f(1).$$

$$\therefore f(x) = \{f(1)\}^x.$$

$f(1)$ is called e and we see that $f(x) = e^x$.

$$\therefore e^x = 1 + x + \frac{x^2}{2!} + \frac{x^3}{3!} + \frac{x^4}{4!} + \ldots.$$

when $$e = 1 + 1 + \frac{1}{2!} + \frac{1}{3!} + \frac{1}{4!} + \ldots.$$

The expansion of e^x is called the Exponential series and is valid *for all values of x.*

The value of e, which is incommensurable, can easily be computed from the above formula to any desired degree of accuracy and equals $2 \cdot 71828 \ldots$.

Changing the sign of x, we have

$$e^{-x} = 1 - x + \frac{x^2}{2!} - \frac{x^3}{3!} + \frac{x^4}{4!} - \ldots.$$

and hence we obtain the expansions for $\cosh x \left(= \dfrac{e^x + e^{-x}}{2}\right)$ and

$\sinh x \left(= \dfrac{e^x - e^{-x}}{2}\right)$.

Now $$e^{x \log a} = e^{\log a^x} = a^x$$

and therefore

$$a^x = e^{x \log a} = 1 + x \log a + \frac{(x \log a)^2}{2!} + \frac{(x \log a)^3}{3!} + \ldots.$$

Putting $(1 + y)$ for a,

$$(1 + y)^x = 1 + x \log (1 + y) + \frac{[x \log (1 + y)]^2}{2!} + \ldots.$$

The right-hand side is a polynomial in x, in which the coefficient of x is $\log (1 + y)$. Therefore $\log (1 + y)$ is equal to the coefficient of x in the expansion of $(1 + y)^x$, which by the Binomial Theorem is

$$1 + xy + \frac{x(x - 1)}{1.2} y^2 + \frac{x(x - 1)(x - 2)}{1.2.3} y^3 + \ldots.$$

and the coefficient of x is

$$y - \tfrac{1}{2}y^2 + \tfrac{1}{3}y^3 - \ldots.$$
$$\therefore\ log\,(1 + y) = y - \tfrac{1}{2}y^2 + \tfrac{1}{3}y^3 - \ldots.$$

Since we have used the Binomial expansion, this is valid only if y lies between -1 and $+1$. Actually y may equal 1 but not -1 and so $-1 < y \leqslant 1$.

This series may be used to evaluate logarithms but it is of little use in practice as the terms converge so slowly. For example to find log 2 to four places of decimals, it would be necessary to consider thousands of terms.

Changing the sign of y,

$$\log\,(1 - y) = - y - \frac{y^2}{2} - \frac{y^3}{3} - \frac{y^4}{4} \ldots. \ -1 \leqslant y < 1.$$

Subtracting the two series,

$$\log \frac{1 + y}{1 - y} = 2\left\{y + \frac{y^3}{3} + \frac{y^5}{5} + \ldots.\right\}.$$

Put $y = \dfrac{m - n}{m + n}$ which must be less than 1 if m and n are positive, so that $\dfrac{1 + y}{1 - y} = \dfrac{m}{n}$ and we have

$$\log \frac{m}{n} = 2\left\{\frac{m - n}{m + n} + \tfrac{1}{3}\left(\frac{m - n}{m + n}\right)^3 + \tfrac{1}{5}\left(\frac{m - n}{m + n}\right)^5 \ldots.\right\}$$

for all positive m and n.

This is the series used to calculate Napierian logarithms (logs to base e), although even using this series, devices are sometimes necessary to avoid lengthy arithmetic.

Example 1. Calculate log 2 to four decimal places.

$$\log \tfrac{2}{1} = 2\{\tfrac{1}{3} + \tfrac{1}{3}(\tfrac{1}{3})^3 + \tfrac{1}{5}(\tfrac{1}{3})^5 + \ldots.\}$$

$\tfrac{1}{3} = \cdot333333$	$\tfrac{1}{3} = \cdot333333$
$(\tfrac{1}{3})^3 = \cdot037037$	$\tfrac{1}{3}(\tfrac{1}{3})^3 = \cdot012346$
$(\tfrac{1}{5})^5 = \cdot004115$	$\tfrac{1}{5}(\tfrac{1}{3})^5 = \cdot000823$
$(\tfrac{1}{3})^7 = \cdot000457$	$\tfrac{1}{7}(\tfrac{1}{3})^7 = \cdot000065$
$(\tfrac{1}{3})^9 = \cdot000051$	$\tfrac{1}{9}(\tfrac{1}{3})^9 = \cdot000006$
	$\overline{\cdot346573}$

$$\therefore\ \log 2 = 2(\cdot346573) = \cdot693146 \doteqdot \cdot6931.$$

Example 2. Calculate log 10 to four decimal places.

$\dfrac{m - n}{m + n}$ is $\tfrac{9}{11}$ and powers of this converge too slowly to be helpful.

We must therefore use some cunning device to avoid the difficulty.

$$\log \tfrac{10}{8} = 2\{\tfrac{1}{9} + \tfrac{1}{3}(\tfrac{1}{9})^3 + \tfrac{1}{5}(\tfrac{1}{9})^5 + \ldots\}$$

$\tfrac{1}{9} = \cdot111111$	$\tfrac{1}{9} = \cdot111111$
$(\tfrac{1}{9})^2 = \cdot012346$	
$(\tfrac{1}{9})^3 = \cdot001372$	$\tfrac{1}{3}(\tfrac{1}{9})^3 = \cdot000457$
$(\tfrac{1}{9})^4 = \cdot000152$	
$(\tfrac{1}{9})^5 = \cdot000017$	$\tfrac{1}{5}(\tfrac{1}{9})^5 = \cdot000003$
	$\overline{\cdot111571}$

$\therefore \quad \log \tfrac{10}{8} = \cdot223142$

$\therefore \quad \log 10 = \cdot223142 + \log 8$

$\qquad\qquad = \cdot223142 + 3 \log 2 \;\; \text{(since } 8 = 2^3)$

$\qquad\qquad = \cdot223142 + 2\cdot079438$

$\qquad\qquad = 2\cdot302580$

$\qquad\qquad \doteqdot 2\cdot3026.$

To calculate logarithms to the base 10 from Napierian logarithms we must use the formula

$$\log_{10} x = \frac{\log_e x}{\log_e 10},$$

which means we must divide the corresponding logarithm by 2·3026

Applications to summing series

The logarithmic and exponential series may be used to sum certain series and there are two types which are of general interest and an example of each is given.

Example 1. Sum to infinity the series

$$\frac{x}{1.2} + \frac{x^2}{2.3} + \frac{x^3}{3.4} + \ldots.$$

Once again, we use Partial Fractions.

The general term is $\dfrac{x^r}{r(r+1)}$.

Now $\dfrac{1}{r(r+1)} = \dfrac{1}{r} - \dfrac{1}{r+1}$ and so $\dfrac{x^r}{r(r+1)} = \dfrac{x^r}{r} - \dfrac{x^r}{r+1}.$

Putting each term in this form, we get

$$S = \left(\frac{x}{1} - \frac{x}{2}\right) + \left(\frac{x^2}{2} - \frac{x^2}{3}\right) + \left(\frac{x^3}{3} - \frac{x^3}{4}\right) + \ldots.$$

$$= \left(\frac{x}{1} + \frac{x^2}{2} + \frac{x^3}{3} + \ldots\right) - \left(\frac{x}{2} + \frac{x^2}{3} + \frac{x^3}{4} \ldots\right)$$

$$= \left(\frac{x}{1} + \frac{x^2}{2} + \frac{x^3}{3} + \ldots\right) - \frac{1}{x}\left(\frac{x^2}{2} + \frac{x^3}{3} + \frac{x^4}{4} + \ldots\right)$$

(arranging each series in the log form)

$$= -\log(1-x) - \frac{1}{x}\{-\log(1-x) - x\} \quad \text{provided} -1 \leqslant x < 1$$

$$= \left(\frac{1}{x} - 1\right)\log(1-x) + 1.$$

Example 2. Sum to infinity

$$1 + \frac{2^2}{2!} + \frac{3^2}{3!} + \frac{4^2}{4!} + \ldots$$

The general term is $\frac{n^2}{n!}$ which equals $\frac{n(n-1)+n}{n!}$.

(*N.B.*—The numerator is arranged so that each term of it will cancel into the denominator $n!$ leaving a numerator 1.)

Therefore $\qquad \frac{n^2}{n!} = \frac{1}{(n-2)!} + \frac{1}{(n-1)!}.$

Expressing each term in this way,

$$\frac{1^2}{1!} = \qquad 1$$

$$\frac{2^2}{2!} = 1 + \frac{1}{1!}$$

$$\frac{3^2}{3!} = \frac{1}{1!} + \frac{1}{2!}$$

$$\frac{4^2}{4!} = \frac{1}{2!} + \frac{1}{3!} \quad \text{etc.}$$

$$\cdot \quad \cdot \quad \cdot \quad \cdot$$

(count 0! as 1 and neglect negative factorials : check the first few terms to see they are correct).

Summing this in columns, we get

$$1 + \frac{2^2}{2!} + \frac{3^2}{3!} + \frac{4^2}{4!} + \ldots = 2e.$$

EXERCISES VI

1. Calculate $\log_e 3$ to 3 decimal places.
2. Expand e^{1+x} as far as the term in x^3.
3. Find the coefficient of x^2 in the expansion of $(1 + x + x^2)e^{-x}$.
4. Find the coefficient of x^3 in the expansion of $(1 + x)\log(1 + x)$.
5. Find the sum to infinity of $\frac{1}{2!} + \frac{2}{3!} + \frac{3}{4!} + \ldots$

6. If $\log_e y = 1 + x + x^2$, show that $y = e(1 + x + \frac{3}{2}x^2)$ as far as the term in x^2.

7. Find the sum to infinity of $\dfrac{x}{2} + \dfrac{x^2}{3} + \dfrac{x^3}{4} + \cdots$.

8. Expand $\dfrac{\log_e (1 + x)}{1 - x}$ as far as the term in x^3.

9. Find the coefficient of x^n in the expansion of $\log (2 + x)$.

10. If $e^{2y} - 3e^y + 2 = 0$, show that $y = 0$ or $\log_e 2$.

THE REMAINDER THEOREM

If a polynomial $f(x)$ is divided by $(x - a)$, the remainder is $f(a)$

The remainder on division by $(x - a)$ will be a number, i.e. will be independent of x. Call this remainder R and then

$$f(x) \equiv (x - a)Q(x) + R,$$

where $Q(x)$ is the quotient. This is an identity and so is true for all values of x.

Putting $x = a$, we get

$$f(a) = R.$$

To find the remainder when $f(x)$ is divided by $(x - a)(x - b)$

The remainder will be linear in x, so suppose it is $Ax + B$.
Then
$$f(x) \equiv (x - a)(x - b)Q(x) + Ax + B$$
where $Q(x)$ is the quotient. Putting $x = a$ and $x = b$ in turn

$$f(a) = Aa + B$$
and
$$f(b) = Ab + B.$$
From these,
$$f(a) - f(b) = A(a - b)$$
and
$$bf(a) - af(b) = B(b - a).$$
Therefore the remainder is

$$\frac{f(a) - f(b)}{a - b}x + \frac{af(b) - bf(a)}{a - b}.$$

The chief use of the Remainder Theorem is when the remainder is zero. If $f(a) = 0$, then $f(x)$ is divisible by $x - a$. This is of much help in factorization and also in solving equations by trial and error, as in the following examples.

Example 1. Factorize

$$a^3(b - c) + b^3(c - a) + c^3(a - b).$$

If we put $b = a$ in this expression, it becomes

$$a^3(a - c) + a^3(c - a) + c^3(0) = 0.$$

Therefore $(a - b)$ must be a factor as must similarly $(b - c)$ and

$(c - a)$. But the expression is of the fourth degree in a, b and c and so the only other factor possible is one of the first degree. It must also be symmetrical in a, b and c and therefore can only be $(a + b + c)$. No other factor except a constant being possible,

$$a^3(b - c) + b^3(c - a) + c^3(a - b) \equiv \lambda(a - b)(b - c)(c - a)(a + b + c)$$

where λ is a constant. λ may be found by equating coefficients (of a^3b for example) or by giving a, b and c special values. Be careful not to give any two equal values, otherwise the equation will become $0 = 0$. Try $a = 0$, $b = 1$ and $c = 2$ and we have

$$0 + 1(2) + 8(- 1) = \lambda(- 1)(- 1)(2)(3)$$
$$\therefore - 6 = + 6\lambda$$

or
$$\lambda = - 1$$

and so

$$a^3(b - c) + b^3(c - a) + c^3(a - b) = - (a - b)(b - c)(c - a)(a + b + c).$$

Example 2. Solve the equation

$$3x^3 + x^2 - 17x + 10 = 0$$

by trial and error.

If $(px + q)$ is a factor of $3x^3 + x^2 - 17x + 10$, then p must be a factor of 3 and q must be a factor of 10. The only rational solutions possible for x are therefore ± 1, ± 2, ± 5, ± 10, $\pm \frac{1}{3}$, $\pm \frac{2}{3}$, $\pm \frac{5}{3}$, $\pm \frac{10}{3}$.

Give x these values in succession to find one solution.

When $x = \frac{2}{3}$,

$$3x^3 + x^2 - 17x + 10 = 3(\tfrac{8}{27}) + \tfrac{4}{9} - 17(\tfrac{2}{3}) + 10$$
$$= \tfrac{8}{9} + \tfrac{4}{9} - \tfrac{34}{3} + 10$$
$$= 0.$$

Therefore $x = \frac{2}{3}$ is a solution and $(3x - 2)$ must be a factor. By division, we get

$$3x^3 + x^2 - 17x + 10 = (3x - 2)(x^2 + x - 5).$$

The other solutions are the solutions of the equation

$$x^2 + x - 5 = 0.$$

Therefore
$$x = \frac{- 1 \pm \sqrt{1 + 20}}{2}$$

and the complete solution is

$$x = \tfrac{2}{3} \quad \text{or} \quad \frac{- 1 \pm \sqrt{21}}{2}.$$

EXERCISES VII

Solve the equations :

1. $x^3 + 3x^2 - 4x - 12 = 0$;   2. $x^3 + 2x^2 - 1 = 0$;

3. $x^3 + x^2 - 4x - 4 = 0$;   **4.** $x^3 + 3x^2 - x - 6 = 0$.

5. Factorize $a^2b - ab^2 + b^2c - c^2b + ac^2 - ca^2$.

6. Factorize $a^4(b - c) + b^4(c - a) + c^4(a - b)$.

ROOTS OF EQUATIONS

The quadratic function

The roots of $ax^2 + bx + c = 0$ are $\dfrac{-b \pm \sqrt{b^2 - 4ac}}{2a}$.

The roots are real therefore if $b^2 > 4ac$ and are equal if $b^2 = 4ac$. This latter condition, therefore, is also the condition that $(ax^2 + bx^2 + c)$ should be a perfect square.

Condition that $(ax^2 + bx + c)$ should be positive for all x

$$ax^2 + bx + c = a\left[x^2 + \frac{b}{a}x\right] + c$$

$$= a\left[x^2 + \frac{b}{a}x + \frac{b^2}{4a^2}\right] + c - \frac{b^2}{4a}$$

$$= a\left(x + \frac{b}{2a}\right)^2 + \frac{4ac - b^2}{4a}.$$

Since $\left(x + \dfrac{b}{2a}\right)^2$ is positive for all values of x, $(ax^2 + bx + c)$ will be positive for all values of x provided that $a > 0$ and that $b^2 < 4ac$. This also infers that $c > 0$ since $4ac$ is positive.

The condition $b^2 < 4ac$ shows that the roots of $ax^2 + bx + c = 0$ must be imaginary : this is obviously necessary since the roots of $ax^2 + bx + c = 0$ are the values of x at the points where the graph of $y = ax^2 + bx + c$ cuts the x-axis. If $(ax^2 + bx + c)$ is always positive, the graph cannot cut the x-axis and so the roots must be imaginary.

Condition for a common root

Suppose that $f(x) = 0$ and $F(x) = 0$ have a common root. Then there must be a value of x, say α, which makes both $f(x)$ and $F(x)$ zero. The condition therefore is obtained by eliminating α between $f(\alpha) = 0$ and $F(\alpha) = 0$; or simply by eliminating x between $f(x) = 0$ and $F(x) = 0$.

Condition for a repeated root

Suppose that $f(x) = 0$ has a repeated root α and that
$$f(x) = (x - \alpha)^2 \phi(x).$$
Then $\qquad f'(x) = 2(x - \alpha)\phi(x) + (x - \alpha)^2 \phi'(x)$

and so $(x - \alpha)$ must be a factor of $f'(x)$. Therefore $f(x) = 0$ and $f'(x) = 0$ have a common root and the condition required is obtained by eliminating x between $f(x) = 0$ and $f'(x) = 0$.

Relations between roots

Suppose the roots of the cubic equation $ax^3 + bx^2 + cx + d = 0$ are α, β and γ.

Then $(x - \alpha)$, $(x - \beta)$ and $(x - \gamma)$ must be factors of $ax^3 + bx^2 + cx + d$, and since the function is a cubic the only other possible factor is a constant.

Therefore
$$ax^3 + bx^2 + cx + d \equiv a(x - \alpha)(x - \beta)(x - \gamma)$$
$$\equiv a\{x^3 - (\alpha + \beta + \gamma)x^2 + (\alpha\beta + \beta\gamma + \gamma\alpha)x - \alpha\beta\gamma\}.$$

Equating coefficients, we have
$$\left.\begin{aligned}
\alpha + \beta + \gamma &= -\frac{b}{a} \\
\beta\gamma + \gamma\alpha + \alpha\beta &= \frac{c}{a} \\
\alpha\beta\gamma &= -\frac{d}{a}
\end{aligned}\right\}$$

Similarly for the quadratic equation $ax^2 + bx + c = 0$, we have
$$\left.\begin{aligned}
\alpha + \beta &= -\frac{b}{a} \\
\alpha\beta &= \frac{c}{a}
\end{aligned}\right\}$$

and for the quartic $ax^4 + bx^3 + cx^2 + dx + e = 0$
$$\left.\begin{aligned}
\alpha + \beta + \gamma + \delta &= -\frac{b}{a} \\
\alpha\beta + \alpha\gamma + \alpha\delta + \beta\gamma + \beta\delta + \gamma\delta &= \frac{c}{a} \\
\beta\gamma\delta + \alpha\gamma\delta + \alpha\beta\delta + \alpha\beta\gamma &= -\frac{d}{a} \\
\alpha\beta\gamma\delta &= \frac{e}{a}
\end{aligned}\right\}$$

To form the equation whose roots are symmetrical functions of each of the roots of a given equation

Example 1. If α, β, γ are the roots of the equation

$$ax^3 + bx^2 + cx + d = 0,$$

form the equation whose roots are $\dfrac{1}{\alpha}$, $\dfrac{1}{\beta}$ and $\dfrac{1}{\gamma}$.

Put $y = \dfrac{1}{x}$ and eliminate x between $y = \dfrac{1}{x}$ and $ax^3 + bx^2 + cx + d = 0$. The only possible values of x are α, β and γ and so the possible values of y are $\dfrac{1}{\alpha}$, $\dfrac{1}{\beta}$, $\dfrac{1}{\gamma}$.

The equation in y is therefore the equation required. It is

$$\frac{a}{y^3} + \frac{b}{y^2} + \frac{c}{y} + d = 0$$

or

$$dy^3 + cy^2 + by + a = 0.$$

Notice that

$$\frac{1}{\alpha} + \frac{1}{\beta} + \frac{1}{\gamma} = -\frac{c}{d}$$

$$\frac{1}{\beta\gamma} + \frac{1}{\gamma\alpha} + \frac{1}{\alpha\beta} = +\frac{b}{d}$$

$$\frac{1}{\alpha}\cdot\frac{1}{\beta}\cdot\frac{1}{\gamma} = -\frac{a}{d}$$

and so the sum of the reciprocals, one at a time, two at a time and three at a time may be obtained from the original equation by applying the normal rules but reversing the coefficients. *This often is a great time saver.*

Example 2. If α, β, γ are the roots of the equation

$$ax^3 + bx^2 + cx + d = 0,$$

form the equation whose roots are α^2, β^2 and γ^2.

By the same reasoning, put $y = x^2$ and eliminate x between this and $ax^3 + bx^2 + cx + d = 0$.

We get

$$ay\sqrt{y} + by + c\sqrt{y} + d = 0.$$

$$\therefore \quad \sqrt{y}(ay + c) = -(by + d).$$

Squaring

$$y(ay + c)^2 = (by + d)^2$$

or

$$a^2y^3 + y^2(2ac - b^2) + y(c^2 - 2bd) - d^2 = 0.$$

This method applies only if each of the new roots is the same function of *one* of the old roots. It can sometimes be adapted to cases in which more than one of the old roots is concerned.

To form the equation whose roots are any symmetrical functions of the roots of a given equation

Example. If α, β, γ are the roots of the equation $x^3 + 3x - 1 = 0$, form the equation whose roots are $\alpha^2 + \alpha$, $\beta^2 + \beta$, $\gamma^2 + \gamma$.

We know that
$$\left.\begin{array}{r} \alpha + \beta + \gamma = 0 \\ \beta\gamma + \gamma\alpha + \alpha\beta = 3 \\ \alpha\beta\gamma = 1 \end{array}\right\}$$

and we set out to find the sum of the new roots one, two and three at a time.

From the above equations, we see
$$\alpha^2 + \beta^2 + \gamma^2 = (\alpha + \beta + \gamma)^2 - 2\Sigma\,\alpha\beta$$
$$= -2(3) = -6.$$

$$\therefore\ (\alpha^2 + \alpha) + (\beta^2 + \beta) + (\gamma^2 + \gamma) = \Sigma\,\alpha^2 + \Sigma\,\alpha = -6 + 0 = -6.$$

$$(\beta^2 + \beta)(\gamma^2 + \gamma) + (\gamma^2 + \gamma)(\alpha^2 + \alpha) + (\alpha^2 + \alpha)(\beta^2 + \beta)$$
$$= \Sigma\,\beta^2\gamma^2 + \Sigma\,\beta^2\gamma + \Sigma\,\beta\gamma.$$

Now $\quad \Sigma\,\beta^2\gamma^2 = (\beta\gamma + \gamma\alpha + \alpha\beta)^2 - 2\alpha\beta\gamma(\alpha + \beta + \gamma) = 9$

and $\quad \Sigma\,\beta^2\gamma = (\beta\gamma + \gamma\alpha + \alpha\beta)(\alpha + \beta + \gamma) - 3\alpha\beta\gamma = -3.$

$$\therefore \Sigma\,(\beta^2 + \beta)(\gamma^2 + \gamma) = 9 - 3 + 3 = 9.$$

Also
$$(\alpha^2 + \alpha)(\beta^2 + \beta)(\gamma^2 + \gamma) = (\alpha^2 + \alpha)(\beta^2\gamma^2 + \beta^2\gamma + \beta\gamma^2 + \beta\gamma)$$
$$= \alpha^2\beta^2\gamma^2 + \Sigma\,\alpha^2\beta^2\gamma + \Sigma\,\alpha^2\beta\gamma + \alpha\beta\gamma$$
$$= \alpha^2\beta^2\gamma^2 + \alpha\beta\gamma\,\Sigma\,\alpha\beta + \alpha\beta\gamma\,\Sigma\,\alpha + \alpha\beta\gamma$$
$$= 1 + 1(3) + 0 + 1$$
$$= 5.$$

Changing the signs of these three results alternately, we shall get the coefficients of our new equation which is therefore
$$x^3 + 6x^2 + 9x - 5 = 0.$$

The sum of the powers of the roots of an equation

We can find the sum of the powers of the roots of a cubic equation, for example, by expressing the sum in terms of $(\alpha + \beta + \gamma)$, $(\beta\gamma + \gamma\alpha + \alpha\beta)$ and $\alpha\beta\gamma$.

A useful identity here is
$$\alpha^3 + \beta^3 + \gamma^3 - 3\alpha\beta\gamma$$
$$= (\alpha + \beta + \gamma)(\alpha^2 + \beta^2 + \gamma^2 - \beta\gamma - \gamma\alpha - \alpha\beta).$$

Example. If α, β, γ are the roots of the equation
$$x^3 - 5x^2 + 7x - 1 = 0, \text{ find } \alpha^3 + \beta^3 + \gamma^3.$$

$$\left.\begin{array}{r} \alpha + \beta + \gamma = 5 \\ \beta\gamma + \gamma\alpha + \alpha\beta = 7 \\ \alpha\beta\gamma = 1 \end{array}\right\}$$
$\qquad \alpha^2 + \beta^2 + \gamma^2 = (\alpha + \beta + \gamma)^2 - 2\Sigma\,\alpha\beta$

$\qquad\qquad\qquad = 25 - 14 = 11.$

$$\therefore \ \alpha^3 + \beta^3 + \gamma^3 - 3\alpha\beta\gamma = (\alpha + \beta + \gamma)(\alpha^2 + \beta^2 + \gamma^2 - \beta\gamma - \gamma\alpha - \alpha\beta)$$
$$= 5(11 - 7) = 20.$$
$$\therefore \ \alpha^3 + \beta^3 + \gamma^3 = 23.$$

This method, however, becomes very laborious for higher powers and it is much better to build up the sums of the powers as in the following example.

Example. If α, β, γ are the roots of $x^3 - 5x^2 + 7x - 1 = 0$, find
(i) $\alpha^3 + \beta^3 + \gamma^3$; (ii) $\alpha^4 + \beta^4 + \gamma^4$; (iii) $\alpha^5 + \beta^5 + \gamma^5$.

We know $\Sigma \alpha = 5$ and $\Sigma \dfrac{1}{\alpha} = 7$ (reversing the coefficients).

Since α is a root, $\quad \alpha^3 - 5\alpha^2 + 7\alpha - 1 = 0 \qquad \bullet \qquad \bullet \qquad \bullet \qquad$ (i)

Dividing by α, $\qquad \alpha^2 - 5\alpha + 7 - \dfrac{1}{\alpha} = 0$

Similarly $\qquad\qquad \beta^2 - 5\beta + 7 - \dfrac{1}{\beta} = 0$

and $\qquad\qquad\qquad \gamma^2 - 5\gamma + 7 - \dfrac{1}{\gamma} = 0$

Adding these equations

$$\Sigma \alpha^2 - 5\Sigma \alpha + 21 - \Sigma \frac{1}{\alpha} = 0.$$
$$\therefore \ \Sigma \alpha^2 - 5(5) + 21 - 7 = 0.$$
$$\therefore \ \Sigma \alpha^2 = 11.$$

Adding the three equations similar to equation (1), we get

$$\Sigma \alpha^3 - 5\Sigma \alpha^2 + 7\Sigma \alpha - 3 = 0.$$
$$\therefore \ \Sigma \alpha^3 - 5(11) + 7(5) - 3 = 0.$$
$$\therefore \ \text{(i)} \ \Sigma \alpha^3 = 23.$$

Multiplying equation (i) by α,
$$\alpha^4 - 5\alpha^3 + 7\alpha^2 - \alpha = 0.$$

Adding the three similar equations,
$$\Sigma \alpha^4 - 5\Sigma \alpha^3 + 7\Sigma \alpha^2 - \Sigma \alpha = 0.$$
$$\therefore \ \Sigma \alpha^4 - 5(23) + 7(11) - (5) = 0.$$
$$\therefore \ \text{(ii)} \ \Sigma \alpha^4 = 43.$$

Multiplying equation (i) by α,
$$\alpha^5 - 5\alpha^4 + 7\alpha^3 - \alpha^2 = 0.$$

Adding the equations of this type
$$\Sigma \alpha^5 - 5\Sigma \alpha^4 + 7\Sigma \alpha^3 - \Sigma \alpha^2 = 0.$$
$$\therefore \ \Sigma \alpha^5 - 5(43) + 7(23) - 11 = 0.$$
$$\therefore \ \text{(iii)} \ \Sigma \alpha^5 = 65.$$

We can proceed indefinitely in this way.

Finding numerical roots

The roots of $f(x) = 0$ are the values of x at the points where the graph of $y = f(x)$ crosses the x-axis.

So if $f(x)$ is a continuous function and if $f(a)$ and $f(b)$ are of opposite signs, there must be a root of $f(x) = 0$ between a and b. This is easily seen from consideration of the graph of $f(x)$.

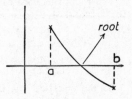

FIG. 1.

If $f(x)$ is a continuous function, between successive roots of $f(x) = 0$, there must be a turning point on the graph and so successive roots of $f(x) = 0$ must be separated by a root of $f'(x) = 0$. This again is easily seen graphically.

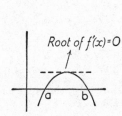

FIG. 2.

The roots of an equation can usually be placed by using a combination of these two results, as in the following examples.

Example 1. Find how many real roots the equation

$$2x^3 - 9x^2 + 12x - 1 = 0 \text{ has.}$$

Let $f(x) = 2x^3 - 9x^2 + 12x - 1$

so $f'(x) = 6x^2 - 18x + 12 = 6(x - 1)(x - 2)$.

$f'(x) = 0$ when $x = 1$ or 2 and so the only roots of $f(x) = 0$ must lie between $-\infty$ and 1, between 1 and 2 and between 2 and ∞.

$f(-\infty)$ is $-$ve (taking the sign of $2x^3$).
$f(1) = 2 - 9 + 12 - 1 = +4$.
$f(2) = 16 - 36 + 24 - 1 = +3$.
$f(\infty)$ is $+$ve (taking the sign of $2x^3$).

As there is only one change of sign, there is only one real root of the equation, which lies between $-\infty$ and 1.

Example 2. Find how many real roots the equation

$$2x^3 - 3x^2 - 12x + 1 = 0 \text{ has.}$$

Let $\qquad f(x) = 2x^3 - 3x^2 - 12x + 1$

so that $\qquad f'(x) = 6x^2 - 6x - 12 = 6(x - 2)(x + 1).$

The roots therefore can only lie in the intervals $-\infty$ to -1, -1 to $+2$ and $+2$ to $+\infty$.

$\qquad f(-\infty)$ is $-$ve (taking the sign of $2x^3$).
$\qquad f(-1) = -2 - 3 + 12 + 1 = +8.$
$\qquad f(2) \quad = 16 - 12 - 24 + 1 = -19.$
$\qquad f(\infty)$ is $+$ve (taking the sign of $2x^3$).

So the equation has three real roots.

The function $\dfrac{ax^2 + bx + c}{Ax^2 + Bx + C}$ when x is real.

Let $\qquad\qquad y = \dfrac{ax^2 + bx + c}{Ax^2 + Bx + C}$

so that $\qquad x^2(Ay - a) + x(By - b) + (Cy - c) = 0.$

If x is real, then "$b^2 > 4ac$" and so

$$(By - b)^2 > 4(Ay - a)(Cy - c)$$

or $\quad y^2(B^2 - 4AC) + 2y(2Ac + 2aC - Bb) + (b^2 - 4ac) > 0.$

Since this has to be positive for all values of y, the equation will give some restriction to the possible values of y.

Example. Consider the possible values of $\dfrac{x^2 + 2x + 3}{x^2 + 3x + 2}.$

Let $\qquad\qquad y = \dfrac{x^2 + 2x + 3}{x^2 + 3x + 2}$

then $\qquad x^2(y - 1) + x(3y - 2) + (2y - 3) = 0.$

x must be real, so

$$(3y - 2)^2 > 4(y - 1)(2y - 3)$$

or $\qquad 9y^2 - 12y + 4 > 8y^2 - 20y + 12$

or $\qquad\qquad y^2 + 8y - 8 > 0.$

Suppose α and β are the roots of $y^2 + 8y - 8 = 0.$

Then $\qquad\qquad y^2 + 8y - 8 = (y - \alpha)(y - \beta)$

$\qquad\qquad \therefore (y - \alpha)(y - \beta) > 0.$

This means that y cannot lie between α and β, i.e. between

$$\frac{-8 \pm \sqrt{64 + 32}}{2},$$

or between $-4 \pm 2\sqrt{6}.$

EXERCISES VIII

1. Find the condition that $x^3 + 3ax^2 + 3bx + 1 = 0$ should have a repeated root.

2. If α, β, γ are the roots of $x^3 - 3x + 1 = 0$, find $\Sigma \alpha^2$ and $\Sigma \alpha^3$.

3. If α, β, γ are the roots of $x^3 - 3x + 1 = 0$, find the equation whose roots are α^2, β^2, γ^2.

4. If α, β, γ are the roots of $x^3 + x^2 + 1 = 0$, find the equation whose roots are $\beta + \gamma$, $\alpha + \gamma$, $\alpha + \beta$.

5. How many real roots has the equation $x^3 - 3x + 1 = 0$.

6. If α, β, γ are the roots of $x^3 + 4x^2 - 1 = 0$, find $\Sigma \alpha^4$.

7. Find the values between which $\dfrac{x^2 + 1}{x^2 - x}$ cannot lie.

8. For what values of a can $\dfrac{x^2 - a}{x - 1}$ take any value ?

9. If α, β, γ are the roots of $x^3 + ax + b = 0$, find the equation whose roots are $(\alpha + 1)$, $(\beta + 1)$ and $(\gamma + 1)$.

10. If α, β, γ are the roots of $x^3 + ax + b = 0$, find the equation whose roots are $-\alpha$, $-\beta$, $-\gamma$.

REVISION PAPER I

1. Find in how many ways a jury of 12 may be chosen from 8 men and 9 women. Show that the number of juries on which women are in the majority is rather more than 3/7 of the total. (L)

2. Write down the first four terms in the expansion of $(1 + x)^8$ in ascending powers of x.

Evaluate $(1 \cdot 001)^8 - (0 \cdot 999)^8$ to 8 significant figures. (C)

3. Find the sum of the first n terms of the series
$$1.3.5 + 3.5.7 + 5.7.9 + \ldots.$$

Prove by induction that the sum of the first n terms of the series
$$\frac{1}{2} + \frac{1.3}{2.4} + \frac{1.3.5}{2.4.6} + \frac{1.3.5.7}{2.4.6.8} + \ldots.$$
is
$$\frac{1.3.5\ldots(2n + 1)}{2.4\ldots(2n)} - 1. \qquad (O \ \& \ C)$$

4. Express as the sum of partial fractions :

(i) $\dfrac{x}{(x - 1)(x - 2)}$, (ii) $\dfrac{x^2}{(x - 1)^2(x - 2)}$, (iii) $\dfrac{x^3}{(x - 1)^3}$. $(O \ \& \ C)$

5. (a) Determine the values between which k must lie in order that the equation in x, $x^2 + 5x - 1 - k(x^2 + 1) = 0$ may have real roots. Find also the values of k for which one root is twice the other.

(b) Find the value of a in order that the coefficient of x in the expansion of $e^{6x-x^2}(1 + ax)^{12}$ may be zero. Find also the coefficient of x^2 when a has this value. (NU)

6. Determine for what ranges of values of x

(i) $x^2 - 4x + 3 > 0$, (ii) $\dfrac{2x^2 - 4x + 5}{x^2 + 2} > 1$,

(iii) $\dfrac{x^2 - 4x + 3}{x - 2} > 0$. (L)

7. (i) If x is sufficiently small for powers of x above the second to be neglected, prove that $\dfrac{1}{1 + e^x} = \frac{1}{4}(2 - x)$.

(ii) Write down the first 5 terms of the series for $\log_e (1 + \frac{1}{2})$ and $\log_e (1 - \frac{1}{2})$ and deduce that $\log_e \sqrt{3} = \dfrac{1}{2} + \dfrac{1}{3} \dfrac{1}{2^3} + \dfrac{1}{5} \dfrac{1}{2^5} + \dots$. Show further that

$$\log_e 2\sqrt{3} = 1 + \left(\frac{1}{2} + \frac{1}{3}\right)\frac{1}{2^2} + \left(\frac{1}{4} + \frac{1}{5}\right)\frac{1}{2^4} + \left(\frac{1}{6} + \frac{1}{7}\right)\frac{1}{2^6} \dots \quad (NU),$$

8. Assuming that x is sufficiently small, find the values of p and q other than zero, for which

$$(1 + x)^p - \log_e (1 + qx) = 1 + ax^3 + \dots.$$

where the terms omitted contain powers of x higher than the third. Determine the value of the coefficient a. (NU)

9. (i) Show that, if the roots of the equation $x^3 - 5x^2 + qx - 8 = 0$ are in geometric progression, then $q = 10$.

(ii) If α, β, γ are the roots of the equation $x^3 - x^2 + 4x + 7 = 0$, find the equation whose roots are $\beta + \gamma$, $\gamma + \alpha$, $\alpha + \beta$. (C)

10. Express the sum and product of the roots of the equation $x^2 - px + q = 0$ in terms of p and q.

If α, β are the roots of the equation $x^2 + x - 1 = 0$, prove that $\alpha^2 = \beta + 2$, $\beta^2 = \alpha + 2$ and find the quadratic equation whose roots are $\dfrac{\alpha + 1}{\beta + 1}, \dfrac{\beta + 1}{\alpha + 1}$. (L)

REVISION PAPER II

1. Find how many different numbers between 100 and 999 can be formed from the digits 0, 4, 5, 6, 7, 8, no digit being used more than once. Now many of these are odd ? (C)

2. State and prove the expansion of $(1 + x)^n$ in ascending powers of x where n is a positive integer.

Find the term independent of x in the expansion of $\left(x^3 + \dfrac{1}{x}\right)^{4n}$ and show that this is the greatest term in the expansion if

$$\frac{n}{3n + 1} < x^4 < \frac{n + 1}{3n}. \qquad (L)$$

3. Find the sum of the series $1^2 + 2^2 + 3^2 + \ldots + n^2$.

Prove that, if n is even, the sum of the first n terms of the series $1^2 + 2 \cdot 2^2 + 3^2 + 2 \cdot 4^2 + 5^2 + 2 \cdot 6^2 + \ldots$ is $\frac{1}{2}n(n + 1)^2$, and find the sum if n is odd. $\qquad (O\ \&\ C)$

4. If m is a positive integer, show that the sum of the arithmetical series $(2m + 1) + (2m + 3) + (2m + 5) + \ldots + (4m - 1)$ is divisible by 3. If m is also even, show that this sum is divisible by 12. $\quad (NU)$

5. (i) How many numbers greater than one million can be formed using as digits the figures 5, 5, 5, 5, 4, 4, 2 ? How many of these numbers are divisible by 4 ?

(ii) Write down the first four terms in the expansion of $(1 - x)^{-\frac{1}{2}}$. By putting $x = \frac{1}{50}$ find the value of $\sqrt{2}$ correct to 5 decimal places. $\qquad (NU)$

6. Solve the quadratic equation $(x - 1)^2 = a^2(x + a)$. Find for what values of a this quadratic has a root in common with the equation $(x - a)^2 = x(a - 1)^2$. $\qquad (L)$

7. Prove if x is so small that its cube and higher powers can be neglected $\sqrt{\dfrac{1 + x}{1 - x}} = 1 + x + \dfrac{x^2}{2}$.

By taking $x = \frac{1}{9}$, prove that $\sqrt{5}$ is approximately equal to $\frac{181}{81}$. $\quad (C)$

8. (i) Expand $(x - 2)^3(x + 2)^4$ in descending powers of x.

(ii) By expressing $\dfrac{x}{(1 - x)(1 - 2x)}$ as the difference of two fractions, show that the expansion of this fraction in ascending powers of x is

$$x + 3x^2 + 7x^3 + \ldots + (2^n - 1)x^n + \ldots \qquad (C)$$

9. Solve the equation $12x^3 - 4x^2 - 5x + 2 = 0$ given that it has two equal roots. $\qquad (C)$

10. If $f(x)$ denotes the polynomial $p_0x^n + p_1x^{n-1} + p_2x^{n-2} + \ldots + p_n$ of degree n, prove that the remainder when $f(x)$ is divided by $x - a$ is $f(a)$.

If $Rx + S$ is the remainder when $f(x)$ is divided by $(x - a)(x - b)$, show that $f(x)$ can be expressed in the form $(x - a)(x - b)\ F(x) + Rx + S$ where $F(x)$ is a polynomial of degree $n - 2$.

When $x^6 + Px + Q$ is divided by $(x - 2)(x + 3)$ the remainder is $2x + 1$. Without dividing out, find the values of P and Q. $\quad (O\ \&\ C)$

CALCULUS

ABBREVIATIONS

The following abbreviations have been used throughout this section:

D.C.	for	Differential coefficient.
w.r.t.	for	with respect to.
y_n	for	nth D.C. of y w.r.t. x.
$f'(x)$, $f''(x)$	for	1st, 2nd....D.C.s of $f(x)$ w.r.t. x.

Logs are to base e unless otherwise stated.

DIFFERENTIATION

Differential Coefficient

If two points P and Q are taken on the curve $y = f(x)$ at which the x coordinates are x and $x + h$, the gradient of the chord PQ is

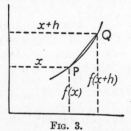

$$\frac{f(x + h) - f(x)}{h}.$$

As $h \to 0$, Q approaches P and the gradient of the chord becomes the gradient of the tangent, commonly called $\frac{dy}{dx}$, $f'(x)$ or the D.C. of y w.r.t. x.

$$\therefore f'(x) = \underset{h \to 0}{\text{Lt}} \frac{f(x + h) - f(x)}{h}.$$

FIG. 3.

Standard Differential Coefficients

Here we assume the normal Algebraic Series and also

$$\underset{x \to 0}{\text{Lt}} \frac{\sin x}{x} = 1.$$

(*N.B.*—x must be in *radians* for this to hold.)

k (constant) $\quad \dfrac{d}{dx}(k) = \underset{h \to 0}{\text{Lt}} \dfrac{k - k}{h} = 0.$

$x^2 \quad\quad\quad \dfrac{d}{dx}(x^2) = \underset{h \to 0}{\text{Lt}} \dfrac{(x + h)^2 - x^2}{h} = \underset{h \to 0}{\text{Lt}} \dfrac{2hx + h^2}{h} = 2x.$

$x^n \quad\quad\quad \dfrac{d}{dx}(x^n) = \underset{h \to 0}{\text{Lt}} \dfrac{(x + h)^n - x^n}{h}$

$$= \underset{h \to 0}{\text{Lt}} \frac{(x^n + nhx^{n-1} + \ldots) - x^n}{h} = nx^{n-1}.$$

36

$\sin x$ $\qquad \dfrac{d}{dx}(\sin x) = \underset{h \to 0}{\text{Lt}} \dfrac{\sin (x + h) - \sin x}{h}$

$$= \underset{h \to 0}{\text{Lt}} \dfrac{2 \cos \left(x + \dfrac{h}{2}\right) \sin \dfrac{h}{2}}{h} = \cos x.$$

$\cos x$ $\qquad \dfrac{d}{dx}(\cos x) = \underset{h \to 0}{\text{Lt}} \dfrac{\cos (x + h) - \cos x}{h}$

$$= \underset{h \to 0}{\text{Lt}} - \dfrac{2 \sin \left(x + \dfrac{h}{2}\right) \sin \dfrac{h}{2}}{h} = - \sin x.$$

e^x $\qquad \dfrac{d}{dx}(e^x) = \underset{h \to 0}{\text{Lt}} \dfrac{e^{x+h} - e^x}{h}$

$$= \underset{h \to 0}{\text{Lt}} \dfrac{e^x(e^h - 1)}{h} = \underset{h \to 0}{\text{Lt}} \dfrac{e^x(h + \dots)}{h} = e^x.$$

$\log x$ $\qquad \dfrac{d}{dx}(\log x) = \underset{h \to 0}{\text{Lt}} \dfrac{\log (x + h) - \log x}{h}$

$$= \underset{h \to 0}{\text{Lt}} \dfrac{\log \left(1 + \dfrac{h}{x}\right)}{h} = \underset{h \to 0}{\text{Lt}} \dfrac{\dfrac{h}{x} + \dots}{h} = \dfrac{1}{x}.$$

Double Function

It is most important to be able to differentiate quickly a function of some expression containing x. For example, we are not often lucky enough to be asked to differentiate $\sin x$—it is generally $\sin 4x$ or $\sin (x^2)$, or even some more complicated expression. How do we set about that ?

Conventionally δx, δy will stand for small increments in the values of $x, y \dots$. These increments may of course be negative but the important thing is that, even if very small, they are *finite*. $\dfrac{\delta y}{\delta x}$, the ratio of the two small quantities, will not necessarily be small and this ratio as δx and $\delta y \to 0$ becomes $\dfrac{dy}{dx}$, the D.C.

If z is a function of y where y itself is some other function of x, it is obvious that $\dfrac{\delta z}{\delta x} = \dfrac{\delta z}{\delta y} \cdot \dfrac{\delta y}{\delta x}$ since these quantities being finite can be cancelled as in Arithmetic. If we now let the quantities concerned tend to zero, taking the limit, we get

$$\frac{dz}{dx} = \frac{dz}{dy} \cdot \frac{dy}{dx}$$

and this shows how to differentiate a double function. For example, let us differentiate $\sin(x^2)$.

Let $\qquad\qquad z = \sin y$ where $y = x^2$,

then $\qquad \dfrac{dz}{dx} = \dfrac{dz}{dy} \cdot \dfrac{dy}{dx} = \cos y \cdot 2x = 2x \cos(x^2)$.

Any double function can be differentiated in this way. With a little practice, it can be done automatically by the following reasoning.

The function is the sine of an angle. The D.C. of sine is cosine and the angle remains unaltered for the moment. Mentally eliminate the sine as we have now dealt with that and we have still to deal with x^2. The D.C. of this is $2x$ and by multiplication the result is $2x \cdot \cos(x^2)$.

This principle must be fully grasped and practised until it is automatic.

Product

If $y = u \cdot v$ where u and v are functions of x, suppose a small change δx occurs in x bringing the corresponding values to $u + \delta u$, $v + \delta v$, $y + \delta y$.

Then $\qquad\qquad y + \delta y = (u + \delta u)(v + \delta v)$,

subtracting $\qquad\qquad \delta y = u\,\delta v + v\,\delta u + \delta u \cdot \delta v$

$$\therefore \frac{\delta y}{\delta x} = u\frac{\delta v}{\delta x} + v\frac{\delta u}{\delta x} + \frac{\delta u \cdot \delta v}{\delta x}.$$

As $\delta x \to 0, \qquad \dfrac{dy}{dx} = u\dfrac{dv}{dx} + v\dfrac{du}{dx}.$

Extension to triple product

If $\qquad\qquad y = u \cdot v \cdot w \cdot = u(v \cdot w)$

$$\frac{dy}{dx} = \frac{du}{dx}(v \cdot w) + u\frac{d}{dx}(v \cdot w)$$

$$= vw\frac{du}{dx} + uw\frac{dv}{dx} + uv\frac{dw}{dx}.$$

Quotient

If
$$y = \frac{u}{v} = u\left(\frac{1}{v}\right)$$

$$\frac{dy}{dx} = \frac{du}{dx}\left(\frac{1}{v}\right) + u\left(-\frac{1}{v^2}\cdot\frac{dv}{dx}\right)$$

$$= \frac{v\dfrac{du}{dx} - u\dfrac{dv}{dx}}{v^2}.$$

To help in getting the sign correct, first square your denominator and then put the denominator unaltered in the numerator.

By using the quotient formula, we easily get:

$$\frac{d}{dx}(\tan x) = \frac{d}{dx}\left(\frac{\sin x}{\cos x}\right) = \sec^2 x.$$

$$\frac{d}{dx}(\operatorname{cosec} x) = \frac{d}{dx}\left(\frac{1}{\sin x}\right) = -\operatorname{cosec} x \cot x.$$

$$\frac{d}{dx}(\sec x) = \frac{d}{dx}\left(\frac{1}{\cos x}\right) = \sec x \tan x.$$

$$\frac{d}{dx}(\cot x) = \frac{d}{dx}\left(\frac{1}{\tan x}\right) = -\operatorname{cosec}^2 x.$$

N.B.—The rate of change of y w.r.t. x is equal to the D.C. of y w.r.t. x. If y decreases as x increases that rate of change will be negative and so the D.C. will be negative. *As the co-ratios are those ratios which decrease as x increases, their D.C.s will be negative.*

Variable Index

To find the D.C. of an expression in which the index is variable *take logs.*

Example 1. Let $y = a^x$,

then $\log y = x \log a$,

differentiating w.r.t. x, $\dfrac{1}{y}\dfrac{dy}{dx} = \log a$.

$$\therefore \frac{d}{dx}(a^x) = y \log a = a^x \log a.$$

Example 2. Let $y = x^x$,

then $\log y = x \log x$,

differentiating, w.r.t. x, $\dfrac{1}{y}\dfrac{dy}{dx} = \log x + 1$.

$$\therefore \frac{d}{dx}(x^x) = (\log x + 1)y = x^x(\log x + 1).$$

This device is also useful for differentiating a continued product.

Example. Let $y = (x - 2)^{\frac{1}{3}}(x - 3)^{\frac{1}{2}}(2x - 1)^{\frac{3}{2}}$,

then $\qquad \log y = \frac{1}{3}\log(x - 2) + \frac{1}{2}\log(x - 3) + \frac{3}{2}\log(2x - 1)$,

Differentiating w.r.t. x,

$$\frac{1}{y}\frac{dy}{dx} = \frac{1}{3(x - 2)} + \frac{1}{2(x - 3)} + \frac{3 \cdot 2}{2(2x - 1)}.$$

$$\therefore \frac{dy}{dx} = \left[\frac{1}{3(x - 2)} + \frac{1}{2(x - 3)} + \frac{3}{(2x - 1)}\right](x - 2)^{\frac{1}{3}}(x - 3)^{\frac{1}{2}}(2x - 1)^{\frac{3}{2}}.$$

Log to base a

Let $\qquad\qquad y = \log_a x = \dfrac{\log x}{\log a}$,

then $\qquad\qquad \dfrac{dy}{dx} = \dfrac{1}{x\log a}$.

Inverse Ratios

Let $\qquad\qquad y = \tan^{-1} x$,

then $\qquad\qquad \tan y = x$,

$$\sec^2 y\frac{dy}{dx} = 1,$$

and so $\qquad \dfrac{dy}{dx} = \dfrac{1}{\sec^2 y} = \dfrac{1}{1 + \tan^2 y} = \dfrac{1}{1 + x^2}$.

Let $\qquad\qquad y = \sin^{-1} x$,

then $\qquad\qquad \sin y = x$,

$$\cos y \cdot \frac{dy}{dx} = 1,$$

and so $\qquad \dfrac{dy}{dx} = \dfrac{1}{\cos y} = \dfrac{1}{\sqrt{1 - \sin^2 y}} = \dfrac{1}{\sqrt{1 - x^2}}$.

We are now in a position to make a table of important functions with their D.C.s. *This must be learnt before progress can possibly be made.*

y	$\dfrac{dy}{dx}$
x^n	nx^{n-1}
$\sin x$	$\cos x$
$\cos x$	$-\sin x$
$\tan x$	$\sec^2 x$
$\operatorname{cosec} x$	$-\operatorname{cosec} x.\cot x$
$\sec x$	$\sec x.\tan x$
$\cot x$	$-\operatorname{cosec}^2 x$
e^x	e^x
$\log x$	$1/x$
a^x	$a^x.\log a$
$\log_a x$	$1/x.\log a$
uv	$u\dfrac{dv}{dx} + v\dfrac{du}{dx}$
u/v	$\left(v\dfrac{du}{dx} - u\dfrac{dv}{dx}\right)/v^2$
$\sin^{-1} x$	$\dfrac{1}{\sqrt{1-x^2}}$
$\tan^{-1} x$	$\dfrac{1}{1+x^2}$

EXERCISES IX

Differentiate :

1. $\sqrt{1+x}$;

2. $\sqrt{\sin x}$;

3. $(3x+1)^4$;

4. $\dfrac{1}{(2x+1)^2}$;

5. $\sqrt{x^2+x+1}$;

6. $\dfrac{x}{x+1}$;

7. $\sin 2x$;

8. $\sin^3 2x$;

9. $\cos(ax+b)$;

10. $\cos^2(ax+b)$;

11. $\sqrt{\sin^{-1} x}$;

12. $\dfrac{1}{\tan^{-1} x}$;

13. e^{ax^2} ;

14. $\log(1+x^3)$;

15. $\log \operatorname{cosec} x$;

16. $x \cot x$;

17. $x^2 \tan^{-1} x$;

18. $\sqrt{\dfrac{x+1}{x-1}}$;

19. $\log \dfrac{x}{x+1}$;

20. $\sec(ax+b)$;

21. $x\, e^x \sin x$;

22. $\cot x\, e^{-x}$;

23. e^{3x^2+4} ;

24. e^{x^2+x+1}

25. $\dfrac{x}{\cos x}$;   **26.** $\dfrac{e^x}{x}$;   **27.** $\sqrt{x^2 + 1}$;

28. $\dfrac{(x - 1)(2x - 1)}{x - 2}$; **29.** $(ax^2 + bx + c)^3$; **30.** $a^{\sin x}$.

MAXIMUM, MINIMUM AND POINT OF INFLEXION

At a maximum, the value of y is larger than at points immediately on either side of it.

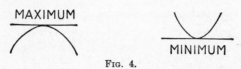

FIG. 4.

At a minimum, the value of y is smaller than at points immediately on either side of it.

N.B.—Maxima and minima are not necessarily the greatest or least values in a range.

At either of these points, it is apparent that $\dfrac{dy}{dx} = 0$.

At a maximum, the value of $\dfrac{dy}{dx}$ is first positive, then zero and finally negative. $\dfrac{dy}{dx}$ is therefore a decreasing function and its D.C. $\left(\text{called } \dfrac{d^2y}{dx^2}\right)$ must be negative.

At a minimum, the value of $\dfrac{dy}{dx}$ is first negative, then zero and finally positive ; $\dfrac{d^2y}{dx^2}$ is therefore positive.

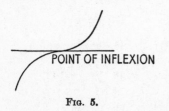

FIG. 5.

If $\dfrac{d^2y}{dx^2} = 0$, the point may be a maximum, minimum or point of inflexion. To discover which, the change in the value of $\dfrac{dy}{dx}$ must be considered. If it changes from negative to positive, the point is a minimum ; if from positive to negative, the point is a maximum ; if there is no change in its sign, the point is a point of inflexion.

Example 1. Consider the origin on the curve $y = x^5$.

$$\frac{dy}{dx} = 5x^4.$$

$\frac{dy}{dx}$ is positive for small values of x, whether positive or negative, and is zero at the origin. The point is therefore a *point of inflexion*.

Example 2. Consider the origin on the curve $y = x^6$.

$\frac{dy}{dx}(= 6x^5)$ is negative for small negative values of x, zero at the origin but positive for small positive values of x. The point is therefore a *minimum*.

Example 3. Find the maximum and minimum points on the curve $y = (x - 1)^3(x + 1)^4$, distinguishing between them.

$$\frac{dy}{dx} = 3(x - 1)^2(x + 1)^4 + 4(x - 1)^3(x + 1)^3$$
$$= (x - 1)^2(x + 1)^3[3x + 3 + 4x - 4]$$
$$= (x - 1)^2(x + 1)^3(7x - 1).$$

The points to be considered are $x = 1$, $x = -1$ and $x = 1/7$.

$x = 1$. When x is near 1, $(x - 1)^2$ is positive and so there is no change of sign in $\frac{dy}{dx}$ as x passes through 1. *This point is a point of inflexion.*

$x = -1$. As $(x + 1)^3$ changes sign from negative to positive when x passes through -1, the value of $\frac{dy}{dx}$ changes from positive to negative. The point is therefore a *maximum*.

$x = 1/7$. $(7x - 1)$ changes sign from negative to positive as x passes through 1/7 and $\frac{dy}{dx}$ changes from negative to positive. The point is therefore a *minimum*.

N.B.—For a point of inflexion, $\frac{dy}{dx}$ is not necessarily 0. $\frac{d^2y}{dx^2} = 0$ is a necessary but not sufficient condition.

EXERCISES X

Investigate the maxima, minima and points of inflexion of:
1. $y = x^4$;   2. $y = (x - 1)^3(x + 1)$;   3. $y = (x - 1)^2(x + 1)^2$;
4. $y = \sin x$;   5. $y = x^3(2x - 1)$.

VELOCITY AND ACCELERATION

$$\text{Velocity} = \frac{ds}{dt}.$$

$$\text{Acceleration} = \frac{d^2s}{dt^2} = \frac{dv}{dt} = \frac{dv}{ds} \cdot \frac{ds}{dt} = v\frac{dv}{ds}.$$

If the coordinates x and y are given in terms of time, $\frac{dx}{dt}$ and $\frac{dy}{dt}$ give the components of velocity along the corresponding axes. The resultant velocity is $\sqrt{\left(\frac{dx}{dt}\right)^2 + \left(\frac{dy}{dt}\right)^2}$.

$\frac{d^2x}{dt^2}$ and $\frac{d^2y}{dt^2}$ give the components of acceleration along the axes and the resultant acceleration is $\sqrt{\left(\frac{d^2x}{dt^2}\right)^2 + \left(\frac{d^2y}{dt^2}\right)^2}$.

TANGENT AND NORMAL

We have already seen that $\frac{dy}{dx}$ gives the gradient of the tangent. The equation of the tangent at (x_1, y_1) to any curve is therefore

$$\frac{y - y_1}{x - x_1} = \left(\frac{dy}{dx}\right)_1.$$

(**Important.** $\frac{dy}{dx}$ gives the general formula for the gradient and so we must be careful to find its value at the particular point.)

The corresponding normal is

$$\frac{y - y_1}{x - x_1} = -\frac{1}{\left(\dfrac{dy}{dx}\right)_1}.$$

PARAMETRIC EQUATIONS

If x and y are given parametrically in terms of a variable t, always work with the parameter and do not attempt by elimination to find the Cartesian equation of the curve.

Example. Find the parameter of the point in which the tangent at the point "t" to the curve $x = at^2$, $y = at^3$ meets the curve again.

$$\frac{dx}{dt} = 2at; \quad \frac{dy}{dt} = 3at^2. \quad \therefore \frac{dy}{dx} = \frac{\dfrac{dy}{dt}}{\dfrac{dx}{dt}} = \frac{3at^2}{2at} = \frac{3t}{2}.$$

[HINT. $\dfrac{dt}{dx} = 1 \bigg/ \dfrac{dx}{dt}; \quad \dfrac{dy}{dx} = \dfrac{dy}{dt} \bigg/ \dfrac{dx}{dt};$

but $\dfrac{d^2t}{dx^2} \neq 1 \bigg/ \dfrac{d^2x}{dt^2}; \quad \dfrac{d^2y}{dx^2} \neq \dfrac{d^2y}{dt^2} \bigg/ \dfrac{d^2x}{dt^2}.$]

Equation of tangent is

$$\frac{y - at^3}{x - at^2} = \frac{3t}{2}$$

or $$2y - 3tx + at^3 = 0.$$

Suppose this meets the curve again at the point (aM^2, aM^3). This point automatically satisfies the curve and so the only condition we get is that it must satisfy the line, i.e.

$$2M^3 - 3tM^2 + t^3 = 0.$$

This is a cubic in M giving the parameters of the three points in which the tangent meets the curve. But it meets the curve in two coincident points at "t" as it is the tangent there and so $(M - t)^2$ must be a factor.

$$\therefore (M^2 - 2Mt + t^2)(2M + t) = 0.$$

So the other value of M is $-\frac{1}{2}t$.

EXERCISES XI

1. If $s = 3t^3 + 2t$, find the acceleration when $t = 2$.

2. If a moving point has coordinates $(e^t \cos t, e^t \sin t)$ after t seconds, find its velocity and acceleration at that time.

3. If a moving point has coordinates $(\cos t, t \sin t)$ at time t, find its velocity and acceleration at that time.

4. Find the equation of the tangent to the curve $y^2 = 2x(x + 1)$ at the point $(1, 2)$.

5. Find the equation of the normal to the curve $y = x^3 + x^2 - x$ at the point $(1, 1)$.

6. Find the equation of the tangent at the point θ to the curve given by $x = a(\theta - \sin \theta)$, $y = a(1 + \cos \theta)$.

7. Find the parameter of the point in which the normal at t to the curve $x = at^2$, $y = 2at$ meets the curve again.

8. Find the equation of the normal at the point t to the curve $x = a \sin^3 t$, $y = a \cos^3 t$.

9. Find the parameter of the point in which the tangent at t to the curve $x = at$, $y = at^3$ meets the curve again.

10. Find the equation of the tangent at the point θ to the curve $x = a \cos \theta$, $y = b \sin \theta$.

DIFFERENTIATION n TIMES

It is sometimes necessary to find the nth D.C. of a function. In the easiest cases, this may be done by finding a general rule, as in the following examples.

$\dfrac{1}{x-a}$ If $y = \dfrac{1}{x-a}$,

$$y_1 = -\frac{1}{(x-a)^2}, \quad y_2 = \frac{(-1)(-2)}{(x-a)^3}$$

and generally, $y_n = \dfrac{(-1)^n n!}{(x-a)^{n+1}}$.

$\log(3x-1)$ $y_1 = \dfrac{3}{3x-1}$;

$$y_2 = \frac{(3)^2(-1)}{(3x-1)^2}$$

and generally, $y_n = \dfrac{(3)^n(-1)^{n-1}(n-1)!}{(3x-1)^n}$.

$\dfrac{1}{x^2-4x+3}$ $\dfrac{1}{(x^2-4x+3)} = \dfrac{1}{(x-1)(x-3)}$

$$= \tfrac{1}{2}\left(\frac{1}{x-3} - \frac{1}{x-1}\right)$$

and now proceed as in the first example.

N.B.—Use partial fractions whenever possible.

$\sin(ax+b)$ $y_1 = a \cos(ax+b)$

$$= a \sin\left(\frac{\pi}{2} + ax + b\right).$$

So differentiation adds $\dfrac{\pi}{2}$ to the angle and introduces the multiplier a.

$$\therefore \ y_n = a^n \sin\left(\frac{n\pi}{2} + ax + b\right).$$

cos $(ax + b)$ Similarly
$$y_n = a^n \cos\left(\frac{n\pi}{2} + ax + b\right).$$

$e^{ax} \sin bx$
$$y_1 = ae^{ax} \sin bx + be^{ax} \cos bx$$
$$= e^{ax}(a \sin bx + b \cos bx)$$
$$= e^{ax}\sqrt{a^2 + b^2}\sin(bx + \alpha),$$

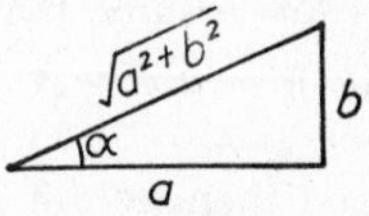

FIG. 6.

using the Auxiliary Angle.

So differentiation adds α to the angle and introduces a multiplier $\sqrt{a^2 + b^2}$.

$$\therefore\ y_n = e^{ax}(a^2 + b^2)^{n/2}\sin(bx + n\alpha)$$

where $\tan \alpha = \dfrac{b}{a}$.

It is worth noting here that if we put $n = -1$, *we shall get the integral of* $e^{ax} \sin bx$.

$$\therefore \int e^{ax}\sin bx\,dx = \frac{e^{ax}}{\sqrt{a^2 + b^2}}(\sin\overline{bx - \alpha})$$
$$= \frac{e^{ax}}{\sqrt{a^2 + b^2}}(\sin bx\cos\alpha - \cos bx\sin\alpha)$$
$$= \frac{e^{ax}}{\sqrt{a^2 + b^2}}\left(\sin bx\,.\,\frac{a}{\sqrt{a^2 + b^2}} - \cos bx\,.\,\frac{b}{\sqrt{a^2 + b^2}}\right)$$
$$= \frac{e^{ax}(a\sin bx - b\cos bx)}{(a^2 + b^2)}.$$

LEIBNITZ' THEOREM

There is one theorem concerned with differentiation n times and this tells us how to differentiate a product n times provided we can so differentiate each factor of the product.

If $y = u\,.\,v$ where u and v are functions of x,
$$y_1 = u_1v + uv_1$$
$$y_2 = (u_2v + u_1v_1) + (u_1v_1 + uv_2)$$
$$= u_2v + 2u_1v_1 + uv_2$$
$$y_3 = (u_3v + u_2v_1) + 2(u_2v_1 + u_1v_2) + (u_1v_2 + uv_3)$$
$$= u_3v + 3u_2v_1 + 3u_1v_2 + uv_3,$$

and we soon suspect that the coefficients are those of the Binomial Theorem. This leads us to Leibnitz' Theorem which we prove by Induction.

$$(uv)_n = u_n v + {}_nC_1 u_{n-1} v_1 + {}_nC_2 u_{n-2} v_2 + \ldots.$$
$$+ {}_nC_r u_{n-r} v_r + {}_nC_{r+1} u_{n-r-1} v_{r+1} + \ldots. + uv_n.$$

We assume that this is true for one value of n—say k, so that
$$(uv)_k = u_k v + {}_kC_1 u_{k-1} v_1 + \ldots.$$
$$+ {}_kC_r u_{k-r} v_r + {}_kC_{r+1} u_{k-r-1} v_{r+1} + \ldots. + uv_k$$
and then we differentiate each side of this equation again w.r.t. x.
$$(uv)_{k+1} = u_{k+1} v + \ldots. + u_{k-r} v_{r+1} ({}_kC_r + {}_kC_{r+1}) + \ldots. + uv_{k+1}.$$
But $\qquad {}_kC_r + {}_kC_{r+1} = {}_{k+1}C_{r+1}$ (see Permutations),

and since this is the same as the original statement with $(k+1)$ replacing k, the theorem must now be true for the value $(k+1)$.

We have already proved the theorem for $n = 1$ and $n = 2$ and so it is generally true.

We can differentiate by this Theorem any product in which one factor is a power of x, as follows :

$x^2 . e^{ax} \qquad y_n = x^2 a^n e^{ax} + n . 2x . a^{n-1} e^{ax} + \dfrac{n(n-1)}{1 . 2} 2 . a^{n-2} e^{ax}$

and all the other terms become zero.

$x^3 . \sin 4x$

$$y_n = x^3 4^n \sin\left(\frac{n\pi}{2} + 4x\right) + n . 3x^2 . 4^{n-1} \sin\left(\overline{\frac{n-1}{2}\pi} + 4x\right)$$
$$+ \frac{n(n-1)}{1 . 2} 6x . 4^{n-2} \sin\left(\overline{\frac{n-2}{2}\pi} + 4x\right)$$
$$+ \frac{n(n-1)(n-2)}{1 . 2 . 3} 6 . 4^{n-3} \sin\left(\overline{\frac{n-3}{2}\pi} + 4x\right)$$

and all the other terms become zero.

EXERCISES XII

Differentiate n times :

1. $\dfrac{1}{(2x - 3)}$;   2. $\dfrac{1}{x^2 - 9}$;   3. $\sin 4x$;

4. $\sin^2 x$;   5. $e^x \cos x$;   6. $y_2 + xy_1$;

7. $(1 - x^2)y_2 - xy_1 + y$;   8. xe^x ;

9. $x^2 \sin x$;   10. $x^2 \cos 2x$.

MACLAURIN'S THEOREM

Leibnitz' Theorem is often used in conjunction with Maclaurin's Theorem which tells us how to expand a function of x as an infinite series in powers of x. We make the fundamental assumption that this can be done provided the function does not tend to infinity as x tends to zero but, this assumption granted, the theorem is not difficult to prove.

Assume $\quad f(x) = A_0 + A_1 x + A_2 \dfrac{x^2}{2!} + A_3 \dfrac{x^3}{3!} + \ldots$

(The factorials need not be introduced here, but, if put in, they lead to simpler coefficients.)

Putting $x = 0$,
$$f(0) = A_0.$$
Differentiating w.r.t. x,
$$f'(x) = A_1 + A_2 x + A_3 \dfrac{x^2}{2!} + \ldots$$

Putting $x = 0$,
$$f'(0) = A_1.$$
Proceeding in this way, we eventually get Maclaurin's Theorem
$$f(x) = f(0) + f'(0)x + f''(0)\dfrac{x^2}{2!} + f'''(0)\dfrac{x^3}{3!} + \ldots$$

N.B.—The values of the differential coefficients when $x = 0$ are the coefficients of x, $\dfrac{x^2}{2!}$ etc. in the expansion.

Examples.

$e^x \qquad y = e^x; \qquad y_1 = e^x; \qquad y_2 = e^x; \qquad y_3 = e^x \ldots$
$\qquad\quad f(0) = 1; \quad f'(0) = 1; \quad f''(0) = 1; \quad f'''(0) = 1 \ldots$
$$\therefore e^x = 1 + x + \frac{x^2}{2!} + \frac{x^3}{3!} + \ldots$$

$\log(1 + x) \qquad y = \log(1 + x); \qquad y_1 = \dfrac{1}{1 + x};$

$$y_2 = -\frac{1}{(1 + x)^2}; \qquad y_3 = \frac{2}{(1 + x)^3} \ldots$$

$\qquad\quad f(0) = 0; \qquad\qquad f'(0) = 1;$
$\qquad\quad f''(0) = -1; \qquad\qquad f'''(0) = 2 \ldots$
$$\therefore \log(1 + x) = x - \frac{x^2}{2} + \frac{x^3}{3} \ldots$$

$\sin x$

$\quad y = \sin x; \quad y_1 = \cos x; \quad y_2 = -\sin x; \quad y_3 = -\cos x \ldots$
$f(0) = 0; \quad f'(0) = 1; \quad f''(0) = 0; \quad f'''(0) = -1 \ldots$
$$\therefore \sin x = x - \frac{x^3}{3!} + \frac{x^5}{5!} \ldots$$

c

cos x

$$y = \cos x; \quad y_1 = -\sin x; \quad y_2 = -\cos x;$$

$$y_3 = +\sin x; \quad y_4 = \cos x \ldots.$$

$$f(0) = 1; \quad f'(0) = 0; \quad f''(0) = -1;$$

$$f'''(0) = 0; \quad f^{IV}(0) = 1 \ldots.$$

$$\cos x = 1 - \frac{x^2}{2!} + \frac{x^4}{4!} - \ldots.$$

To get the general term other than by intuition it is necessary to find the zero value of the nth D.C. and to do this it is important to be able to differentiate n times w.r.t. x an equation of the type

$$x^2 y_2 + x y_1 + y = 0.$$

(Such an equation is called *a differential equation*.)

Here we use Liebnitz to get the following result—

$$\left[x^2 y_{n+2} + n.2x.y_{n+1} + \frac{n(n-1)}{1.2}.2.y_n \right]$$

$$+ [x y_{n+1} + n.1.y_n] + y_n = 0$$

and then we must collect terms.

TAYLOR'S THEOREM

Taylor's Theorem is a more general form of Maclaurin's and states that—

$$f(x + h) = f(x) + h f'(x) + \frac{h^2}{2!} f''(x) + \frac{h^3}{3!} f'''(x) + \ldots.$$

It is especially useful for finding the difference columns in books of tables.

For example, find sin $30°$ $1'$ to 4 places of decimals.

$$\sin (x + h) = \sin x + h \cos x + \frac{h^2}{2!}(-\sin x) + \frac{h^3}{3!}(-\cos x)\ldots.$$

Here $\quad \sin x = \sin 30° = \frac{1}{2}; \quad \cos x = \frac{\sqrt{3}}{2}.$

$h = 1'$, which must be in radians, remember.

$$= \frac{1}{60} \frac{\pi}{180}.$$

$$\therefore \sin (30° \; 1') = \frac{1}{2} + \frac{\pi}{60.180}.\frac{\sqrt{3}}{2} + \frac{\pi^2}{60^2.180^2.2}\left(-\frac{1}{2}\right)\ldots.$$

The third term is roughly $\dfrac{10}{60^2 \times 180^2 \times 4}$ which will not affect the fourth decimal place.

$$\frac{\pi\sqrt{3}}{60.180.2} = \frac{5\cdot4414}{60.180.2} = \frac{0\cdot027207}{6.18} = 0\cdot000252.$$

$$\therefore \sin 30° \ 1' = 0\cdot5003.$$

EXERCISES XIII

Expand as far as the term in x^3 :

1. $\tan x$; **2.** a^x ; **3.** $\tan^{-1} x$;

4. $e^x \cos x$; **5.** $\log (1 + \sin x)$.

INTEGRATION

To integrate a function is to find another function which when differentiated gives the original. Since a constant when differentiated is zero, every integral will contain an arbitrary constant. This, for brevity, will be omitted in the examples given here. We can, from our differentiation table, immediately get a corresponding integration table.

y	$\int y \, . \, dx$
x^n	$x^{n+1}/(n + 1)$ $\quad(n \neq -1)$
$\sin x$	$-\cos x$
$\cos x$	$\sin x$
$1/x$	$\log x$
a^x	$a^x/\log a$
e^x	e^x
$\dfrac{1}{\sqrt{1 - x^2}}$	$\sin^{-1} x$
$\dfrac{1}{1 + x^2}$	$\tan^{-1} x$

HINT. If x is replaced by $(px + q)$ in the left-hand column where p and q are constants, replace x by $(px + q)$ in the right-hand column, but also divide by p.

Example. $\displaystyle\int \sin (3x + 4)dx = -\tfrac{1}{3} \cos (3x + 4)$.

It is also important to note that the integral of a function in which the numerator is the D.C. of the denominator is *log (denominator)*.

$$\int \cot x \, dx = \int \frac{\cos x}{\sin x} dx = \log (\sin x)$$

$$\int \tan x \, dx = - \int \frac{-\sin x}{\cos x} dx = - \log (\cos x) \text{ or } \log (\sec x);$$

in general $\qquad \int \frac{f'(x)}{f(x)} dx = \log f(x).$

Also since $\int \frac{du}{\sqrt{u}} = 2\sqrt{u}$, whenever the numerator is the D.C. of

the expression under a square root in the denominator, the integral is 2 *(denominator)*.

Algebraic Integration

There are four standard formulae on which most of the algebraic integrals we consider are based.

I. $\qquad \int \frac{dx}{a^2 - x^2} = \int \frac{1}{2a}\left(\frac{1}{a-x} + \frac{1}{a+x}\right)dx = \frac{1}{2a} \log \frac{a+x}{a-x}.$

II. $\qquad \int \frac{dx}{a^2 + x^2} = \frac{1}{a^2} \int \frac{dx}{1 + x^2/a^2} = \frac{a}{a^2} \tan^{-1} \frac{x}{a} = \frac{1}{a} \tan^{-1} \frac{x}{a}.$

III. $\quad \int \frac{dx}{\sqrt{a^2 - x^2}} = \frac{1}{a} \int \frac{dx}{\sqrt{1 - x^2/a^2}} = \frac{a}{a} \sin^{-1} \frac{x}{a} = \sin^{-1} \frac{x}{a}.$

IV (TRICKY). $\int \frac{dx}{\sqrt{a^2 + x^2}}.$

Put $\qquad y^2 = a^2 + x^2.$

Then $\qquad y\frac{dy}{dx} = x. \quad \therefore \frac{dy}{x} = \frac{dx}{y} = \frac{dx + dy}{x + y}$

by adding numerators and denominators.

$$\therefore \int \frac{dx}{\sqrt{a^2 + x^2}} = \int \frac{dx}{y} = \int \frac{dx + dy}{x + y}$$
$$= \log (x + y) \quad \text{[Top D.C. of bottom]}$$
$$= \log (x + \sqrt{a^2 + x^2}).$$

Similarly $\qquad \int \frac{dx}{\sqrt{x^2 - a^2}} = \log (x + \sqrt{x^2 - a^2}).$

N.B.—*dx* counts as one unit of length so that I and II are − 1 dimensions and III and IV of zero dimensions. This is an aid in remembering which of the integrals has a constant outside.

We shall now consider the integral of any algebraic expression with a quadratic denominator.

Type A.
$$\int \frac{dx}{ax^2 + 2bx + c} = \frac{1}{a}\int \frac{dx}{x^2 + \frac{2b}{a}x + \frac{c}{a}}$$

$$= \frac{1}{a}\int \frac{dx}{\left(x + \frac{b}{a}\right)^2 + \frac{c}{a} - \frac{b^2}{a^2}}.$$

This reduces to I or II as $\left(\frac{c}{a} - \frac{b^2}{a^2}\right)$ is negative or positive.

Example.
$$\int \frac{dx}{3x^2 + 4x + 2} = \frac{1}{3}\int \frac{dx}{x^2 + \frac{4}{3}x + \frac{2}{3}}$$
$$= \frac{1}{3}\int \frac{dx}{(x + \frac{2}{3})^2 + \frac{2}{9}} = \frac{1}{3}\cdot\frac{3}{\sqrt{2}}\tan^{-1}\frac{x + \frac{2}{3}}{\frac{\sqrt{2}}{3}} = \frac{1}{\sqrt{2}}\tan^{-1}\frac{3x + 2}{\sqrt{2}}.$$

Type B (linear numerator).
$$\int \frac{px + q}{ax^2 + 2bx + c}dx$$
$$= \frac{p}{2a}\int \frac{2ax + 2b}{ax^2 + 2bx + c}dx + \left(q - \frac{pb}{a}\right)\int \frac{dx}{ax^2 + 2bx + c}.$$

HINT. The numerator of the first integral in this line is the D.C. of the denominator and its multiplier is such that the coefficient of x is the same as in the original expression. The second integral balances the constant coefficient.

The first integral is $\log(ax^2 + 2bx + c)$ and the second is of Type A.

Example.
$$\int \frac{2x + 1}{3x^2 + 4x + 2}dx$$
$$= \frac{1}{3}\int \frac{6x + 4}{3x^2 + 4x + 2}dx - \frac{1}{3}\int \frac{dx}{3x^2 + 4x + 2}$$
$$= \tfrac{1}{3}\log(3x^2 + 4x + 2) - \frac{1}{3\sqrt{2}}\tan^{-1}\frac{3x + 2}{\sqrt{2}}.$$

Type C. If the numerator is of equal or higher degree than the denominator, DIVIDE and we shall then reduce the integral to Type B.

Example.
$$\int \frac{6x^2 + 10x + 5}{3x^2 + 4x + 2}dx$$

$$= \int \left(2 + \frac{2x + 1}{3x^2 + 4x + 2}\right)dx$$

$$= 2x + \tfrac{1}{3}\log(3x^2 + 4x + 2) - \frac{1}{3\sqrt{2}}\tan^{-1}\frac{3x + 2}{\sqrt{2}}.$$

N.B.—If the denominator factorizes, it is generally easier to use *Partial Fractions*.

We shall now consider the corresponding cases when the denominator is the square root of a quadratic expression.

Type D.
$$\int \frac{dx}{\sqrt{ax^2 + 2bx + c}}$$

$$= \frac{1}{\sqrt{a}}\int \frac{dx}{\sqrt{x^2 + 2\dfrac{b}{a}x + \dfrac{c}{a}}} \quad (a > 0)$$

$$= \frac{1}{\sqrt{a}}\int \frac{dx}{\sqrt{\left(x + \dfrac{b}{a}\right)^2 + \dfrac{c}{a} - \dfrac{b^2}{a^2}}},$$

which reduces to IV.

If a is negative, it reduces to III.

Example.
$$\int \frac{dx}{\sqrt{2 + 4x - 3x^2}}$$

$$= \frac{1}{\sqrt{3}}\int \frac{dx}{\sqrt{\tfrac{2}{3} + \tfrac{4}{3}x - x^2}} = \frac{1}{\sqrt{3}}\int \frac{dx}{\sqrt{\tfrac{10}{9} - (x - \tfrac{2}{3})^2}}$$

$$= \frac{1}{\sqrt{3}}\sin^{-1}\frac{x - \tfrac{2}{3}}{\sqrt{\tfrac{10}{9}}} = \frac{1}{\sqrt{3}}\sin^{-1}\frac{3x - 2}{\sqrt{10}}.$$

Type E.
$$\int \frac{px + q}{\sqrt{ax^2 + 2bx + c}}dx$$

$$= \frac{p}{2a}\int \frac{2ax + 2b}{\sqrt{ax^2 + 2bx + c}}dx + \left(q - \frac{pb}{a}\right)\int \frac{dx}{\sqrt{ax^2 + 2bx + c}}$$

(cf. Type B)

The first integral is $2\sqrt{ax^2 + 2bx + c}$ $\left(\text{cf. }\int \frac{du}{\sqrt{u}}\right)$ and the second is of Type D.

Example.
$$\int \frac{1 + x}{\sqrt{2 + 4x - 3x^2}} dx$$

$$= -\frac{1}{6} \int \frac{4 - 6x}{\sqrt{2 + 4x - 3x^2}} dx + \frac{5}{3} \int \frac{dx}{\sqrt{2 + 4x - 3x^2}}$$

$$= -\tfrac{1}{3} \sqrt{2 + 4x - 3x^2} + \frac{5}{3\sqrt{3}} \sin^{-1} \frac{3x - 2}{\sqrt{10}}.$$

Integrals of this type with the numerator of higher degree than the first are generally beyond the scope of this book.

Powers of cos and sine

$\int \cos^m \theta . \sin^n \theta . d\theta$ *can readily be solved if either m or n is odd (or both).*

Example 1.
$$\int \cos^3 \theta \sin^4 \theta \, d\theta$$

$$= \int \cos^2 \theta \sin^4 \theta (\cos \theta \, d\theta) \quad \text{[Take one of the odd index with } d\theta.\text{]}$$

$$= \int (1 - \sin^2 \theta) \sin^4 \theta \, d(\sin \theta)$$

$$= \int (\sin^4 \theta - \sin^6 \theta) \, d(\sin \theta) \qquad = \frac{\sin^5 \theta}{5} - \frac{\sin^7 \theta}{7}.$$

Example 2.
$$\int \sin^3 \theta . d\theta$$

$$= \int \sin^2 \theta \, (\sin \theta . d\theta) = \int (1 - \cos^2 \theta) d(-\cos \theta) = -\cos \theta + \frac{\cos^3 \theta}{3}.$$

If m and n are both even, the integrand must be expressed in multiple angles.

Example.
$$\int \cos^2 \theta \sin^4 \theta \, d\theta.$$

$$\cos^2 \theta \sin^4 \theta = (\cos^2 \theta \sin^2 \theta) \sin^2 \theta = \frac{\sin^2 2\theta}{4}\left(\frac{1 - \cos 2\theta}{2}\right)$$

$$= \frac{1 - \cos 4\theta}{8} . \frac{1 - \cos 2\theta}{2}$$

$$= \tfrac{1}{16}(1 - \cos 2\theta - \cos 4\theta + \cos 2\theta . \cos 4\theta)$$

$$= \tfrac{1}{16}\left(1 - \cos 2\theta - \cos 4\theta + \frac{\cos 2\theta + \cos 6\theta}{2}\right)$$

$$= \tfrac{1}{32}(2 - \cos 2\theta - 2 \cos 4\theta + \cos 6\theta)$$

$$\therefore \int \cos^2 \theta \sin^4 \theta \, d\theta = \tfrac{1}{32}\left(2\theta - \frac{\sin 2\theta}{2} - \frac{2 \sin 4\theta}{4} + \frac{\sin 6\theta}{6}\right).$$

Useful Substitutions

If $\sqrt{a^2 - x^2}$ occurs, try $x = a.\sin\theta$.

Example.

$$\int \frac{dx}{(a^2 - x^2)^{\frac{3}{2}}}$$

Put $x = a\sin\theta$

so that $dx = a\cos\theta\, d\theta$

and $a^2 - x^2 = a^2\cos^2\theta.$

$$= \int \frac{a\cos\theta\, d\theta}{a^3\cos^3\theta}$$

$$= \frac{1}{a^2}\int \sec^2\theta\, d\theta = \frac{1}{a^2}\tan\theta$$

$$= \frac{1}{a^2}\cdot\frac{x}{\sqrt{a^2 - x^2}}.$$

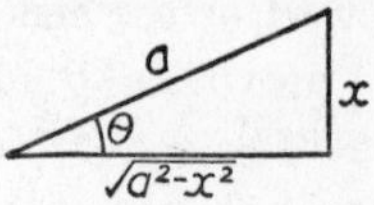

FIG. 7.

If $\sqrt{a^2 + x^2}$ occurs, try $x = a.\tan\theta$.

Example.

$$\int \frac{dx}{(a^2 + x^2)^{\frac{3}{2}}}$$

Put $x = a\tan\theta$

so that $dx = a\sec^2\theta\, d\theta$

and $a^2 + x^2 = a^2\sec^2\theta.$

$$= \int \frac{a\sec^2\theta\, d\theta}{a^3\sec^3\theta}$$

$$= \frac{1}{a^2}\int \cos\theta\, d\theta$$

$$= \frac{1}{a^2}\sin\theta$$

$$= \frac{1}{a^2}\cdot\frac{x}{\sqrt{a^2 + x^2}}.$$

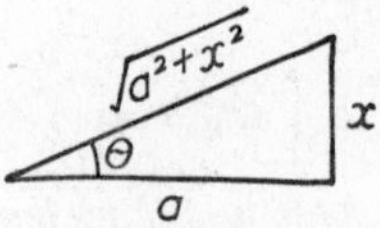

FIG. 8.

In $\displaystyle\int \frac{dx}{x\sqrt{ax^2 + 2bx + c}}$, *put* $x = \dfrac{1}{y}$.

If $x = \dfrac{1}{y}$, $dx = -\dfrac{1}{y^2}.dy$

$$\int \frac{dx}{x\sqrt{ax^2 + 2bx + c}} = -\int \frac{\dfrac{1}{y^2}.dy}{\dfrac{1}{y}\sqrt{\dfrac{a}{y^2} + \dfrac{2b}{y} + c}} = -\int \frac{dy}{\sqrt{a + 2by + cy^2}}$$

which is of Type D.

If $(a - x)$ and $(x - b)$ occur, try $x = a\cos^2\theta + b\sin^2\theta$.

Example.

$$\int \frac{dx}{(a-x)^{\frac{1}{2}}(x-b)^{\frac{3}{2}}}$$

If $\quad x = a\cos^2\theta + b\sin^2\theta$

$$dx = 2(b-a)\cos\theta\sin\theta\,d\theta$$

$$= \int \frac{2(b-a)\cos\theta\sin\theta\,d\theta}{(a-b)^{\frac{1}{2}}\sin\theta(a-b)^{\frac{3}{2}}\cos^3\theta}$$

$$\left.\begin{array}{l} a-x = (a-b)\sin^2\theta \\ x-b = (a-b)\cos^2\theta \end{array}\right\}$$

$$= -\frac{2}{a-b}\int \sec^2\theta\,d\theta$$

$$\frac{a-x}{x-b} = \tan^2\theta.$$

$$= \frac{2}{b-a}.\tan\theta = \frac{2}{b-a}\sqrt{\frac{a-x}{x-b}}.$$

In trigonometrical integrals, try $t = \tan\dfrac{\theta}{2}$.

Example 1.

$$\int \operatorname{cosec}\theta\,d\theta$$

Put $\quad t = \tan\dfrac{\theta}{2}$

$$= \int \frac{1}{\sin\theta}d\theta$$

$$dt = \tfrac{1}{2}.\sec^2\frac{\theta}{2}d\theta$$

$$= \int \frac{1+t^2}{2t}.\frac{2dt}{1+t^2}$$

$$\therefore d\theta = \frac{2dt}{1+t^2}.$$

$$= \int \frac{1}{t}dt$$

Also $\quad \sin\theta = \dfrac{2t}{1+t^2}$

$$= \log\left(\tan\frac{\theta}{2}\right)$$

$$\cos\theta = \frac{1-t^2}{1+t^2}.$$

$$\log\left(\tan\frac{\theta}{2}\right) = \log\frac{\sin\dfrac{\theta}{2}}{\cos\dfrac{\theta}{2}} = \log\frac{2\sin^2\dfrac{\theta}{2}}{2\sin\dfrac{\theta}{2}.\cos\dfrac{\theta}{2}} = \log\frac{1-\cos\theta}{\sin\theta}$$

$$= \log(\operatorname{cosec}\theta - \cot\theta). \quad \text{(An alternative form.)}$$

Example 2. $\quad \displaystyle\int \sec\theta\,d\theta$ $\qquad$ Use the same substitution.

$$= \int \frac{1}{\cos\theta}d\theta$$

$$= \int \frac{1+t^2}{1-t^2}.\frac{2dt}{1+t^2} = \int \frac{2dt}{1-t^2}$$

$$= \log\frac{1+t}{1-t} = \log\frac{1+\tan\dfrac{\theta}{2}}{1-\tan\dfrac{\theta}{2}} = \log\tan\left(\frac{\pi}{4}+\frac{\theta}{2}\right).$$

The alternative form is $\log(\sec\theta + \tan\theta)$.

We can now complete our integral table, *which must be learnt.*

y	$\int y \, . \, dx$
x^n	$x^{n+1}/n + 1 \quad (n \neq -1)$
$\sin x$	$-\cos x$
$\cos x$	$\sin x$
$\tan x$	$\log \sec x$
$\operatorname{cosec} x$	$\log \tan \dfrac{x}{2}$ or $\log (\operatorname{cosec} x - \cot x)$
$\sec x$	$\log \tan \left(\dfrac{\pi}{4} + \dfrac{x}{2} \right)$ or $\log (\sec x + \tan x)$
$\cot x$	$\log \sin x$
e^x	e^x
$1/x$	$\log x$
$1/(a^2 - x^2)$	$\dfrac{1}{2a} \log \dfrac{a + x}{a - x}$
$1/(a^2 + x^2)$	$\dfrac{1}{a} \tan^{-1} \dfrac{x}{a}$
$1/\sqrt{a^2 - x^2}$	$\sin^{-1} \dfrac{x}{a}$
$1/\sqrt{a^2 + x^2}$	$\log (x + \sqrt{a^2 + x^2})$
a^x	$a^x/\log a$

Integration by Parts

From the product formula

$$\frac{d}{dx}(uv) = u\frac{dv}{dx} + v\frac{du}{dx}.$$

$$\therefore \ u\frac{dv}{dx} = \frac{d}{dx}(uv) - v\frac{du}{dx}.$$

$$\therefore \int u\frac{dv}{dx}dx = uv - \int v\frac{du}{dx}.dx,$$

or, alternatively, $\quad \displaystyle\int u \, dv = uv - \int v \, du.$

This is very useful for integrating products.

First type. Products of powers of x with $\sin x$, $\cos x$ or e^x. Leave the power of x unaltered.

Example.
$$\int x^2 e^x dx$$

$$= \int x^2 d(e^x) = x^2 e^x - \int e^x d(x^2)$$

$$= x^2 e^x - 2 \int x e^x dx$$

$$= x^2 e^x - 2 \int x . d(e^x)$$

$$= x^2 e^x - 2 \left[x e^x - \int e^x d(x) \right] \quad \text{By Parts, again.}$$

$$= x^2 e^x - 2x e^x + 2e^x.$$

Second type. Products of powers of x with $\sin^{-1} x$, $\log x$ or $\tan^{-1} x$. Integrate the power of x.

Example.
$$\int x \tan^{-1} x \, dx$$

$$= \int \tan^{-1} x \, d\left(\frac{x^2}{2}\right)$$

$$= \frac{x^2}{2} \tan^{-1} x - \int \frac{x^2}{2} d(\tan^{-1} x)$$

$$= \frac{x^2}{2} \tan^{-1} x - \frac{1}{2} \int \frac{x^2}{1 + x^2} dx$$

$$= \frac{x^2}{2} \tan^{-1} x - \frac{1}{2} \int \left(1 - \frac{1}{1 + x^2}\right) dx$$

$$= \frac{x^2}{2} \tan^{-1} x - \tfrac{1}{2} x + \tfrac{1}{2} \tan^{-1} x.$$

Third type. $\sin^{-1} x$, $\tan^{-1} x$, $\log x$ alone.

Example.
$$\int \log x \, dx$$

$$= x \log x - \int x \, d(\log x) = x \log x - \int x . \frac{1}{x} \, dx = x \log x - x.$$

Fourth Type. Forming an equation. Examples of this type are $e^{ax} . \sin bx$, $\sec^3 x$, $\sqrt{a^2 + x^2}$.

Example.
$$\int \sec^3 x \, dx$$

$$= \int \sec x \, d(\tan x)$$

$$= \sec x \tan x - \int \tan x \, d(\sec x)$$

$$= \sec x \tan x - \int \tan^2 x . \sec x \, dx$$

$$= \sec x \tan x - \int (\sec^2 x - 1) \sec x \, dx$$

$$= \sec x \tan x - \int \sec^3 x \, dx + \log (\sec x + \tan x).$$

$$\therefore \ 2 \int \sec^3 x . dx = \sec x \tan x + \log (\sec x + \tan x)$$

and $\quad \int \sec^3 x \, dx = \frac{1}{2} \sec x \tan x + \frac{1}{2} \log (\sec x + \tan x).$

DEFINITE INTEGRALS

If the indefinite integral of $f(x)$ is $F(x)$, then
$$\int_a^b f(x)dx = F(b) - F(a),$$
and note that the arbitrary constant has now disappeared.

INTEGRAL OF $1/x$

There is one common trap for the unwary in definite integrals. Consider
$$\int_2^3 \frac{dx}{x-5} = \left| \log (x-5) \right|_2^3 = \log (-2) - \log (-3).$$
But the log of a negative quantity is meaningless and so our integration has gone astray.

The integral of $1/x$ might be considered as follows—
$$\int \frac{dx}{x} = \int \frac{-dx}{-x} = \log (-x)$$

and so the integral of $\frac{1}{x}$ is $\log x$ or $\log (-x)$ whichever gives a real value.

So our example should have read

$$\int_2^3 \frac{dx}{x-5} = \left| \log(5-x) \right|_2^3 = \log 2 - \log 3$$

$$= \log 2/3.$$

(*N.B.*—If we had continued with our previous answer,

$$\log(-2) - \log(-3) = \log(-2)/(-3) = \log 2/3$$

and we arrive at the correct result.)

EXERCISES XIV

Integrate :

1. $\sin(3-x)$; 2. $\tan 2x$; 3. $\cot \frac{1}{2}x$;

4. e^{1-x} ; 5. $\dfrac{1}{ax+b}$; 6. $(2x+3)\sqrt{x^2+3x+2}$;

7. $\dfrac{\cos x}{(1+\sin x)^2}$; 8. $x\sqrt{a^2-x^2}$; 9. $\sin^3 x$;

10. $\cos^4 x$; 11. $\sin^2 x \cos^3 x$; 12. $\dfrac{1}{\sqrt{16-x^2}}$;

13. $\dfrac{1}{16+x^2}$; 14. $\dfrac{1}{\sqrt{16+9x^2}}$; 15. $\dfrac{1}{x^2+4x+5}$;

16. $\dfrac{1}{\sqrt{x^2+4x+5}}$; 17. $\dfrac{x}{x^2+4x+5}$; 18. $\dfrac{x}{\sqrt{x^2+4x+5}}$;

19. $\dfrac{1}{\sqrt{2x-x^2}}$; 20. $\dfrac{1}{\sqrt{2x+x^2}}$; 21. $\dfrac{x^2}{x-1}$;

22. $\dfrac{2x-5}{(x-2)(x-3)}$; 23. $x^2 \cos x$; 24. $x \tan^{-1} x$;

25. $x(\log x)^2$; 26. $x^3 e^{-x}$; 27. $\dfrac{1}{\sin x + \cos x}$;

28. $\dfrac{1}{5+3\cos x}$; 29. $\dfrac{1}{3+2\sin x}$; 30. $\tan^3 x$.

AREA, VOLUME AND CENTRE OF GRAVITY

Consider the area between the curve $y = f(x)$, the ordinates $x = a$, $x = b$ and the x-axis.

The area of an elemental strip as shown is $y\delta x$.

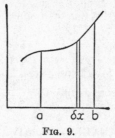

Fig. 9.

Therefore $\delta A = y \cdot \delta x$ and, in the limit, $\dfrac{dA}{dx} = y$.

$$\therefore A(\text{the area}) = \int_a^b y \cdot dx.$$

Volume of Rotation about the x-axis

The volume obtained by revolving the strip is $\pi y^2 \cdot \delta x$.

$$\therefore V = \pi \int_a^b y^2 \cdot dx.$$

Centre of Gravity

If $\bar{x}$, $\bar{y}$ are the coordinates of the Centre of Gravity of the area, the moment of the strip about the y-axis is $y\,\delta x \cdot x$.

$$\therefore A\bar{x} = \int_a^b xy\,dx.$$

(We have, for convenience, considered the mass per unit area to be unity.)

The moment of the strip about the x-axis is $y\,\delta x \cdot \dfrac{y}{2}$ (C.G. half-way up).

$$\therefore A\bar{y} = \frac{1}{2}\int_a^b y^2 \cdot dx.$$

From these formulae, it follows immediately that
$$V/A \cdot \bar{y} = 2\pi \quad \text{or} \quad V = 2\pi A \cdot \bar{y}.$$

This is Guldinus' first Theorem. Expressed in words: "The volume obtained by revolving an area about an axis not cutting the area is equal to the area times the distance moved by the centre of gravity of the area."

EXERCISES XV

1. Evaluate

(a) $\displaystyle\int_0^2 x^2 dx$, (b) $\displaystyle\int_0^4 \sqrt{x}\, dx$, (c) $\displaystyle\int_0^{\pi/2} \cos x\, dx$, (d) $\displaystyle\int_1^e \frac{1}{x} dx$, (e) $\displaystyle\int_2^3 \frac{1}{1-x} dx$.

2. Find the area of the segment cut off by the x-axis from
$$y = (x - 1)(x - 2).$$

3. Find the area bounded by the curve $y = \sin x$ and the x-axis between $x = 0$ and $x = \pi$.

4. Find the area between the curves $y^2 = x$ and $x^2 = 8y$.

5. Find the area bounded by the curve $y^2 = x^3$ and the line $x = 1$.

6. That part of the curve $y = \sin x$ between $x = 0$ and $x = \pi$ is rotated about the axis of x. Find the volume of revolution.

7. That part of the curve $y = \sin x$ between $x = 0$ and $x = \pi$ is rotated about the axis of y. Find the volume generated.

8. That part of the curve $xy = 6$ between $x = 2$ and $x = 3$ is rotated about the x-axis. Find the volume generated.

9. Find the position of the centre of gravity of that part of the curve $y = (x - 1)(x - 2)$ which lies below the x-axis.

10. Find the centre of gravity of that part of the curve $y^2 = 12x$ cut off by the line $x = 3$.

ARCS

The formulae used to find the length of arc (s) are
$$\left(\frac{ds}{dx}\right)^2 = 1 + \left(\frac{dy}{dx}\right)^2 ;$$
$$\left(\frac{ds}{d\theta}\right)^2 = \left(\frac{dx}{d\theta}\right)^2 + \left(\frac{dy}{d\theta}\right)^2$$

if x and y are expressed in terms of a parameter θ.

Hence
$$s = \int \sqrt{1 + \left(\frac{dy}{dx}\right)^2} . dx.$$

To find the centre of gravity of an arc, we consider the moment of a small length of arc δs about each of the axes in turn, and we get

$$s\,\bar{x} = \int x\, ds$$

$$s\,\bar{y} = \int y\, ds.$$

Considering the surface area of the frustum formed by rotating the element about the x-axis, the surface area of revolution

$$(S) = 2\pi \int y \, ds.$$

Therefore $\qquad\qquad S = 2\pi s . \bar{y}.$

This is Guldinus' second Theorem.

" The surface area of revolution of an arc about an axis not cutting the arc is equal to the length of arc times the distance moved by the centre of gravity of the arc."

Now a few examples of the use of the two Theorems of Guldinus.

Example 1. A cone is formed by the revolution of a generator about its axis. Therefore the surface area of the cone equals $\pi r l$ where l is the length of the slant edge.

Example 2. A frustum is formed by the revolution of a generator about its axis. The distance of the centre of gravity of the generator from the axis is $\frac{1}{2}(r_1 + r_2)$ and so the surface area of the frustum is $\pi(r_1 + r_2)l$ where l is the slant edge of the frustum.

Example 3. By rotating a semicircular arc about its bounding diameter we get a sphere. If the distance of the centre of gravity of the arc from the diameter is x, by Guldinus' Theorem

$$\pi r(2\pi x) = 4\pi r^2. \quad \therefore x = \frac{2r}{\pi}.$$

Therefore the distance of the centre of gravity of a semicircular arc from its bounding diameter is $\frac{2r}{\pi}$.

It follows that the coordinates of the centre of gravity of an arc in the form of a quadrant are $\left(\dfrac{2r}{\pi}, \dfrac{2r}{\pi}\right)$.

Example 4. If a semicircle is rotated about its bounding diameter, we get a sphere of volume $\frac{4}{3}\pi r^3$. If x is the distance of the C.G. of the semicircle from the diameter

$$\frac{\pi r^2}{2}(2\pi x) = \frac{4}{3}\pi r^3. \quad \therefore x = \frac{4r}{3\pi}.$$

The distance of the C.G. of a semicircle from its bounding diameter is $\frac{4r}{3\pi}$ and the coordinates of the C.G. of a quadrant are $\left(\dfrac{4r}{3\pi}, \dfrac{4r}{3\pi}\right)$.

POLAR COORDINATES

From the figure, the area of an elemental triangle is $\frac{1}{2}r^2 \, \delta\theta$.

$$A = \frac{1}{2}\int_\theta^{\theta_2} r^2 \, \delta\theta.$$

The moment of this area about the y-axis is $\frac{1}{2}r^2\,\delta\theta \cdot \frac{2}{3}r\cos\theta$ and therefore

$$A\bar{x} = \frac{1}{3}\int_{\theta_1}^{\theta_2} r^3 \cos\theta\,d\theta.$$

Similarly, $$A\bar{y} = \frac{1}{3}\int_{\theta_1}^{\theta_2} r^3 \sin\theta\,d\theta.$$

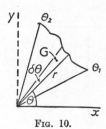

FIG. 10.

By Guldinus, the volume of rotation about the x-axis is $A.2\pi\,\bar{y}$,

whence $$V = \frac{2\pi}{3}\int_{\theta_1}^{\theta_2} r^3 \sin\theta\,.d\theta.$$

The length of arc in Polar Coordinates is

$$\int_{\theta_1}^{\theta_2}\sqrt{r^2 + \left(\frac{dr}{d\theta}\right)^2}.d\theta.$$

EXERCISES XVI

1. Find the length of that part of the curve $x^2 + y^2 = a^2$ in the first quadrant lying between $x = 0$ and $x = \frac{1}{2}a$.

2. Find the length of the arc of $y^2 = 8x^3$ from $x = 0$ to $x = \frac{4}{9}$.

3. Find the area enclosed by $r = a\cos\theta$.

4. Find the area of one loop of $r^2 = a^2 \cos 2\theta$.

5. Find the surface area generated by the parabola $y^2 = 4x$ when that part between $(0, 0)$ and $(1, 2)$ revolves about the x-axis.

MOMENTS OF INERTIA

The Moment of Inertia of a body about an axis is the sum of each element of mass times the square of its distance from the axis.

There are two general theorems:

1. If Ox, Oy, Oz are three mutually perpendicular lines, Ox and Oy being in the plane of a lamina, and if I_x, I_y, I_z are respectively the Moments of Inertia of the lamina about these axes, then

$$I_z = I_x + I_y.$$

If the coordinates of an element of mass m are (x, y) then

$$I_z = \sum m(x^2 + y^2)$$
$$I_y = \sum mx^2$$
$$I_x = \sum my^2.$$
$$\therefore I_z = I_x + I_y.$$

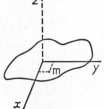

FIG. 11.

2. The Moment of Inertia of a body about an axis not through its C.G. is equal to its Moment of Inertia about a parallel axis through its C.G. $+ M.d^2$, where M is the mass of the body and d is the distance between the parallel axes.

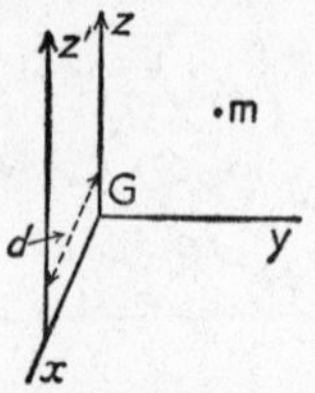

Take the C.G. at the origin and the z-axis and the parallel through $(d, 0, 0)$ to be the two axes of inertia.

Then
$$I_z = \Sigma\, m(x^2 + y^2)$$
$$I_z{}' = \Sigma\, m[(x - d)^2 + y^2]$$
$$= \Sigma\, m(x^2 + y^2) - 2d \Sigma\, mx + d^2 \Sigma\, m$$
$$= I_z + M.d^2$$

Fig. 12.

$(\Sigma\, mx = 0,$ property of C.G.$)$.

M.I. of uniform bar, mass M, length $2a$ about axis through C.G. perpendicular to the bar

If m is the mass per unit length, the M.I. of an element of length δx distant x from the mid point is $m\,\delta x\,.x^2$.

$$\therefore\ I = \int_{-a}^{a} mx^2 dx = \left| \frac{mx^3}{3} \right|_{-a}^{a} = \tfrac{2}{3}ma^3 = \tfrac{1}{3}Ma^2 \quad (M = 2ma).$$

M.I. of circular disc, mass M, radius a about an axis through its centre perpendicular to its plane

Consider an elemental ring of thickness δx and radius x.
M.I. of ring $= 2\pi\, mx.\delta x.x^2$.

$$\therefore\ I = 2\pi m \int_{0}^{a} x^3 dx = 2\pi m.\frac{a^4}{4} = \frac{Ma^2}{2} \quad (M = \pi ma^2).$$

By Theorem 1, $M.I.$ about a diameter $= \dfrac{Ma^2}{4}$.

M.I. of sphere about diameter

Consider an elemental disc perpendicular to the diameter, thickness δx and radius y.

$$\text{M.I. of disc} = m.\pi y^2 dx.\frac{y^2}{2} \quad \text{(by last formula).}$$

$$\therefore\ I = 2\pi m \int_{0}^{a} \frac{y^4}{2} dx = \pi m \int_{0}^{a} (a^2 - x^2)^2 dx \quad \text{since } x^2 + y^2 = a^2$$

$$= \pi m \left| a^4 x - 2a^2.\frac{x^3}{3} + \frac{x^5}{5} \right|_{0}^{a} = \pi m a^5 (1 - \tfrac{2}{3} + \tfrac{1}{5})$$

$$= \tfrac{8}{15}\, \pi m a^5 = \tfrac{2}{5}\, Ma^2 (M = \tfrac{4}{3}\pi ma^3).$$

Solid of revolution about axis

Rotate an elemental strip to form a disc.

$$\text{M.I. of disc} = \pi m y^2 . \delta x . \frac{y^2}{2}.$$

$$\therefore I = \frac{\pi m}{2} \int y^4 dx.$$

Fig. 13.

Most of these formulae can be summed up in one rule, called *Routh's Rule*:

The Moment of Inertia of a symmetrical body about one of its principal axes is equal to

$$M . \frac{\text{sum of squares on other two principal semi-axes}}{3, 4 \text{ or } 5}.$$

The denominator is 3 if the body is rectangular;

,, ,, ,, 4 ,, ,, ,, ,, circular or elliptical;
,, ,, ,, 5 ,, ,, ,, ,, spherical or ellipsoidal.

EXERCISES XVII

Find the moment of inertia of :

1. A uniform rod, mass M, length $2a$, about a perpendicular through one end ;

2. A disc, mass M, radius a, about a tangent ;

3. A sphere, mass M, radius a, about a tangent ;

4. A square, mass M, side $2a$, about one of the sides ;

5. A cone, mass M, radius of base a, about the axis ;

6. That part of the parabola, $y^2 = 4x$, between $x = 0$ and $x = 2$ about the x-axis ;

7. The solid formed by rotating that part of the parabola specified in question 6 round the x-axis about that axis.

REDUCTION FORMULAE

Consider $\int \cos^n \theta \, d\theta.$

$$\int \cos^n \theta \, d\theta = \int \cos^{n-1} \theta \, d(\sin \theta)$$

$$= \cos^{n-1} \theta \sin \theta - (n-1) \int \cos^{n-2} \theta (-\sin \theta) \sin \theta \, d\theta$$

[by parts]

$$= \cos^{n-1}\theta \sin\theta + (n-1)\int \cos^{n-2}\theta(1-\cos^2\theta)\,d\theta$$

$$= \cos^{n-1}\theta \sin\theta + (n-1)\int \cos^{n-2}\theta\,d\theta$$

$$-\,(n-1)\int \cos^n\theta\,d\theta.$$

$$\therefore n\int \cos^n\theta\,d\theta = \cos^{n-1}\theta \sin\theta + (n-1)\int \cos^{n-2}\theta\,d\theta.$$

Such a relation is called a reduction formula and it can be used to find $\int \cos^n\theta\,d\theta$ for any value of n.

Putting $n = 3$,

$$3\int \cos^3\theta\,d\theta = \cos^2\theta \sin\theta + 2\int \cos\theta\,d\theta$$

$$= \cos^2\theta \sin\theta + 2\sin\theta$$

and, by a similar method, we find $\int \cos^5\theta\,d\theta$, $\int \cos^7\theta\,d\theta$, etc.

Also knowing that $\int \cos^0\theta\,d\theta = \theta$, we can find $\int \cos^2\theta\,d\theta$, $\int \cos^4\theta.d\theta$, etc.

These integrals are most important between the limits of 0 and $\dfrac{\pi}{2}$. At both these limits $\cos^{n-1}\theta \sin\theta$ is 0.

$$\therefore n\int_0^{\pi/2} \cos^n\theta.d\theta = (n-1)\int_0^{\pi/2} \cos^{n-2}\theta.d\theta,$$

or if I_n stands for $\displaystyle\int_0^{\pi/2} \cos^n\theta\,d\theta$:

$$n.I_n = (n-1)I_{n-2}.$$

But $\qquad\qquad I_1 = \displaystyle\int_0^{\pi/2} \cos\theta\,d\theta = 1.$

$\therefore$ Using the formula, $I_3 = \frac{2}{3}$; $\quad I_5 = \frac{4}{5}I_3$

$$= \tfrac{4}{5}.\tfrac{2}{3} \text{ etc.}$$

$$\therefore I_n = \frac{(n-1)(n-3)\ldots.2}{n(n-2)\ldots.3} \quad (n \text{ odd}).$$

Also
$$I_0 = \int_0^{\pi/2} \cos^0 \theta . d\theta = \frac{\pi}{2}$$

$$\therefore \text{ Using the formula, } I_2 = \tfrac{1}{2}.\frac{\pi}{2}; \ I_4 = \tfrac{3}{4} I_2$$

$$= \tfrac{3}{4}.\tfrac{1}{2}.\frac{\pi}{2} \text{ etc.}$$

$$\therefore I_n = \frac{(n-1)(n-3)\ldots.3}{n(n-2)\ldots.2}.\frac{\pi}{2} \quad (n \text{ even}).$$

HINT. The factor $\frac{\pi}{2}$ occurs only when n is even.

The same two formulae hold also for $\int_0^{\pi/2} \sin^n \theta \, d\theta$. This is proved by the substitution $\theta = \frac{\pi}{2} - \phi$.

Then
$$d\theta = -\, d\phi$$

and
$$\int_0^{\pi/2} \cos^n \theta \, d\theta = -\int_{\pi/2}^0 \sin^n \phi . d\phi = \int_0^{\pi/2} \sin^n \phi \, d\phi.$$

Using these formulae, $\int_0^{\pi/2} \cos^m \theta \sin^n \theta \, d\theta$ can readily be calculated if either m or n is even.

Example.
$$\int_0^{\pi/2} \cos^2 \theta \sin^4 \theta \, d\theta$$

$$= \int_0^{\pi/2} (1 - \sin^2 \theta) \sin^4 \theta \, d\theta = \int_0^{\pi/2} \sin^4 \theta \, d\theta - \int_0^{\pi/2} \sin^6 \theta \, d\theta$$

$$= \frac{3.1}{4.2}\frac{\pi}{2} - \frac{5.3.1}{6.4.2}.\frac{\pi}{2} = \frac{3\pi}{16}\left(1 - \frac{5}{6}\right) = \frac{\pi}{32}.$$

Since both $\cos \theta$ and $\sin \theta$ take the same numerical values in all four quadrants, the limits in these integrals can be adapted to any multiples of $\frac{\pi}{2}$. It is necessary only to consider the sign of the integrand in the quadrants concerned.

Example 1.
$$\int_0^\pi \cos^9 \theta \, d\theta.$$

Between 0 and $\frac{\pi}{2}$, $\cos^9 \theta$ is +ve.

Between $\dfrac{\pi}{2}$ and π, $\cos^9 \theta$ is $-$ve.

$$\therefore \int_0^\pi \cos^9 \theta \, d\theta = 0.$$

Example 2. $\displaystyle\int_0^{3\pi/2} \cos^2 \theta \sin^4 \theta \, d\theta.$

$\cos^2 \theta \sin^4 \theta$ is positive in each of the three quadrants between 0 and $\dfrac{3\pi}{2}$

$$\therefore \int_0^{3\pi/2} \cos^2 \theta \sin^4 \theta \, d\theta = 3 \int_0^{\pi/2} \cos^2 \theta \sin^4 \theta \, d\theta = \frac{3\pi}{32}.$$

EXERCISES XVIII

Evaluate :

1. $\displaystyle\int_0^{\pi/2} \cos^3 \theta \, d\theta$;

2. $\displaystyle\int_0^{\pi/2} \sin^4 \theta \, d\theta$;

3. $\displaystyle\int_0^{\pi/2} \cos^2 \theta \sin^2 \theta \, d\theta$;

4. $\displaystyle\int_0^\pi \cos^3 \theta \, d\theta$;

5. $\displaystyle\int_0^\pi \sin^4 \theta \, d\theta$;

6. $\displaystyle\int_0^\pi \cos^2 \theta \sin^2 \theta \, d\theta$;

7. $\displaystyle\int_0^{3\pi/2} \cos^6 \theta \, d\theta$;

8. $\displaystyle\int_0^{2\pi} \sin^4 \theta \, d\theta$;

9. $\displaystyle\int_{\pi/2}^\pi \sin^3 \theta \, d\theta$;

10. $\displaystyle\int_{\pi/2}^{3\pi/2} \sin^2 \theta \, d\theta.$

HYPERBOLIC FUNCTIONS

The definitions of the hyperbolic functions, $\cosh x$, $\sinh x$ and $\tanh x$ are :

$$\cosh x = \frac{e^x + e^{-x}}{2} \; ; \quad \sinh x = \frac{e^x - e^{-x}}{2} \; ; \quad \tanh x = \frac{\sinh x}{\cosh x}.$$

The following formulae follow simply :

$$\frac{d}{dx}(\cosh x) = \sinh x \, ;$$

$$\frac{d}{dx}(\sinh x) = \cosh x \, ;$$

$$\cosh^2 x - \sinh^2 x = \left(\frac{e^x + e^{-x}}{2}\right)^2 - \left(\frac{e^x - e^{-x}}{2}\right)^2 = 1.$$

This last formula is useful in providing alternative forms for

$$\int \frac{dx}{\sqrt{x^2 - a^2}} \quad \text{and} \quad \int \frac{dx}{\sqrt{x^2 + a^2}}$$

$\int \dfrac{dx}{\sqrt{x^2 - a^2}}.$

Putting	$x = a \cosh \theta$
so that	$dx = a \sinh \theta . d\theta$
and	$x^2 - a^2 = a^2 \sinh^2 \theta.$

$$\int \frac{dx}{\sqrt{x^2 - a^2}} = \int \frac{a \sinh \theta . d\theta}{a \sinh \theta} = \theta = \cosh^{-1} \frac{x}{a}.$$

$\int \dfrac{dx}{\sqrt{x^2 + a^2}}.$

Putting	$x = a \sinh \theta$
so that	$dx = a \cosh \theta . d\theta$
and	$x^2 + a^2 = a^2 \cosh^2 \theta.$

$$\int \frac{dx}{\sqrt{x^2 + a^2}} = \int \frac{a \cosh \theta . d\theta}{a \cosh \theta} = \theta = \sinh^{-1} \frac{x}{a}.$$

EXERCISES XIX

1. Differentiate $\cosh 2x$, $\sinh^2 x$, $\sqrt{\cosh x}$, $\operatorname{cosech} x$, $\tanh x$.

2. Integrate

$$\frac{1}{\sqrt{x^2 - 4}}, \quad \frac{1}{\sqrt{x^2 + 4}}, \quad \frac{1}{\sqrt{4x^2 - 9}}, \quad \frac{1}{\sqrt{4x^2 + 9}}, \quad \frac{1}{\sqrt{x^2 + 2x + 2}}.$$

DIFFERENTIAL EQUATIONS

In conclusion, we shall consider the three easiest types of differential equations.

Type 1. Variables separable

If a differential equation between x and y can be transposed so that all the x terms (including the dx) are on one side and all the y terms on the other, the solution is straightforward.

Example. Solve $\qquad x\dfrac{dy}{dx} = y^2 + 1.$

Here $\qquad\qquad\qquad \dfrac{dx}{x} = \dfrac{dy}{y^2 + 1}$

$$\therefore \int \frac{dx}{x} = \int \frac{dy}{y^2 + 1}$$

and $\qquad\qquad\qquad \log x = \tan^{-1} y + C.$

Type 2. Integrating factor

The equation $\dfrac{dy}{dx} + Py = Q$, where P and Q are functions of x, can be integrated by multiplying throughout by $e^{\int P dx}$.

Example. $\dfrac{dy}{dx} + \tan x . y = \cos x.$

Multiply throughout by

$$e^{\int \tan x \, dx} = e^{\log \sec x} = \sec x.$$

Then $\sec x . \dfrac{dy}{dx} + \sec x . \tan x . y = 1.$

The left-hand side will now always be a perfect differential.

$$\frac{d}{dx}(y \sec x) = 1$$

$$\therefore \ y \sec x = x + C.$$

Type 3. Equations of second order with constant coefficients

$$\frac{d^2y}{dx^2} + a\frac{dy}{dx} + by = 0$$

where a and b are constants, generally written

$$(D^2 + aD + b)y = 0.$$

Try for a solution

$$y = e^{mx}; \quad \text{then } \frac{dy}{dx} = me^{mx}, \ \ \frac{d^2y}{dx^2} = m^2 e^{mx}$$

and so $m^2 + am + b = 0.$

(a) *If the roots are real*, say m_1 and m_2.

Then $y = e^{m_1 x}$ and $y = e^{m_2 x}$ are both solutions.

The general solution is

$$y = Ae^{m_1 x} + Be^{m_2 x}.$$

Example. $\dfrac{d^2y}{dx^2} - 3\dfrac{dy}{dx} + 2y = 0.$

Here $(m^2 - 3m + 2) = 0. \ \ \therefore \ m = 1$ or $2.$

General solution is $y = Ae^x + Be^{2x}.$

(b) *If the roots are equal*, say to m.

Then $y = (A + Bx)e^{mx}$ is the general solution.

Example. $\dfrac{d^2y}{dx^2} - 4\dfrac{dy}{dx} + 4y = 0.$

Here $(m^2 - 4m + 4) = 0. \ \ \therefore \ m = 2$ (repeated root).

General solution is $y = (A + Bx)e^{2x}$.

(c) *If the roots are imaginary, say* $(p + iq)$ *and* $(p - iq)$.

Then $y = e^{px} (A \cos qx + B \sin qx)$ is the general solution.

Example. $\dfrac{d^2y}{dx^2} - 4\dfrac{dy}{dx} + 7y = 0.$

Here

$$(m^2 - 4m + 7) = 0. \quad \therefore \ m = \frac{4 \pm \sqrt{16 - 28}}{2} = 2 \pm 3i.$$

General solution is

$$y = e^{2x}(A \cos 3x + B \sin 3x).$$

[*N.B.*—This is the equation for damped Simple Harmonic Motion.]

Two important particular cases of this equation with their solutions

1. Simple Harmonic Motion.

If $\dfrac{d^2x}{dt^2} = - n^2x$

then $x = A \sin nt + B \cos nt.$

2. If $\dfrac{d^2x}{dt^2} = + n^2x$

then $x = Ae^{nt} + Be^{-nt}.$

EXERCISES XX

Solve the differential equations :

1. $(x + 1)\dfrac{dy}{dx} = y$;

2. $\dfrac{dy}{dx} = ky$;

3. $\dfrac{dy}{dx} + \dfrac{y}{x} = 1$;

4. $\dfrac{dy}{dx} + y \cot x = 1$;

5. $\dfrac{dy}{dx} + xy = e^{-x^2/2}$;

6. $\dfrac{d^2y}{dx^2} - 5\dfrac{dy}{dx} + 4y = 0$;

7. $\dfrac{d^2y}{dx^2} - 2\dfrac{dy}{dx} + y = 0$;

8. $\dfrac{d^4y}{dx^4} = y$;

9. $\dfrac{d^2y}{dx^2} - 2\dfrac{dy}{dx} + 2y = 0$;

10. $\dfrac{d^3y}{dx^3} = \dfrac{dy}{dx}.$

REVISION PAPER III

1. (a) Find the differential coefficient with respect to x of

$$\cos\left(\frac{\pi}{6} - 3x\right), \quad \log_e (x^3 - 2x^2).$$

(b) If $y = xe^{x - x^2}$, prove that y increases as x increases from $-\frac{1}{2}$ to 1.

(NU)

2. Find the x and y coordinates of the turning points and points of inflexion of the curve $y = \dfrac{x}{x^2 + 1}$.

Sketch the curve and mark the above points on it. (C)

3. Find the equation of the tangent at the point $(2t^3, 3t^2)$ on the curve $4y^3 = 27x^2$.

Prove that the locus of the intersection of perpendicular tangents to the curve is $y = x^2 + 1$. (L)

4. State Leibnitz' theorem for the nth differential coefficient of the product of two functions.

If $y = e^x \log x$, show that

$$x\frac{d^2y}{dx^2} - (2x - 1)\frac{dy}{dx} + (x - 1)y = 0. \qquad (O \& C)$$

Find the equation obtained by differentiating this equation n times.

5. Evaluate the integrals

(i) $\displaystyle\int \frac{(x + 1)^2}{x} dx$,   (ii) $\displaystyle\int \frac{dx}{x^2 + 4x + 7}$,   (iii) $\displaystyle\int_1^2 \log_e 2x \, dx$. (NU)

6. Sketch the curve $y^2 = \dfrac{x}{2 - x}$.

Find the area bounded by the curve, the axis of y and the line $y = 1$.

If the portion of the curve in the first quadrant between $x = 0$ and $x = 1$ performs a complete revolution about the axis of x, prove that the volume generated is $\pi(2 \log_e 2 - 1)$. (NU)

7. Write down Maclaurin's series for the expansion of $f(x)$ in ascending powers of x.

If $f(x) = e^{\sin x}$, show that $f(0) = f'(0) = f''(0) = 1$, and evaluate $f'''(0)$ and $f''''(0)$. Hence obtain the expansion of $f(x)$ in ascending powers of x as far as the term in x^4. (C)

8. (i) A curve passes through the point $(2, 0)$ and its gradient at the point (x, y) is $x^2 - 2x$ for all values of x. Find the equation of the curve, and the maximum and minimum values of y.

(ii) Evaluate the integrals

$$\int_0^{\pi/6} \sin x \cos 3x \, dx \quad \text{and} \quad \int_0^{\pi/3} \sin^3 x \, dx. \qquad (L)$$

9. A chord of a circle of radius r subtends an angle 2α at the centre. The minor segment cut off by this chord is revolved about the chord through an angle 2π. Prove that the volume of the solid so formed is

$$2\pi r^3 (\sin \alpha - \tfrac{1}{3} \sin^3 \alpha - \alpha \cos \alpha). \qquad (L)$$

10. Prove that

$$\int_0^\pi \cos^2 \theta \, d\theta = \tfrac{1}{2}\pi, \qquad \int_0^\pi \cos^4 \theta \, d\theta = \tfrac{3}{8}\pi.$$

Find the area bounded by the curve $r = a(1 + \cos \theta)$ and determine the position of the centre of gravity of the area. $(O \ \& \ C)$

REVISION PAPER IV

1. Find the derivatives with respect to x of the functions

    (i) $6(x^3 + 1) \log (x + 1) - 2x^3 + 3x^2 - 6x$,

    (ii) $(x^2 + 2) \sqrt{1 - x^2} + 3x^3 \sin^{-1} x$. (NU)

2. (i) Differentiate with respect to x,

$$e^{-x} \cos 2x \quad \text{and} \quad \tan^{-1} \frac{1}{\sqrt{x - 1}}.$$

(ii) Express $\dfrac{4x}{4x^2 - 9}$ in partial fractions and hence find its nth

differential coefficient with respect to x. (C)

3. The area of the complete surface of a right pyramid standing on a square base is 18 cm². If the length of a side of the base is x cm, prove that the volume of the pyramid is

$$x \sqrt{9 - x^2} \text{ cm}^3.$$

Prove that the greatest volume of the pyramid is $4\tfrac{1}{2}$ cm³. (C)

4. If the tangent at the point P (at^2, at^3) on the curve $ay^2 = x^3$ meets the curve again at Q, find the coordinates of Q.

If N is the foot of the perpendicular from P to the x-axis, R is the point where the tangent at P cuts the y-axis, and O is the origin prove that OQ and RN are equally inclined to the x-axis. (L)

5. (i) Find the coordinates of the point P on the curve $y = 2x^2 + \dfrac{8}{x}$,

the tangent at which passes through the origin. Obtain also the coordinates of the point Q where the tangent at P meets the curve again.

(ii) Find the maximum value of the function $2 \sin x + \sin 2x$. *(L)*

6. (i) If $y = \sin(m \sin^{-1} x)$, prove that

$$(1 - x^2)\frac{d^2y}{dx^2} - x\frac{dy}{dx} + m^2y = 0.$$

(ii) Find $\int \log_e x \, dx$ and $\int e^x \sin 2x \, dx$.

(iii) Evaluate $\int_0^1 x^3(1 - x^2)^{\frac{1}{2}}dx$. *(L)*

7. A particle moves in a plane so that its coordinates at time t are given by $x = e^t \cos t$, $y = e^t \sin t$. Find the magnitude of the velocity and of the acceleration at time t and prove that the acceleration always acts at right angles to the radius vector. *(O & C)*

8. Prove that the area enclosed between the line $y = 3$ and the portion of the curve $y = 6 \sin x$ for which x lies between 0 and π is $6\sqrt{3} - 2\pi$.

Find the volume generated by a complete revolution of this area about the line $y = 0$. *(C)*

9. (a) Prove that $\int_0^a x \cos x \, dx = a \sin a + \cos a - 1$, and evaluate $\int_0^{\pi/2} x^2 \sin x \, dx$.

(b) Prove that $\int_0^1 \frac{x^2 + 6}{(x^2 + 4)(x^2 + 9)}dx = \frac{\pi}{20}$. *(NU)*

10. If $\cos y = \cos \alpha \cos x$ where x, y and α lie between 0 and $\frac{\pi}{2}$ radians and α is constant, find the values of y, $\frac{dy}{dx}$ and $\frac{d^2y}{dx^2}$ when x is 0.

Taking x to be so small that x^3 and higher powers of x are negligible, use Maclaurin's theorem to show that $y = \alpha + \frac{1}{2}x^2 \cot \alpha$.

Hence calculate y in degrees, correct to 0·001° if $\alpha = 45°$ and $x = 1° \ 48'$. *(O & C)*

ANALYTICAL GEOMETRY

ABBREVIATIONS USED

The point A has coordinates (x_1, y_1).
The point B has coordinates (x_2, y_2).
The point C has coordinates (x_3, y_3).
w.r.t. stands for " with respect to ".

THE STRAIGHT LINE

THE distance between the points A and B is, by Pythagoras,
$$\sqrt{(x_1 - x_2)^2 + (y_1 - y_2)^2}.$$
The gradient of the line AB is $(y_2 - y_1)/(x_2 - x_1)$.

To find the coordinates of the point dividing the join of A and B in the ratio $\lambda : \mu$.

Suppose the coordinates of the point P required are (X, Y). Then by parallels,
$$\frac{x_2 - X}{X - x_1} = \frac{\mu}{\lambda}$$

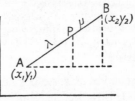

and so $\quad X(\lambda + \mu) = \lambda x_2 + \mu x_1.$

Similarly for the y coordinate and so P is
$$\left[\frac{\lambda x_2 + \mu x_1}{\lambda + \mu}, \quad \frac{\lambda y_2 + \mu y_1}{\lambda + \mu} \right].$$

Fig. 14.

N.B.—If P is not between A and B, the ratio AP/PB is negative and the same formula holds provided that μ is taken to be negative.

As a particular example, putting $\lambda = \mu = 1$, we see that the *mid point* of AB is $[\frac{1}{2}(x_1 + x_2), \frac{1}{2}(y_1 + y_2)]$.

Centre of gravity of the triangle ABC

If A' is the mid point of BC,
$$A' \equiv [\tfrac{1}{2}(x_3 + x_2), \tfrac{1}{2}(y_3 + y_2)].$$
But G divides AA' in the ratio $2/1$. The x coordinate of G therefore is

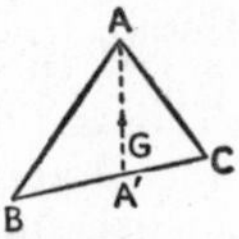

Fig. 15.

$$\frac{2\left(\dfrac{x_3 + x_2}{2}\right) + x_1}{3} = \tfrac{1}{3}(x_1 + x_2 + x_3).$$

The y coordinate follows in a similar manner and so *each coordinate of the centre of gravity of a triangle is one third of the sum of the coordinates of the vertices.*

The area of the triangle ABC

From the figure, we see that

$$ABC = \text{trapezium } APRC + \text{trapezium } CRQB - \text{trapezium } APQB.$$
$$= \tfrac{1}{2}(y_3 + y_1)(x_3 - x_1) + \tfrac{1}{2}(y_2 + y_3)(x_2 - x_3)$$
$$- \tfrac{1}{2}(y_1 + y_2)(x_2 - x_1)$$
$$= \tfrac{1}{2}(x_1y_2 - x_2y_1 + x_2y_3 - x_3y_2 + x_3y_1 - x_1y_3).$$

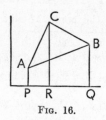

Fig. 16.

N.B.—If you can remember $x_1y_2 - x_2y_1$ the other terms are got by changing the suffixes cyclically, i.e. $1 \rightarrow 2 \rightarrow 3 \rightarrow 1$.

It is often helpful to use the particular case of this formula when C becomes the origin, i.e. $x_3 = y_3 = 0$. The area of this triangle is $\tfrac{1}{2}(x_1y_2 - x_2y_1)$.

Equation of a straight line

If (x, y) is a point on the line joining (x_1, y_1) and (x_2, y_2), the area of the triangle formed by these three points is zero. Therefore

$$x_1y_2 - x_2y_1 + x_2y - xy_2 + xy_1 - x_1y = 0$$

or

$$x_2(y - y_1) - y_2(x - x_1) = yx_1 - xy_1$$
$$= x_1(y - y_1) - y_1(x - x_1).$$

Therefore

$$(x_2 - x_1)(y - y_1) = (y_2 - y_1)(x - x_1)$$

or

$$\frac{y - y_1}{x - x_1} = \frac{y_2 - y_1}{x_2 - x_1}.$$

This is therefore the equation of the straight line joining the points A and B and since it is of the first degree in x and y, it also shows that *any straight line* must be represented by an equation of *the first degree.*

Since $(y_2 - y_1)/(x_2 - x_1)$ is the gradient of the line, its equation may also be written $\dfrac{y - y_1}{x - x_1} = m$, where m is the gradient of the line.

Intercept form

To find the equation of the line which makes intercepts a and b on the axes.

We want the line joining $(a, 0)$ to $(0, b)$. The equation is therefore

$$\frac{y - 0}{x - a} = \frac{b - 0}{0 - a}$$

or
$$- ay = bx - ba$$

or
$$x/a + y/b = 1.$$

Gradient-intercept form

To find the equation of a straight line of gradient m, making an intercept c on the y-axis.

The intercepts are obviously c and $- c/m$ and so the equation is

$$- \frac{x}{c/m} + \frac{y}{c} = 1$$

or
$$y = mx + c.$$

(p, α) form

To find the equation of a straight line such that the perpendicular from the origin is of length p and makes an angle α with the x-axis.

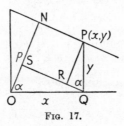

Fig. 17.

If (x, y) are the coordinates of any point on the line, from the figure we see that

$$ON = OS + PR.$$

Therefore
$$p = x \cos \alpha + y \sin \alpha.$$

This, then, is the equation required.

The angle between two lines

To find the angle between two lines of gradients m and t.

From the figure, we see

$$\theta = \beta - \alpha.$$

Therefore $$\tan \theta = \tan (\beta - \alpha)$$
$$= \frac{\tan \beta - \tan \alpha}{1 + \tan \beta \tan \alpha}.$$

But $\tan \beta = m$, $\tan \alpha = t$ and so

$$\tan \theta = \frac{m - t}{1 + mt}$$

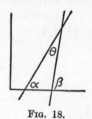

and *the angle between the lines is* $\tan^{-1} \dfrac{m - t}{1 + mt}.$

FIG. 18.

If the lines are parallel, since $\tan 0°$ is zero,

$$m = t.$$

If the lines are perpendicular, since $\tan 90°$ is infinite,

$$mt = -1.$$

The product of the gradients of perpendicular lines is -1.

Example. Write down the equations of the lines through $(1, 2)$ which are parallel and perpendicular to $3x - 4y = 7$.

(i) For the parallel line, keep the x and y terms unaltered. The equation is $3x - 4y = C$ and since the line passes through $(1, 2)$, the value of C is found by substituting $x = 1$, $y = 2$ in the left-hand side. Therefore $C = 3(1) - 4(2) = -5$ and the parallel line is

$$3x - 4y = -5.$$

(ii) For the perpendicular line, interchange the coefficients of x and y and alter the sign between them. The line becomes $4x + 3y = K$ and K is found by substituting $x = 1$, $y = 2$ in the equation. The equation of the perpendicular is then

$$4x + 3y = 10.$$

EXERCISES XXI

Write down the equations of the following lines:

1. The join of $(1, 3)$ and $(-2, 4)$;

2. Through $(1, -1)$ of gradient 2;

3. Making intercepts 2 and 3 on the axes;

4. Such that the perpendicular to it from the origin is of length 3 and makes an angle of $30°$ with the x-axis;

5. Through $(2, -1)$ making $45°$ with the x-axis;

6. The join of $(0, 2)$ and $(-1, 3)$;

7. Through $(1, 2)$ parallel to $3x + 4y = 7$;

8. Through (1, 2) perpendicular to $2x - 5y = 8$;

9. Through (2, -3) parallel to $2x - y = 1$;

10. Through (1, -7) perpendicular to $x + 2y = 5$;

11. Through (x', y') parallel to $lx + my + n = 0$;

12. Through (x', y') perpendicular to $y = mx + c$.

13. Find the area of the triangle formed by the points (0, 0), (2, 4) and (3, 1).

14. Find the area of the triangle formed by the points (1, 1), (2, 2) and (3, 5).

15. If A is (1, 2), B is (3, 1) and $AP/PB = 2/3$, where P is on AB find the coordinates of P.

16. If A is (2, 1), B is $(-4, 3)$ and $AP/PB = -3/2$ (i.e. P is on AB produced), find the coordinates of P.

17. Find the angle between the lines $y = 2x - 3$ and $x + y = 4$.

18. Find the angle between $3x + y = 7$ and $x - y = 0$.

19. Find the length of the perpendicular from the origin to $2x + 3y = 4$.

20. Find the length of the perpendicular from the origin to $3x - 4y = 5$.

The length of the perpendicular

To find the length of the perpendicular from (x', y') to $ax + by + c = 0$.

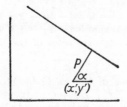

Fig. 19.

Suppose the perpendicular makes α with the x-axis. If the length of the perpendicular is p, then the coordinates of its foot are $x' + p \cos \alpha$, $y' + p \sin \alpha$. This point lies on $ax + by + c = 0$, and therefore

$$a(x' + p \cos \alpha) + b(y' + p \sin \alpha) + c = 0$$

or $$p(a \cos \alpha + b \sin \alpha) = -(ax' + by' + c).$$

D

But since the product of the gradients of perpendicular lines is -1,

$$\tan \alpha(-a/b) = -1$$

and therefore $\qquad \tan \alpha = b/a.$

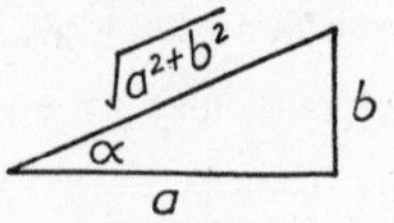

Fig. 20.

So $\qquad a \cos \alpha + b \sin \alpha = a \cdot \dfrac{a}{\sqrt{a^2 + b^2}} + b \cdot \dfrac{b}{\sqrt{a^2 + b^2}}$

$$= \sqrt{a^2 + b^2}.$$

Therefore $\qquad p = -\dfrac{ax' + by' + c}{\sqrt{a^2 + b^2}}.$

The minus sign is of no great significance in itself (since we have a square root in the denominator) but the comparison between the signs of the perpendiculars from two points to the same line is of the utmost importance. If these perpendiculars are of the same sign, the points are on the same side of the line; if of different signs, the points are on opposite sides. The square root of the denominator is assumed to have its positive value throughout and so will not affect the comparison. Hence all we need to do is to substitute the points in the lines themselves.

Example. Are $(1, 2)$ and $(3, 1)$ on the same side or on opposite sides of the line $3x - 4y - 1 = 0$?

If $x = 1$, $y = 2$, the value of $3x - 4y - 1$ is $3 - 8 - 1$, i.e. is $-$ve.

If $x = 3$, $y = 1$, the value of $3x - 4y - 1$ is $9 - 4 - 1$, i.e. is $+$ve.

So the points are on opposite sides of the line.

Angle bisectors

To find the equations of the angle bisectors between the lines $ax + by + c = 0$ and $Ax + By + C = 0$, we use the geometrical property that the perpendiculars from any point on either angle bisector to the two lines are equal.

Therefore $\qquad \dfrac{ax + by + c}{\sqrt{a^2 + b^2}} = \pm \dfrac{Ax + By + C}{\sqrt{A^2 + B^2}}.$

gives the required pair of lines.

It is sometimes necessary to distinguish which of these is the internal bisector and which the external bisector and a method of doing this is illustrated in the following example.

Example. Find the incentre of the triangle formed by the lines
$x + 2y - 10 = 0$, $2x + y - 9 = 0$, $x - 2y - 2 = 0$.

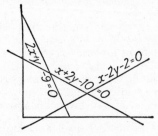

FIG. 21.

It is helpful to draw a diagram showing the relative positions of the lines. If (x, y) is the incentre, the length of the perpendicular from (x, y) to $2x + y - 9 = 0$ is $\dfrac{2x + y - 9}{\sqrt{5}}$.

If we substitute the coordinates of the origin in this, we get a negative quantity, but (x, y) and the origin are on opposite sides of the line and so $\dfrac{2x + y - 9}{\sqrt{5}}$ is positive.

The perpendicular from (x, y) to $x - 2y - 2 = 0$ is of length $\dfrac{x - 2y - 2}{\sqrt{5}}$. The origin substituted in this will give a negative expression and as (x, y) and the origin are on the same side of the line $\dfrac{x - 2y - 2}{\sqrt{5}}$ is negative.

The perpendicular from (x, y) to $x + 2y - 10 = 0$ is $\dfrac{x + 2y - 10}{\sqrt{5}}$. The origin substituted in this expression gives a negative quantity but again (x, y) and the origin are on the same side of the line and therefore $\dfrac{x + 2y - 10}{\sqrt{5}}$ is negative.

Therefore
$$\frac{2x + y - 9}{\sqrt{5}} = -\frac{x - 2y - 2}{\sqrt{5}} = -\frac{x + 2y - 10}{\sqrt{5}}$$

from which $3x - y = 11$ and $3x + 3y = 19$.

So the incentre is $(4\tfrac{1}{3}, 2)$.

Taking the alternative signs in the equations will give the ex-centres.

A line through the intersection of two given lines

If $l = 0$ and $l' = 0$ are the equations of any two straight lines, then $l + \lambda l' = 0$ will represent a line passing through their point of intersection for all values of λ.

Since l and l' are expressions of the first degree so must be $l + \lambda l'$ and therefore $l + \lambda l' = 0$ must be a straight line. The coordinates of the point of intersection of l and l' will make $l = 0$ and also $l' = 0$ and so will also make $(l + \lambda l')$ zero. Therefore $l + \lambda l' = 0$ passes through the point of intersection of l and l'.

This is particularly useful in finding the equation of a line joining the point of intersection of two given lines to the origin.

Example. Find the equation of the line joining the point of intersection of $2x + y - 3 = 0$ and $x + 3y + 8 = 0$ to the origin.

Choose multiples of the lines so that on addition the constant term will vanish. The equation we get is

$$8(2x + y - 3) + 3(x + 3y + 8) = 0.$$

This represents a straight line through the intersection of the two given lines and it certainly passes through the origin.

Therefore $19x + 17y = 0$ is the equation required.

EXERCISES XXII

Write down the lengths of the perpendiculars from the following points to the following lines :

1. $(2, 1)$ to $3x + 4y = 7$.

2. $(3, -1)$ to $12x + 5y = 8$.

3. $(1, 0)$ to $y = mx + c$.

4. (x', y') to $x/a + y/b = 1$.

5. Are $(1, 3)$ and $(2, -1)$ on the same side of $3x - 2y = 7$?

6. Find the equations of the angle bisectors between $3x + 4y = 7$ and $5x + 12y = 13$.

7. Find the equation of the line joining the origin to the intersection of $x + 2y - 2 = 0$ and $3x - 5y + 1 = 0$.

8. Find the coordinates of the incentre of the triangle formed by the axes and the line $3x + 4y = 12$.

9. Find the coordinates of the image of the point $(1, 2)$ in the line $x + y = 4$.

10. A line joining points P and Q on the axes is of constant length $2l$. Find the equation of the locus of the mid point of PQ.

PAIRS OF STRAIGHT LINES

Any two lines through the origin may be written $y = mx$ and $y = tx$ where m and t are their gradients.

So $(y - mx)(y - tx) = 0$, giving either $y - mx = 0$ or $y - tx = 0$, must represent the pair.

The general form of this equation is $ax^2 + 2hxy + by^2 = 0$, so this equation must represent a pair of straight lines, real or imaginary, through the origin.

Writing this as $b\left(\dfrac{y}{x}\right)^2 + 2h\left(\dfrac{y}{x}\right) + a = 0$, since $\dfrac{y}{x}$ is the gradient of a line through the origin, we see that the roots of this equation are the gradients of the lines, m and t.

Therefore
$$m + t = -\frac{2h}{b} \qquad \cdots \qquad \text{(i)}$$

and
$$mt = \frac{a}{b} \qquad \cdots \qquad \text{(ii)}$$

The angle between the lines $ax^2 + 2hxy + by^2 = 0$

Suppose $ax^2 + 2hxy + by^2 = 0$ represents the lines $y = mx$ and $y = tx$.

If the angle between them is θ, then

$$\tan\theta = \frac{m - t}{1 + mt}$$

$$= \frac{\sqrt{(m + t)^2 - 4mt}}{1 + mt}$$

$$= \frac{\sqrt{4h^2/b^2 - 4a/b}}{1 + a/b} \quad \text{using (i) and (ii)}$$

$$= \frac{2\sqrt{h^2 - ab}}{a + b}.$$

N.B.—The lines will be perpendicular if the value of this fraction becomes infinite, i.e. if $a + b = 0$.

To find the equation of the angle bisectors

Supposing that $ax^2 + 2hxy + by^2 = 0$ represents the lines $y = mx$ and $y = tx$, the bisectors are

$$\frac{y - mx}{\sqrt{1 + m^2}} = \pm\frac{y - tx}{\sqrt{1 + t^2}}$$

or $\qquad (1 + t^2)(y - mx)^2 = (1 + m^2)(y - tx)^2$

or $\quad x^2(m^2 - t^2) - 2xy(m + mt^2 - t - tm^2) + y^2(t^2 - m^2) = 0.$

Dividing by $(m - t)$, since m is not equal to t,

$$x^2(m + t) - 2xy(1 - mt) - y^2(m + t) = 0.$$

Substituting for $(m + t)$ and mt,

$$x^2(- 2h/b) - 2xy(1 - a/b) - y^2(- 2h/b) = 0$$

or $$(x^2 - y^2).(- 2h) = 2xy(b - a).$$

Therefore $\dfrac{x^2 - y^2}{xy} = \dfrac{a - b}{h}$ is the equation required.

Notice that this pair of lines is perpendicular since the sum of the coefficients of x^2 and y^2 is zero.

To find the equation of the pair of lines joining the points of intersection of $ax^2 + 2hxy + by^2 + 2gx + 2fy + c = 0$ and $lx + my + n = 0$ to the origin

From the linear equation, express 1 as a linear function of x and y, i.e. $1 = - (lx + my)/n$. Use this to build up every term of the quadratic equation to the second degree and we get,

$$ax^2 + 2hxy + by^2 + (2gx + 2fy)\left(- \frac{lx + my}{n} \right) + c\left(- \frac{lx + my}{n} \right)^2 = 0.$$

Every term here is of the second degree and since any point which satisfies both

$$- (lx + my)/n = 1 \text{ and } ax^2 + 2hxy + by^2 + 2gx + 2fy + c = 0$$

must also satisfy this new equation, it must represent the required pair of lines.

To find the condition that the general equation of the second degree should represent a pair of straight lines

We have so far considered only pairs of straight lines through the origin. The equation of the pair of lines $ax + by + c = 0$ and $lx + my + n = 0$ is obviously

$$(ax + by + c)(lx + my + n) = 0$$

and it is worth noting that

$$a(x - \alpha)^2 + 2h(x - \alpha)(y - \beta) + b(y - \beta)^2 = 0$$

represents a pair of straight lines through the point (α, β) and parallel to the pair $ax^2 + 2hxy + by^2 = 0$. The general equation of the second degree

$$ax^2 + 2hxy + by^2 + 2gx + 2fy + c = 0$$

will represent a pair of straight lines *if it factorizes*.

Expanding the equation as a quadratic in x, we get

$$ax^2 + 2x(hy + g) + (by^2 + 2fy + c) = 0.$$

When we solve for x, we shall get an expression containing a square root. If the equation represents a pair of lines, x must be expressible as one or other of two linear expressions in x and y, so that this square root must be rational.

Therefore $(hy + g)^2 - a(by^2 + 2fy + c)$ must be a perfect square. The condition for this is

$$(hg - af)^2 = (h^2 - ab)(g^2 - ac)$$

which simplified becomes

$$af^2 + bg^2 + ch^2 = 2fgh + abc.$$

EXERCISES XXIII

1. Find the angle between the pair $3x^2 - 4xy - 7y^2 = 0$.

2. Write down the equation of the angle bisectors between the lines $3x^2 - 4xy - 7y^2 = 0$.

3. Find the equation of the pair of lines joining the points of intersection of $3x^2 - y^2 - 2x = 1$ and $x = 3 - y$ to the origin.

4. Find the angle between the lines joining the origin to the points of intersection of $x^2 + y^2 - 2x - 4y + 4 = 0$ and $x + 2y = 4$.

5. Find the value of λ if $3x^2 - 2xy - y^2 - 2x - 4y + \lambda = 0$ represents a line pair.

6. Find the length of the intercept cut from $x + y = 1$ by the line pair $ax^2 + 2hxy + by^2 = 0$.

7. Find the coordinates of the centre of gravity of the triangle formed by $x + y = 1$ and $ax^2 + 2hxy + by^2 = 0$.

8. Find the coordinates of the orthocentre of the triangle in question 7.

THE CIRCLE

If (x, y) is a point on a circle, centre (a, b) radius r, then

$$(x - a)^2 + (y - b)^2 = r^2.$$

This is an equation of the second degree in which the coefficients of x^2 and y^2 are equal and the xy term is missing. The general equation of a circle, then, may be put in the form

$$x^2 + y^2 + 2gx + 2fy + c = 0.$$

This can be rearranged as

$$(x + g)^2 + (y + f)^2 = g^2 + f^2 - c$$

from which we see that the centre is $(-g, -f)$ and the radius $\sqrt{g^2 + f^2 - c}$.

To find the equation of the tangent of gradient m to the circle $x^2 + y^2 = a^2$

Suppose the tangent is $y = mx + c$. The length of the perpendicular from the centre $(0, 0)$ must be a.

$$\therefore \frac{x_0 + c + y_0}{\sqrt{1 + m^2}} = a.$$

The tangent of gradient m is

$$y = mx + a\sqrt{1 + m^2}.$$

(It is easier to use this simple geometrical property of the circle than to use the method used for the other conics.)

To find the tangent at (x', y') to the circle $x^2 + y^2 + 2gx + 2fy + c = 0$

The gradient of the line joining (x', y') to the centre $(-g, -f)$ is $(y' + f)/(x' + g)$. The gradient of the tangent is therefore $-(x' + g)/(y' + f)$ and so its equation is

$$\frac{y - y'}{x - x'} = -\frac{x' + g}{y' + f}.$$

This rearranged is

$$xx' + yy' + gx + fy = x'^2 + y'^2 + gx' + fy'.$$

But since (x', y') lies on the circle,

$$x'^2 + y'^2 + 2gx' + 2fy' + c = 0$$

or

$$x'^2 + y'^2 + gx' + fy' = -gx' - fy' - c.$$

So the equation of the tangent may be written

$$xx' + yy' + g(x + x') + f(y + y') + c = 0.$$

To find the polar of (x', y') w.r.t. $x^2 + y^2 + 2gx + 2fy + c = 0$

Let the points of contact be (x_1, y_1) and (x_2, y_2). The tangent at (x_1, y_1) is

$$xx_1 + yy_1 + g(x + x_1) + f(y + y_1) = c = 0.$$

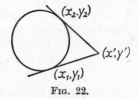

FIG. 22.

This passes through (x', y') and so

$$x'x_1 + y'y_1 + g(x' + x_1) + f(y' + y_1) + c = 0.$$

But this is equally the condition that (x_1, y_1) should lie on the line

$$xx' + yy' + g(x + x') + f(y + y') + c = 0.$$

By symmetry (x_2, y_2) also lies on this line but as the line joining two points is unique, this line must be the polar of (x', y').

To find the condition that $x^2 + y^2 + 2gx + 2fy + c = 0$ and $x^2 + y^2 + 2Gx + 2Fy + C = 0$ should cut orthogonally

If the circles cut at P, then $A\widehat{P}B$ must be a right angle.

FIG. 23.

Therefore $AP^2 + PB^2 = AB^2$,

or AB^2 must equal the sum of the squares of the radii.

Therefore

$$(G - g)^2 + (F - f)^2 = G^2 + F^2 - C + g^2 + f^2 - c$$

or $\quad 2Gg + 2Ff = C + c.$

The length of the tangent from (x', y') to
$\quad x^2 + y^2 + 2gx + 2fy + c = 0$

By Pythagoras,

$$t^2 = (x' + g)^2 + (y' + f)^2 - (g^2 + f^2 - c)$$
$$= x'^2 + y'^2 + 2gx' + 2fy' + c.$$

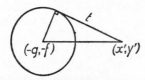

FIG. 24.

N.B.—To find the square of the tangent from a point to a circle, simply substitute the coordinates of the point in the equation of the circle. This only applies however when *the coefficients of x^2 and y^2 are unity*. The length of the tangent from (x', y') to

$$ax^2 + ay^2 + 2gx + 2fy + c = 0$$

is $\quad \sqrt{\dfrac{ax'^2 + ay'^2 + 2gx' + 2fy' + c}{a}}.$

Coaxal circles and radical axis

Let $\quad S = x^2 + y^2 + 2gx + 2fy + c$

and $\quad S' = x^2 + y^2 + 2Gx + 2Fy + C.$

Let (x', y') be a point so that the tangents from it to the two circles $S = 0$ and $S' = 0$ are equal. Then

$$x'^2 + y'^2 + 2gx' + 2fy' + c = x'^2 + y'^2 + 2Gx' + 2Fy' + C$$

and so $S = S'$ gives the locus of such points.

This is a line which is perpendicular to the line of centres and is called the radical axis of the two circles.

What will the circle $S + \lambda S' = 0$ represent?

Let (x', y') be any point on the radical axis of S and S' and let t be the length of the tangent from (x', y') to either of these circles. Let T be the length of the tangent from the same point to the circle $S + \lambda S' = 0$.

(It will represent a circle because the coefficients of x^2 and y^2 are equal and there is no term in xy.)

Then

$$t^2 = x'^2 + y'^2 + 2gx' + 2fy' + c = x'^2 + y'^2 + 2Gx' + 2Fy' + C$$

But

$$T^2 = \frac{(x'^2 + y'^2 + 2gx' + 2fy' + c) + \lambda(x'^2 + y'^2 + 2Gx' + 2Fy' + C)}{1 + \lambda}$$

$$= \frac{t^2 + \lambda t^2}{1 + \lambda}$$

$$= t^2.$$

So all circles of the form $S + \lambda S' = 0$ will have a common radical axis which is also the radical axis of $S = 0$ and $S' = 0$.

Circles of a coaxal system

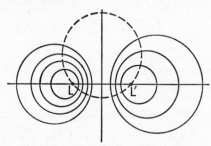

Fig. 25.

The diagram represents a coaxal system of circles.

The circles of the system of zero radius are called the limiting points L and L'. The dotted circle is one of a system of circles orthogonal to the coaxal system. Such circles will all pass through L and L'.

If S and S' do intersect,

$S + \lambda S' = 0$ represents a system of circles all passing through the common points of S and S';

$S - S' = 0$ represents their common chord.

EXERCISES XXIV

1. Find the centre and radius of $x^2 + y^2 - 4x + 2y - 4 = 0$.

2. Find the equation of the tangent at $(-1, -6)$ to
$$x^2 + y^2 + 2x + 6y + 1 = 0.$$

3. Find the polar of the origin with respect to
$$x^2 + y^2 + 2x + 6y + 1 = 0.$$

4. Find the equation of the circle, centre the origin, which cuts $x^2 + y^2 + 2x + 6y + 1 = 0$ orthogonally.

5. Find the length of the tangent from the origin to
$$x^2 + y^2 + 2x + 6y + 1 = 0.$$

6. Find the radical axis of
$$x^2 + y^2 + 2x + 6y + 1 = 0 \text{ and } x^2 + y^2 - 2x - 6y + 1 = 0.$$

7. Find the equation of the circle coaxal with the two circles in question 6 and passing through the point $(1, 1)$.

8. Find the equation of the circle through the points $(0, 1)$, $(1, 2)$ and $(3, 1)$.

9. Find the equations of the circles which touch the x-axis, touch the line $3y = 4x$ and pass through the point $(1, 1)$.

10. Find the locus of points from which tangents to the two circles $x^2 + y^2 + 2x + 6y + 1 = 0$ and $x^2 + y^2 - 2x - 6y - 1 = 0$ are in the ratio $2 : 1$.

THE PARABOLA

A conic is defined by the focus-directrix property, i.e. as the locus of a point which moves so that its distance from a fixed point is in a constant ratio to its distance from a fixed line. The fixed point is called the focus, the fixed line the directrix and the constant ratio the eccentricity.

For the parabola, the eccentricity is 1;
for the ellipse, the eccentricity is less than 1;
for the hyperbola, the eccentricity is greater than 1.

If S is the fixed point and X the foot of the perpendicular from S to the fixed line, the parabola will obviously be symmetrical about SX and there will be one point only on SX on the locus, i.e. the mid point of SX, A. Let $SA = a$ and take AS to be the x-axis and A the origin. If P (x, y) is any point on the locus, $PS^2 = PK^2$ and therefore

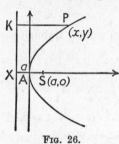

FIG. 26.

$$(x - a)^2 + y^2 = (x + a)^2$$

or $$y^2 = 4ax$$

is the equation of the parabola.

To find the tangent of gradient m

Let $y = mx + c$ be the tangent. It meets the parabola where
$$(mx + c)^2 = 4ax$$

i.e. where $$m^2x^2 + 2x(mc - 2a) + c^2 = 0 \quad . \quad . \quad . \quad (i)$$

For a tangent, the roots of this must be coincident and therefore
$$4(mc - 2a)^2 = 4m^2c^2$$

or $$c = a/m.$$

The tangent of gradient m is $y = mx + \dfrac{a}{m}$

Equation (i) becomes
$$m^2x^2 - 2ax + a^2/m^2 = 0$$
or $$(mx - a/m)^2 = 0$$

and so $x = a/m^2$ and by substitution $y = 2a/m$.

So the point $(a/m^2, 2a/m)$ is a parametric expression for a point on the parabola for all values of m and the gradient of its tangent there is m. By writing $1/m$ for m, it is seen that the point $(am^2, 2am)$ also lies on the parabola and the following table can easily be written down:

Point	Gradient of tangent	Gradient of normal
$(a/m^2, \ 2a/m)$	$+ \, m$	$- \, 1/m$
$(am^2, \ 2am)$	$+ \, 1/m$	$- \, m$
$(am^2, \ - 2am)$	$- \, 1/m$	$+ \, m$

The normal

The normal at $(am^2, 2am)$ for example may be written down from the knowledge that its gradient is $-m$.

Its equation must be of the form $y + mx = C$ and as it passes through the point $(am^2, 2am)$, $C = 2am + am^3$, and so the equation of the normal is

$$y + mx = 2am + am^3.$$

Usually, express your point parametrically in the form $(am^2, 2am)$.

If you are specially interested in the gradient of the tangent, express your point as $(a/m^2, 2a/m)$.

If you are specially interested in the gradient of the normal, express your point as $(am^2, -2am)$.

Equation of chord joining $(am^2, 2am)$ and $(at^2, 2at)$

The equation is

$$\frac{y - 2am}{x - am^2} = \frac{2am - 2at}{am^2 - at^2}$$

$$\left\{ m = \frac{2am - 2at}{am^2 - at^2} \right\}$$

$$= \frac{2}{m + t}.$$

Therefore $(m + t)y - 2am^2 - 2amt = 2x - 2am^2$

or $\qquad\qquad (m + t)y - 2x = 2amt.$

The tangent at (x', y')

Differentiating $y^2 = 4ax$ w.r.t. x, we get

$$2y\frac{dy}{dx} = 4a$$

and therefore $\qquad\qquad \dfrac{dy}{dx} = 2a/y.$

The gradient of the tangent at (x', y') is therefore $2a/y'$ and its equation

$$\frac{y - y'}{x - x'} = \frac{2a}{y'}.$$

or $\qquad\qquad yy' - y'^2 = 2ax - 2ax'$

or $\qquad\qquad\qquad yy' = 2a(x + x')$

since $\qquad\qquad\qquad y'^2 = 4ax'$

The locus of the foot of the perpendicular from the focus to a tangent

$y = mx + a/m$ is any tangent.

The perpendicular to this through $(a, 0)$ is

$$my + x = a.$$

We find the locus by eliminating m between the two equations

$$my - m^2x = a$$

and $$my + x = a.$$

Subtracting $$x(1 + m^2) = 0$$

or $$x = 0, \textit{ the tangent at the vertex.}$$

The locus of the intersection of perpendicular tangents

The tangent of gradient m is

$$y = mx + a/m\,;$$

the tangent of gradient $-1/m$ is

$$y = -(1/m)x - am.$$

The locus is found by eliminating m between

$$my - m^2x = a$$

and $$my + x = -am^2.$$

By subtraction $$x(1 + m^2) = -a(1 + m^2)$$

or $$x = -a, \textit{ the directrix.}$$

The polar of (x', y')

Suppose the points of contact of the tangents are (x_1, y_1) and (x_2, y_2). Then the tangent at (x_1, y_1), $yy_1 = 2a(x + x_1)$ passes through (x', y').

Therefore $$y'y_1 = 2a(x' + x_1).$$

But this is equally the condition that the line $yy' = 2a(x + x')$ should pass through (x_1, y_1). By symmetry, this line also passes through (x_2, y_2). But since there is a unique line joining two points, $yy' = 2a(x + x')$ must be the polar of (x', y').

The feet of the normals from a point to the parabola

Suppose the normal at $(am^2, 2am)$ passes through the given point (h, k). Then (h, k) satisfies the equation

$$y + mx = 2am + am^3.$$

Therefore $$am^3 + m(2a - h) - k = 0.$$

This is a cubic in m, giving three values of m, i.e. there are, in general, three normals passing through a given point. Moreover, since a cubic has either three or one real roots, there must be either three or one real normals.

As the term in m^2 is missing, the sum of the roots is zero. Therefore the sum of the ordinates of the feet is zero and so the centre of gravity of the triangle formed by the feet of the normals from any point lies on the axis.

The circle through the feet of the normals

Consider the intersections of the parabola with the general circle

$$x^2 + y^2 + 2gx + 2fy + c = 0.$$

If they meet at the point $(am^2, 2am)$,

$$a^2m^4 + 4a^2m^2 + 2gam^2 + 4fam + c = 0.$$

This is a quartic in m and since the term in m^3 is missing the sum of the roots is zero. Therefore the sum of the ordinates of the points of intersection of the parabola $y^2 = 4ax$ with any circle is zero.

Since the sum of the ordinates of the feet of the normals is already zero, the circle through the three feet of the normals from any point to the parabola must pass through the origin.

The locus of the mid points of parallel chords

Suppose (x', y') is the mid point of a chord of the parabola which makes an angle θ with the positive direction of the x-axis where $\tan \theta = m$. A point distant r from (x', y') along the line has coordinates $(x' + r \cos \theta, y' + r \sin \theta)$. This point lies on the parabola if

$$(y' + r \sin \theta)^2 = 4a(x' + r \cos \theta).$$

This is a quadratic in r whose roots are the distances from (x', y') to the parabola along the chord. These distances are equal in magnitude but opposite in sign and so the sum of the roots of the equation is zero. This means that the coefficient of r must be zero and so

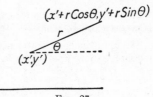

Fig. 27.

$$2y' \sin \theta = 4a \cos \theta.$$

The locus is therefore $y = 2a/m$. This is a diameter of the parabola (a line parallel to the axis) and we can remember its equation by noticing that the point of contact of the tangent of gradient m, $(a/m^2, 2a/m)$, must lie on the locus.

Equation of the chord whose mid point is (x', y')

Suppose the chord is of gradient m. The locus of the mid points of chords parallel to this is $y = 2a/m$ and the point (x', y') must lie on this locus. So the gradient of the chord is $2a/y'$ and its equation

$$\frac{y - y'}{x - x'} = \frac{2a}{y'}.$$

EXERCISES XXV

1. Find the equation of the normal at $(3, 6)$ to the parabola $y^2 = 12x$ and find the point in which it meets the curve again.

2. If the chord joining the points $(am^2, 2am)$ and $(at^2, 2at)$ passes through the focus of $y^2 = 4ax$, prove that $mt = -1$.

3. Find the locus of the mid point of a focal chord of $y^2 = 4ax$

4. Find the locus of the intersection of perpendicular normals to $y^2 = 4ax$.

5. Find the equation of the chord of the parabola $y^2 = 8x$ whose mid point is $(1, 2)$.

6. Find the pole of the line $2x + 3y = 1$ with respect to the parabola $y^2 = 4x$.

7. A chord of the parabola $y^2 = 4ax$ passes through the point $(2a, 0)$ Find the locus of the intersection of the tangents at the ends of the chord.

8. Find the condition that $lx + my = 1$ should be a normal to $y^2 = 4ax$.

9. Find the condition that $lx + my + n = 0$ should touch $y^2 = 4ax$. If it does touch, what are the coordinates of its point of contact ?

10. Find the coordinates of the mid point of the polar of $(-1, -2)$ with respect to the parabola $y^2 = 4x$.

THE ELLIPSE AND THE HYPERBOLA

Much of the work for the ellipse and the hyperbola is almost identical and to emphasize this similarity, the two conics are, for the most part, considered side by side.

ELLIPSE

If S is a focus and SX the perpendicular to the directrix, there will be two points, A and A', on the ellipse lying on SX.

Since $e < 1$, one will be between S and X and the other will be on XS produced.

Let C be the mid point of AA' and call the length of AA' $2a$. Take C as the origin of coordinates and CA' as the x-axis.

HYPERBOLA

If S is a focus and SX the perpendicular to the directrix, there will be two points, A and A', on the hyperbola lying on SX.

Since $e > 1$, one will be between S and X and the other will be on SX produced.

Let C be the mid point of AA' and call the length of AA' $2a$. Take C as the origin of coordinates and CA as the x-axis.

ELLIPSE

Since A and A' are on the ellipse,

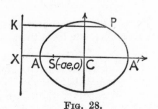

FIG. 28.

$$SA = e.AX$$
and $$SA' = e.A'X.$$

Adding,
$$2a = e(AX + A'X)$$
$$= e(CX - a + CX + a)$$
$$= 2e.CX.$$

Therefore $CX = a/e.$

But $CA + AX = CX$

so $$AX = a/e - a,$$

and since $SA = e.AX$

$$SA = a - ae,$$

and $$CS = a - SA$$

or $$CS = ae.$$

If $P(x, y)$ is any point on the ellipse,
$$PS^2 = (e.PK)^2$$

or
$$(x + ae)^2 + y^2 = [e(x + a/e)]^2.$$

So $$x^2 + 2aex + a^2e^2 + y^2$$
$$= e^2x^2 + 2aex + a^2$$
$$x^2(1 - e^2) + y^2 = a^2(1 - e^2)$$

or $$x^2/a^2 + y^2/a^2(1 - e^2) = 1.$$

So
$$x^2/a^2 + y^2/a^2(1 - e^2) = 1$$

HYPERBOLA

Since A and A' are on the hyperbola,

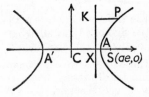

FIG. 29.

$$SA = e.AX$$
and $$SA' = e.A'X.$$

Subtracting,
$$2a = e(A'X - AX)$$
$$= e(a + CX - a + CX)$$
$$= 2e.CX.$$

Therefore $CX = a/e.$

But $CA - AX = CX$

so $$AX = a - a/e,$$

and since $SA = e.AX$

$$SA = ea - a,$$

and $$CS = a + SA$$

or $$CS = ae.$$

If $P(x, y)$ is any point on the hyperbola,
$$PS^2 = (e.PK)^2$$

or
$$(x - ae)^2 + y^2 = [e(x - a/e)]^2.$$

So $$x^2 - 2aex + a^2e^2 + y^2$$
$$= e^2x^2 - 2aex + a^2$$
$$x^2(e^2 - 1) - y^2 = a^2(e^2 - 1)$$

or $$x^2/a^2 - y^2/a^2(e^2 - 1) = 1.$$

So
$$x^2/a^2 - y^2/a^2(e^2 - 1) = 1$$

ELLIPSE

or, putting

$$b^2 = a^2(1 - e^2)$$
$$x^2/a^2 + y^2/b^2 = 1.$$

HYPERBOLA

or, putting

$$b^2 = a^2(e^2 - 1)$$
$$x^2/a^2 - y^2/b^2 = 1.$$

The difference between the equations of the two conics is only in the sign of b^2; so all equations are deducible, one from the other, by changing the sign of b^2.

The ellipse is by its equation symmetrical about both axes. We deduce therefore the existence of two foci and two directrices similarly placed.

Putting $x = 0$, we see that the ellipse cuts the y-axis at points whose distances from the origin are b. This is called the length of the semi-minor axis and can be shown on the figure.

The hyperbola is by its equation symmetrical about both axes. We deduce therefore the existence of two foci and two directrices similarly placed.

Putting $x = 0$, we see that the hyperbola cuts the y-axis where $y^2 = -b^2$. b is still called the semi-minor axis but its length cannot be indicated on the figure.

The equation of the tangent of gradient m

Suppose the tangent is

$$y = mx + c.$$

This line cuts the ellipse where

$$x^2/a^2 + (mx + c)^2/b^2 = 1$$

or

$$(b^2 + a^2m^2)x^2$$
$$+ 2a^2mcx + a^2(c^2 - b^2) = 0.$$

For this line to be a tangent, the equation must have equal roots.

$$4a^4m^2c^2$$
$$= 4(b^2 + a^2m^2)a^2(c^2 - b^2)$$
$$\therefore a^2m^2c^2 = b^2c^2 - b^4$$
$$+ a^2m^2c^2 - a^2m^2b^2$$
$$\therefore c^2 = a^2m^2 + b^2.$$

So the tangent of gradient m is

$$y = mx + \sqrt{a^2m^2 + b^2}.$$

Suppose the tangent is

$$y = mx + c.$$

This line cuts the hyperbola where

$$x^2/a^2 - (mx + c)^2/b^2 = 1$$

or

$$(b^2 - a^2m^2)x^2$$
$$- 2a^2mcx - a^2(c^2 + b^2) = 0.$$

For this line to be a tangent, the equation must have equal roots.

$$4a^4m^2c^2$$
$$= 4(b^2 - a^2m^2)(-a^2)(c^2 + b^2)$$
$$\therefore a^2m^2c^2 = -b^2c^2 - b^4$$
$$+ a^2m^2c^2 + a^2m^2b$$
$$\therefore c^2 = a^2m^2 - b^2.$$

So the tangent of gradient m is

$$y = mx + \sqrt{a^2m^2 - b^2}.$$

ELLIPSE   HYPERBOLA

The auxiliary circle

To find the locus of the foot of the perpendicular from the focus to a tangent.

The tangent of gradient m is

$$y = mx + \sqrt{a^2m^2 + b^2}.$$

The perpendicular from the focus $(ae, 0)$ is

$$my + x = ae.$$

To find the locus, we must eliminate m between

$$(y - mx)^2 = a^2m^2 + b^2$$

and

$$(my + x)^2 = a^2e^2 = a^2 - b^2.$$

Adding,

$$y^2(1 + m^2) + x^2(1 + m^2) = a^2(1 + m^2)$$

and so the locus is

$$x^2 + y^2 = a^2.$$

The tangent of gradient m is

$$y = mx + \sqrt{a^2m^2 - b^2}.$$

The perpendicular from the focus $(ae, 0)$ is

$$my + x = ae.$$

To find the locus, we must eliminate m between

$$(y - mx)^2 = a^2m^2 - b^2$$

and

$$(my + x)^2 = a^2e^2 = a^2 + b^2.$$

Adding,

$$y^2(1 + m^2) + x^2(1 + m^2) = a^2(1 + m^2)$$

and so the locus is

$$x^2 + y^2 = a^2.$$

The director circle

To find the locus of the intersection of perpendicular tangents.

The tangent of gradient m is

$$y = mx + \sqrt{a^2m^2 + b^2}.$$

The tangent of gradient $(-1/m)$ is

$$y = (-1/m)x + \sqrt{a^2(-1/m)^2 + b^2}.$$

To find the locus, we eliminate m between

$$(y - mx)^2 = a^2m^2 + b^2$$

and $(my + x)^2 = a^2 + b^2m^2.$

Adding,

$$y^2(1 + m^2) + x^2(1 + m^2) = a^2(1 + m^2) + b^2(1 + m^2)$$

and so the locus is

$$x^2 + y^2 = a^2 + b^2.$$

The tangent of gradient m is

$$y = mx + \sqrt{a^2m^2 - b^2}.$$

The tangent of gradient $(-1/m)$ is

$$y = (-1/m)x + \sqrt{a^2(-1/m)^2 - b^2}.$$

To find the locus, we eliminate m between

$$(y - mx)^2 = a^2m^2 - b^2$$

and $(my + x)^2 = a^2 - b^2m^2.$

Adding,

$$y^2(1 + m^2) + x^2(1 + m^2) = a^2(1 + m^2) - b^2(1 + m^2)$$

and so the locus is

$$x^2 + y^2 = a^2 - b^2.$$

ELLIPSE	HYPERBOLA

The tangent at (x', y')

From
$$x^2/a^2 + y^2/b^2 = 1,$$
differentiating w.r.t. x,
$$2x/a^2 + (2y/b^2)\,\frac{dy}{dx} = 0.$$

Therefore $\frac{dy}{dx}$ at the point (x', y') is $- b^2x'/a^2y'$.

The equation of the tangent is therefore
$$\frac{y - y'}{x - x'} = - \frac{b^2x'}{a^2y'}$$
or
$$a^2yy' - a^2y'^2 + b^2xx' - b^2x'^2 = 0.$$
Dividing by a^2b^2,
$$xx'/a^2 + yy'/b^2 = x'^2/a^2 + y'^2/b^2$$
or $xx'/a^2 + yy'/b^2 = 1,$
since (x', y') lies on the ellipse.

From
$$x^2/a^2 - y^2/b^2 = 1,$$
differentiating w.r.t. x,
$$2x/a^2 - (2y/b^2)\,\frac{dy}{dx} = 0.$$

Therefore $\frac{dy}{dx}$ at the point (x', y') is $+ b^2x'/a^2y'$.

The equation of the tangent is therefore
$$\frac{y - y'}{x - x'} = + \frac{b^2x'}{a^2y'}$$
or
$$a^2yy' - a^2y'^2 = b^2xx' - b^2x'^2.$$
Dividing by a^2b^2,
$$xx'/a^2 - yy'/b^2 = x'^2/a^2 - y'^2/b^2$$
or $xx'/a^2 - yy'/b^2 = 1,$
since (x', y') lies on the hyperbola.

The normal at (x', y')

The gradient of the normal must be $+ a^2y'/b^2x'$ and its equation,
$$xy'/b^2 - yx'/a^2$$
$$= x'y'/b^2 - x'y'/a^2$$
or
$$a^2xy' - b^2yx' = (a^2 - b^2)x'y'.$$

The gradient of the normal must be $- a^2y'/b^2x'$ and its equation,
$$xy'/b^2 + yx'/a^2$$
$$= x'y'/b^2 + x'y'/a^2$$
or
$$a^2xy' + b^2yx' = (a^2 + b^2)x'y'.$$

The polar of (x', y')

Suppose the points of contact of the tangents from (x', y') are (x_1, y_1) and (x_2, y_2).
The tangent at (x_1, y_1),
$$xx_1/a^2 + yy_1/b^2 = 1,$$
passes through (x', y') and so
$$x'x_1/a^2 + y'y_1/b^2 = 1.$$

Suppose the points of contact of the tangents from (x', y') are (x_1, y_1) and (x_2, y_2).
The tangent at (x_1, y_1),
$$xx_1/a^2 - yy_1/b^2 = 1,$$
passes through (x', y') and so
$$x'x_1/a^2 - y'y_1/b^2 = 1.$$

ELLIPSE

But this is equally the condition that the line

$$xx'/a^2 + yy'/b^2 = 1$$

should pass through (x_1, y_1).

Similarly it passes through (x_2, y_2) and as the line joining two points is unique, the equation of the polar must be

$$xx'/a^2 + yy'/b^2 = 1.$$

The pole of $lx + my + n = 0$

Suppose the pole of

$$lx + my + n = 0$$

is (α, β).

Then the polar of (α, β)

$$x\alpha/a^2 + y\beta/b^2 = 1$$

and $lx + my + n = 0$

must represent the same line.

The coefficients are therefore proportional and so

$$\frac{\alpha/a^2}{l} = \frac{\beta/b^2}{m} = -\frac{1}{n}.$$

Hence $\alpha = -a^2l/n$

and $\beta = -b^2m/n$,

and the pole of the line is

$$(-a^2l/n, -b^2m/n).$$

N.B.—If the line

$$lx + my + n = 0$$

is a tangent to the ellipse, its pole must lie on the line itself. Therefore

$$l(-a^2l/n) + m(-b^2m/n) + n = 0$$

or $a^2l^2 + b^2m^2 = n^2$

is the condition for

$$lx + my + n = 0$$

to be a tangent to the ellipse.

HYPERBOLA

But this is equally the condition that the line

$$xx'/a^2 - yy'/b^2 = 1$$

should pass through (x_1, y_1).

Similarly it passes through (x_2, y_2) and as the line joining two points is unique, the equation of the polar must be

$$xx'/a^2 - yy'/b^2 = 1.$$

Suppose the pole of

$$lx + my + n = 0$$

is (α, β).

Then the polar of (α, β)

$$x\alpha/a^2 - y\beta/b^2 = 1$$

and $lx + my + n = 0$

must represent the same line.

The coefficients are therefore proportional and so

$$\frac{\alpha/a^2}{l} = -\frac{\beta/b^2}{m} = -\frac{1}{n}.$$

Hence $\alpha = -a^2l/n$

and $\beta = b^2m/n$,

and the pole of the line is

$$(-a^2l/n, +b^2m/n).$$

N.B.—If the line

$$lx + my + n = 0$$

is a tangent to the hyperbola, its pole must lie on the line itself. Therefore

$$l(-a^2l/n) + m(b^2m/n) + n = 0$$

or $a^2l^2 - b^2m^2 = n^2$

is the condition for

$$lx + my + n = 0$$

to be a tangent to the hyperbola.

ELLIPSE	HYPERBOLA

If it is a tangent, its point of contact must be

$$(- a^2l/n, - b^2m/n).$$

If it is a tangent, its point of contact must be

$$(- a^2l/n, + b^2m/n).$$

The locus of the mid points of parallel chords

Suppose (x', y') is the mid point of a chord which makes an angle θ with the positive x direction where $\tan \theta = m$. Then a point along the line distant r from (x', y') has co-ordinates

$$(x' + r \cos \theta, y' + r \sin \theta).$$

This lies on the ellipse if

$$\frac{(x' + r \cos \theta)^2}{a^2} + \frac{(y' + r \sin \theta)^2}{b^2} = 1.$$

The roots of this quadratic in r are the distances from (x', y') to the ellipse along the chord and these are equal in magnitude but opposite in sign. The sum of the roots is then zero and so the coefficient of r in the equation must be zero.

Therefore

$$\frac{2x' \cos \theta}{a^2} + \frac{2y' \sin \theta}{b^2} = 0.$$

So the locus of the mid points is

$$y = - b^2x/a^2m.$$

Diameters such that each bisects all chords parallel to the other are called *conjugate diameters*.

The product of the gradients of conjugate diameters is

$$- b^2/a^2.$$

Suppose (x', y') is the mid point of a chord which makes an angle θ with the positive x direction where $\tan \theta = m$. Then a point along the line distant r from (x', y') has co-ordinates

$$(x' + r \cos \theta, y' + r \sin \theta).$$

This lies on the hyperbola if

$$\frac{(x' + r \cos \theta)^2}{a^2} - \frac{(y' + r \sin \theta)^2}{b^2} = 1.$$

The roots of this quadratic in r are the distances from (x', y') to the hyperbola along the chord and these are equal in magnitude but opposite in sign. The sum of the roots is then zero and so the coefficient of r in the equation must be zero.

Therefore

$$\frac{2x' \cos \theta}{a^2} - \frac{2y' \sin \theta}{b^2} = 0.$$

So the locus of the mid points is

$$y = + b^2x/a^2m.$$

Diameters such that each bisects all chords parallel to the other are called *conjugate diameters*.

The product of the gradients of conjugate diameters is

$$+ b^2/a^2.$$

Conjugate points are, in general, points such that the polar of one passes through the other.

ELLIPSE

HYPERBOLA

Conjugate lines are such that the pole of one lies on the other. Conjugate diameters hold to this definition as the pole of a diameter is a point at infinity in the conjugate direction.

N.B.—Whenever a question introduces the mid point of a chord, *use conjugate diameters.*

Equation of the chord whose mid point is (x', y')

The diameter through (x', y') bisects this chord and, therefore, all chords parallel to it. The gradient of this diameter is y'/x'. So the gradient of the conjugate diameter which must be parallel to the chord required is

$$- b^2 x'/a^2 y'.$$

The equation of the chord is

$$\frac{y - y'}{x - x'} = - \frac{b^2 x'}{a^2 y'}.$$

The diameter through (x', y') bisects this chord and, therefore, all chords parallel to it. The gradient of this diameter is y'/x'. So the gradient of the conjugate diameter which must be parallel to the chord required is

$$+ b^2 x'/a^2 y'.$$

The equation of the chord is

$$\frac{y - y'}{x - x'} = + \frac{b^2 x'}{a^2 y'}.$$

EXERCISES XXVI

1. Find the coordinates of the foci and the eccentricity of
$$4x^2 + 9y^2 = 36.$$

2. Find the pole of $3x - 4y = 1$ with respect to $\dfrac{x^2}{3} - \dfrac{y^2}{4} = 1$.

3. Find the condition that $lx + my = 1$ should be a tangent to
$$\frac{x^2}{a^2} + \frac{y^2}{b^2} = 1.$$

4. Find the equation of the normal at $(1, 1)$ to $2x^2 - y^2 = 1$.

5. Find the equation of the chord of $\dfrac{x^2}{4} + \dfrac{y^2}{25} = 1$ whose mid point is $(1, 2)$.

6. Find the equation of the chord of $\dfrac{x^2}{a^2} - \dfrac{y^2}{b^2} = 1$ whose mid point is (α, β).

7. A chord of $3x^2 - 2y^2 = 1$ passes through $(1, 2)$. Find the locus of its mid point.

8. Find the condition that $px^2 + 2qxy + ry^2 = 0$ should be a pair of conjugate diameters of $\dfrac{x^2}{a^2} + \dfrac{y^2}{b^2} = 1$.

9. Prove that the product of the lengths of the perpendiculars from the foci to any tangent to $\dfrac{x^2}{a^2} + \dfrac{y^2}{b^2} = 1$ is constant and equal to b^2.

10. If P is any point on the hyperbola $x^2 - y^2 = 1$ and C is the centre, find the locus of the mid point of PC.

THE ELLIPSE

The eccentric angle of the ellipse

Consider the ellipse with its auxiliary circle. If Q is a point on the circle such that $ACQ = \theta$, then the coordinates of Q are $(a \cos \theta,$ $a \sin \theta)$. If P is a point on the ellipse such that QP is perpendicular to CA, then the x coordinate of P is $a \cos \theta$.

Therefore

$$(a \cos \theta)^2/a^2 + y^2/b^2 = 1,$$

and so

$$y^2 = b^2 \sin^2 \theta.$$

FIG. 30.

So the coordinates of the point P in the first quadrant are $(a \cos \theta, b \sin \theta)$ where θ is called the eccentric angle of P. The geometrical significance of the angle is not often required but the parametric representation of a point as $(a \cos \theta, b \sin \theta)$ is very important.

The line joining α and β

The equation of the line joining α and β is

$$\frac{y - b \sin \alpha}{x - a \cos \alpha} = \frac{b(\sin \alpha - \sin \beta)}{a(\cos \alpha - \cos \beta)}$$

$$= \frac{b \cdot 2 \cos \frac{1}{2}(\alpha + \beta) \sin \frac{1}{2}(\alpha - \beta)}{- a \cdot 2 \sin \frac{1}{2}(\alpha + \beta) \sin \frac{1}{2}(\alpha - \beta)}$$

$$= - \frac{b \cdot \cos \frac{1}{2}(\alpha + \beta)}{a \cdot \sin \frac{1}{2}(\alpha + \beta)}.$$

Therefore

$$ay \sin \tfrac{1}{2}(\alpha + \beta) + bx \cos \tfrac{1}{2}(\alpha + \beta)$$

$$= ab(\cos \alpha \cos \tfrac{1}{2}(\alpha + \beta) + \sin \alpha \sin \tfrac{1}{2}(\alpha + \beta)$$

$$= ab \cos \tfrac{1}{2}(\alpha - \beta)$$

or $$x/a \cdot \cos \tfrac{1}{2}(\alpha + \beta) + y/b \cdot \sin \tfrac{1}{2}(\alpha + \beta) = \cos\frac{\alpha - \beta}{2}.$$

The eccentric angles at the ends of conjugate diameters

If θ and ϕ are the eccentric angles of the points P and Q which are ends of conjugate diameters of the ellipse, the gradient of CP is $b \sin \theta / a \cos \theta$ and the gradient of CQ is $b \sin \phi / a \cos \phi$.

Therefore $(b/a . \tan \theta)(b/a . \tan \phi) = - b^2/a^2$

and so $\tan \phi = - \cot \theta = \tan\left(\dfrac{\pi}{2} + \theta\right).$

The general solution of this equation is

$$\phi = n\pi + \frac{\pi}{2} + \theta.$$

Therefore $\phi - \theta = (2n + 1)\dfrac{\pi}{2}$

and so the eccentric angles at the ends of conjugate diameters differ by an odd multiple of $\dfrac{\pi}{2}$.

The coordinates of the ends of the two diameters are shown in the diagram.

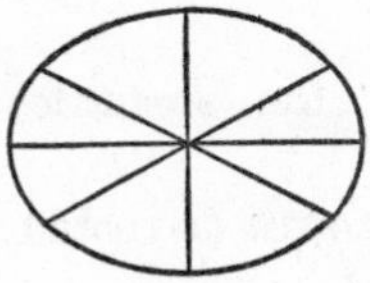

$(- a \sin \theta, b \cos \theta)$ $(a \cos \theta, b \sin \theta)$

$(- a \cos \theta, - b \sin \theta)$ $(a \sin \theta, - b \cos \theta)$

Fig. 31.

THE HYPERBOLA

The asymptotes of the hyperbola

There is nothing in the hyperbola corresponding to the eccentric angle of the ellipse although there are various ways (none very convenient) of expressing a point on the hyperbola parametrically.   The three most useful are

$$(a \sec \theta, \ b \tan \theta) ;$$
$$(a \cosh \theta, \ b \sinh \theta) ;$$
$$[\tfrac{1}{2}a(t + 1/t), \tfrac{1}{2}b(t - 1/t)].$$

The tangent at the last of these points is

$$(x/2a) . (t + 1/t) - (y/2b) . (t - 1/t) = 1.$$

This can be rearranged as

$$(x/2a) . (t^2 + 1) - (y/2b)(t^2 - 1) = t$$

and becomes

$$x/a + y/b = 0 \quad \text{when } t = 0.$$

The tangent can also be re-written,

$$(x/2a).(1 + 1/t^2) - (y/2b)(1 - 1/t^2) = 1/t$$

and when $1/t = 0$ this becomes

$$x/a - y/b = 0.$$

But the values $t = 0$ and $1/t = 0$ both make the coordinates of the original point $[\frac{1}{2}a(t + 1/t),\ \frac{1}{2}b(t - 1/t)]$ infinite, and so $x/a = \pm y/b$ are the "tangents at infinity" or the asymptotes of the hyperbola.

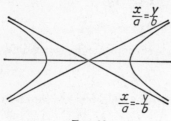

Any line parallel to an asymptote will cut the hyperbola at one finite point only. If $a = b$, the asymptotes become $x = y$ and $x = -y$ and since these two lines are at right angles, the hyperbola is called *a rectangular hyperbola*. Its equation referred to the axes of the hyperbola is $x^2 - y^2 = a^2$.

FIG. 32.

Since $b^2 = a^2(e^2 - 1)$, the eccentricity of any rectangular hyperbola is $\sqrt{2}$.

Showing how to turn the axes of coordinates through an angle θ

Suppose the equation of a curve is given referred to rectangular axes Ox and Oy and we wish to find its equation referred to new rectangular coordinates OX and OY where $xOX = \theta$. Let any point P have coordinates (x, y) and (X, Y) referred respectively to the two sets of axes.

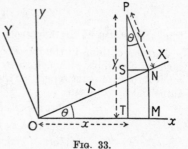

$$x = OT = OM - SN$$
$$= X \cos \theta - Y \sin \theta.$$
$$y = PT = NM + PS$$
$$= X \sin \theta + Y \cos \theta.$$

So if the equation is given as a connection between x and y

FIG. 33.

all we need to do is to make these substitutions for x and y to get the equation between X and Y.

THE RECTANGULAR HYPERBOLA

The equation of a rectangular hyperbola referred to its asymptotes

The equation of a rectangular hyperbola referred to its axes as coordinate axes is $x^2 - y^2 = a^2$. Let us now turn the axes through $-45°$ so that the asymptotes become the axes of coordinates.

We write
$$x = X \cos(-45°) - Y \sin(-45°)$$
$$= (X + Y)/\sqrt{2}$$

and
$$y = X \sin(-45°) + Y \cos(-45°)$$
$$= (Y - X)/\sqrt{2}.$$

$$x^2 - y^2 = a^2$$

becomes
$$(X + Y)^2/2 - (Y - X)^2/2 = a^2$$

or
$$XY = \tfrac{1}{2}a^2.$$

Writing $c^2 = \tfrac{1}{2}a^2$, and reverting to the more usual x and y for current coordinates, the equation of a rectangular hyperbola may be written

$$xy = c^2.$$

N.B.—The axes were turned through $-45°$ and not $45°$ in order to get part of the curve in the first quadrant.

The tangent at (x', y')

If $xy = c^2$, then differentiating w.r.t. x,

$$x\frac{dy}{dx} + y = 0.$$

Therefore at the point (x', y'),

$$\frac{dy}{dx} = -y'/x',$$

and so the equation of the tangent is

$$\frac{y - y'}{x - x'} = -\frac{y'}{x'}$$

or
$$xy' + yx' = 2x'y'$$

or
$$xy' + yx' = 2c^2$$

since (x', y') lies on the hyperbola.

The polar of (x', y')

If the points of contact of the tangents from (x', y') are (x_1, y_1) and (x_2, y_2), the tangent at (x_1, y_1) which is $xy_1 + yx_1 = 2c^2$ passes through (x', y') and so

$$x'y_1 + y'x_1 = 2c^2.$$

But this is equally the condition that the line $xy' + yx' = 2c^2$ should pass through (x_1, y_1). Similarly the line passes through (x_2, y_2) but as the line joining two points is unique, this line must be the polar of (x', y').

Line joining the points m and t

Any point on the hyperbola can conveniently be represented parametrically as $(cm, c/m)$.

The gradient of the line joining the points m and t is

$$\frac{c/m - c/t}{cm - ct} = -\frac{1}{mt}.$$

The equation of the line is therefore

$$\frac{y - c/t}{x - ct} = -\frac{1}{mt}$$

or

$$mty - cm = -x + ct$$

or

$$x + mty = c(m + t).$$

The locus of the mid points of parallel chords

If (x', y') is the mid point of a chord making θ with the positive x direction where $\tan \theta = m$, a point distant r from (x', y') along the chord will have coordinates $x' + r \cos \theta$ and $y' + r \sin \theta$. This lies on the hyperbola if $(x' + r \cos \theta)(y' + r \sin \theta) = c^2$. But since (x', y') is the mid point, the roots of this equation in r must be equal and opposite and so the sum of the roots is zero.

Therefore

$$x' \sin \theta + y' \cos \theta = 0.$$

The locus required is $y = -mx$.

Conjugate diameters of a rectangular hyperbola are therefore equally inclined to the asymptotes.

N.B.—The product of the gradients of conjugate diameters is no longer b^2/a^2. This formula applies only when the axes of coordinates are the axes of the hyperbola.

The equation of the chord whose mid point is (x', y')

The diameter joining (x', y') to the centre will bisect the chord and therefore all chords parallel to it. The gradient of this diameter is y'/x' and so the gradient of the conjugate diameter is $-y'/x'$. The equation of the chord is therefore

$$\frac{y - y'}{x - x'} = -\frac{y'}{x'}.$$

The equation of a conic with given asymptotes

Since $xy = c^2$ is the equation of a hyperbola having $x = 0$ and $y = 0$ as asymptotes, the equation of a general hyperbola having asymptotes $ax + by + c = 0$ and $lx + my + n = 0$ is

$$(ax + by + c)(lx + my + n) = k.$$

So the equation of a hyperbola and the equation of its asymptotes differ only in the constant term.

EXERCISES XXVII

1. If P and Q are two points of an ellipse, eccentric angles α and β, and PQ is of fixed gradient, prove that $\alpha + \beta$ is constant.

2. If CP and CD are conjugate radii of an ellipse, prove that

$$CP^2 + CD^2 = a^2 + b^2.$$

3. If PQR are three points on the rectangular hyperbola $xy = c^2$, prove that the orthocentre of PQR also lies on the curve.

4. Find the pole of the line $3x - y = 2$ with respect to $xy = c^2$.

5. Find the equation of the chord of the hyperbola $xy = 4$, whose mid point is $(1, 1)$.

6. Find the equation of the hyperbola which passes through the point $(1, 1)$ and whose asymptotes are $x + y = 1$ and $x - y = 1$.

7. Find the locus of the point whose polar with respect to

$$x^2 - 2xy - y^2 = 4x.$$

is perpendicular to the polar of $(1, 1)$ in the same conic.

8. A chord of the hyperbola $xy = c^2$ passes through the fixed point (h, k). Find the locus of the mid point of the chord.

9. Find the condition that $lx + my = 1$ should be a normal to $xy = c^2$.

10. If the normal at P of eccentric angle θ on $\dfrac{x^2}{a^2} + \dfrac{y^2}{b^2} = 1$ passes through Q of eccentric angle ϕ, prove that

$$\tan \theta \tan \frac{\theta + \phi}{2} = -\frac{b^2}{a^2}.$$

THE GENERAL CONIC

A few important results for the general conic are given in conclusion.

(1) $ax^2 + 2hxy + by^2 + 2gx + 2fy + c = 0$ represents

a circle if $a = b$ and $h = 0$.
a pair of straight lines if $af^2 + bg^2 + ch^2 = 2fgh + abc$.
a parabola if $h^2 = ab$.
an ellipse if $h^2 < ab$.
a hyperbola if $h^2 > ab$.
a rectangular hyperbola if $a + b = 0$.

(2) If $S = 0$, $S' = 0$ are any two conics, then $S + \lambda S' = 0$ represents a system of conics passing through the points of intersection
of S and S'

As S and S' are of the second degree, so is $S + \lambda S'$. Therefore
$S + \lambda S' = 0$ must represent a conic.

Any point of intersection of S and S' will make $S = 0$ and $S' = 0$
and so must also make $S + \lambda S'$ zero. Therefore $S + \lambda S' = 0$ passes
through all the points of intersection of S and S'.

(3) **To find the polar of** (x', y') **with respect to the general conic**

In the equation of the general conic, replace

$$
\begin{array}{lll}
x^2 & \text{by} & xx' \\
y^2 & \text{by} & yy' \\
2xy & \text{by} & xy' + yx' \\
2x & \text{by} & x + x' \\
2y & \text{by} & y + y' \\
c & \text{by} & c \text{ (if } c \text{ is a constant).}
\end{array}
$$

This will in all cases give the polar of (x', y') and if the point (x', y')
lies on the conic, it will give the tangent at the point.

REVISION PAPER V

1. (a) The coordinates of the points A, B, C are (3, 0), (0, 5), (4, 4)
and N is the foot of the perpendicular from C to AB. If CN is produced through N to D so that $ND = 3CN$, calculate the coordinates
of D.

(b) A carriage spring is in the shape of part of an ellipse. Referred
to the principal axes of the ellipse, the coordinates of the ends of the
spring are (16, 9) and $(-16, 9)$ and the tangents to the ellipse at
these points are at right angles. Find the lengths of the axes of the
ellipse. (NU)

2. Obtain the equation of the locus of a point P which moves so
that $PB = 2PA$ where A, B are respectively (1, 0), $(-1, 0)$. Show
that the locus is a circle and determine the radius and the coordinates
of the centre.

Verify that $y = 4/3$ is a tangent to the circle and determine the
equation of the other tangent that passes through the point $(-1,
4/3)$. (NU)

3. Show that the equation of the line joining the points $(ap^2, 2ap)$,
$(aq^2, 2aq)$ is $(p + q)y = 2x + 2apq$.

The chord PQ of the parabola $y^2 = 4ax$ passes through the fixed point $(b, 0)$ and the chord PR passes through the fixed point $(c, 0)$. Show that, as P varies, the locus of the mid point of QR is

$$(b^2 + c^2)y^2 = 2a(b + c)^2x. \qquad (NU)$$

4. Find the radius and centre of the circle

$$x^2 + y^2 - 2x - 8y + 8 = 0.$$

Show by calculation that the point $(2 \cdot 9, 6 \cdot 4)$ lies outside this circle and calculate the length of the tangent to this circle from this point.

(C)

5. Find the equation of the normal at the point $(at^2, 2at)$ on the parabola $y^2 = 4ax$.

The point O is the origin of coordinates, the point P is the point $(at^2, 2at)$ and the point Q on the parabola is such that OP and PQ are equally inclined in opposite senses to the axis of the parabola. Prove that the circumcentre of the triangle OPQ lies on the normal at P. (C)

6. (i) Find the equation of the circle which passes through the three points $(0, 0)$, $(0, 1)$, $(2, 3)$.

(ii) Find the equations of the two circles which touch the lines $x + 2y = 1$, $x = 0$, $y = 0$ and have their centres on the line $x = y$.

$(O \& C)$

7. Find the equation of the normal at the point $P(x', y')$ on the ellipse $\dfrac{x^2}{a^2} + \dfrac{y^2}{b^2} = 1$.

The normal at P meets the x-axis at G. If Q is the point of intersection of the line through G parallel to the y-axis and the line joining P to the centre of the ellipse, show that the equation of the locus of Q is

$$\frac{x^2}{a^2} + \frac{y^2}{b^2} = \frac{(a^2 - b^2)^2}{a^4}. \qquad (L)$$

8. Show that the coordinates of a point on the hyperbola $\dfrac{x^2}{a^2} - \dfrac{y^2}{b^2} = 1$ can be expressed in terms of a parameter t by means of the relations

$$\frac{x - a}{at^2} = \frac{x + a}{a} = \frac{y}{bt}.$$

Show also that if any point P on the hyperbola be joined to the ends A, A' of the axis along $y = 0$, the line through A at right angles to PA meets PA' on a fixed line. (C)

9. Prove that the equation of the tangent to the parabola $y^2 = 4ax$ at the point (x', y') on it, is $yy' = 2a(x + x')$.

This parabola and the circle $x^2 + y^2 = 32a^2$ meet at the point P in the first quadrant. The tangent to the parabola at P meets the

y-axis at T and the normal to the parabola at P meets this axis at R. The foot of the perpendicular from P to the x-axis is N. Prove that $OR = 3ON = 6OT$ where O is the origin. (NU)

10. Find the equation of the tangent to the rectangular hyperbola $xy = c^2$ at the point $(ct, c/t)$.

Prove that the rectangular hyperbolas $xy = c^2$ and $x^2 - y^2 = a^2$ have two real common tangents and that the points of contact of either common tangent subtend a right angle at the origin of coordinates. $(O \& C)$

REVISION PAPER VI

1. A square $ABCD$ has its opposite vertices A and C at $(2, -5)$ and $(-4, 3)$. Find the coordinates of B and D and the equations of the lines which contain the sides of the square. (L)

2. A is the point $(4, 4)$, B is $(5, 3)$ and C is $(6, 0)$. Find the equations of the perpendicular bisectors of AB and BC. Hence calculate the coordinates of the circumcentre and the length of the circumradius of the triangle ABC. (L)

3. The straight line $lx + my + n = 0$ cuts the parabola $y^2 = 4ax$ in two points P, Q. Show that the coordinates of the mid point of the chord PQ are $\dfrac{2am^2 - ln}{l^2}, \; -\dfrac{2ma}{l}$.

A variable tangent to the parabola $y^2 = 4bx$ meets the parabola $y^2 = 4ax$ in P, Q. Show that the locus of the mid point of PQ is a similar parabola $y^2 = 4cx$ and express c in terms of a and b. (NU)

4. Show that the equation of the normal to the ellipse $\dfrac{x^2}{a^2} + \dfrac{y^2}{b^2} = 1$ at the point $P(a \cos \theta, \; b \sin \theta)$ is

$$\frac{ax}{\cos \theta} - \frac{by}{\sin \theta} = a^2 - b^2.$$

If the normal meets the y-axis in Q, and if S is either focus, determine PQ^2 and SQ^2 in terms of θ and show that SQ/PQ is independent of θ. (NU)

5. Prove that the centroid of the triangle whose vertices are (x_1, y_1), (x_2, y_2) and (x_3, y_3) is the point $\left(\dfrac{x_1 + x_2 + x_3}{3}, \dfrac{y_1 + y_2 + y_3}{3} \right)$.

P is the point $(at^2, 2at)$ on the curve $y^2 = 4ax$. The tangent and normal at P meet the x-axis at T and G respectively. Show that as t varies, the centroid of the triangle PTG describes the curve

$$9y^2 = 12ax - 8a^2. \qquad (L)$$

6. Prove that if the equation $ax^2 + 2hxy + by^2 + 2gx + 2fy + c = 0$ represents two straight lines, then $abc + 2fgh - af^2 - bg^2 - ch^2 = 0$.

Find the equation of the third pair of lines through the four points of intersection of the line pairs

$x^2 - 3xy + 2y^2 = 0$; $2x^2 + 3xy - 2y^2 - 27x + 6y + 36 = 0$. $(O \& C)$

7. Prove that the equation of the chord joining the points $(a \cos \theta,$ $b \sin \theta)$ and $(a \cos \phi, b \sin \phi)$ on the ellipse $\dfrac{x^2}{a^2} + \dfrac{y^2}{b^2} = 1$ is

$$\frac{x}{a} \cos \frac{\theta + \phi}{2} + \frac{y}{b} \sin \frac{\theta + \phi}{2} = \cos \frac{\theta - \phi}{2}.$$

A quadrilateral $ABCD$ is inscribed in an ellipse. From any point P on the ellipse a chord PQ is drawn parallel to AB, a chord QR is drawn parallel to BC and a chord RS parallel to CD. Prove that SP is parallel to DA. (C)

8. Find the equation of the tangent and of the normal at the point $(ct, c/t)$ on the hyperbola $xy = c^2$.

Show that the straight line whose equation is

$$(x + y - 2c) \sec \alpha - (x - y) \tan \alpha = 0$$

is a tangent to the hyperbola $xy = c^2 \sec^2 \alpha$ and a normal to the hyperbola $xy = -\dfrac{c^2 \cot^2 \alpha}{4}$. (C)

9. Find the equation of the circle on PQ as diameter where P is the point (x_1, y_1) and Q is the point (x_2, y_2).

A variable circle is drawn through the fixed point $A(h, k)$ to touch the axis of x. Find the equation of the locus of the other extremity of the diameter through A. (NU)

10. Find the equation of the chord joining the points $(cp, c/p)$, $(cq, c/q)$ on the rectangular hyperbola $xy = c^2$.

Prove that if $PQRS$ is a rectangle inscribed in the hyperbola, then the parameters of its vertices can be taken as $p, 1/p, -p, -1/p$ respectively. (No credit will be given for a proof of the converse that these points are vertices of a rectangle.)

Deduce that it is impossible to describe a square in a rectangular hyperbola. $(O \& C)$

PURE GEOMETRY

ABBREVIATIONS USED

I stands for the incentre of the triangle *ABC*.
O stands for the circumcentre of the triangle *ABC*.
G stands for the centre of gravity of the triangle *ABC*.
H stands for the orthocentre of the triangle *ABC*.
N stands for the nine-point centre of the triangle *ABC*.
A' stands for the mid point of the side *BC*.
B' stands for the mid point of the side *CA*.
C' stands for the mid point of the side *AB*.
D stands for the foot of the perpendicular from *A* to *BC*.
E stands for the foot of the perpendicular from *B* to *CA*.
F stands for the foot of the perpendicular from *C* to *AB*.

PLANE GEOMETRY

The incentre

The locus of points equidistant from two given lines is the pair of angle bisectors. If the internal bisectors of *B* and *C* meet at *I*, and *IX*, *IY*, *IZ* are the perpendiculars to the sides :

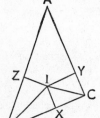

Fig. 34.

$$IX = IZ \; (I \text{ on bisector of } B);$$
$$IX = IY \; (I \text{ on bisector of } C)$$

and therefore $IZ = IY$ and consequently *I* is on the angle bisector of *A*. Also a circle can be drawn with centre *I* and radius *IX* to touch the sides of the triangle.

Therefore the three angle bisectors of a triangle are concurrent and meet at the incentre.

The circumcentre

The locus of points equidistant from two given points is the perpendicular bisector of the line joining them. If the perpendicular bisectors of *AB* and *AC* meet at *O*, then

$OA = OB$ (*O* is on the perpendicular bisector of *AB*);
$OA = OC$ (*O* is on the perpendicular bisector of *AC*).

Therefore $OB = OC$ and so *O* must be on

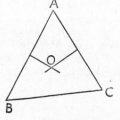

Fig. 35.

114

the perpendicular bisector of *BC*. Also we may draw a circle centre *O*, radius *OA* to pass through *ABC*.

The three perpendicular bisectors of the sides of a triangle are concurrent and meet at the circumcentre.

The orthocentre

Draw through each vertex of the triangle *ABC* a line parallel to the opposite side to form a triangle *XYZ*. Then *BCAZ* and *BCYA* are parallelograms and so *ZA = BC = AY*. Therefore *A* is the mid point of *ZY* and since *ZY* and *BC* are parallel, the altitude through *A* of the triangle *ABC* will be the perpendicular bisector of the side *ZY*. But the three perpendicular bisectors of the sides of a triangle are concurrent and so the altitudes of the triangle *ABC* must be concurrent.

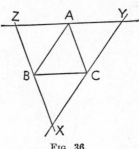

FIG. 36.

The altitudes of a triangle are concurrent and meet at the orthocentre. This is *not* the centre of any well-known circle.

The centre of gravity

Let *BB'* meet *AA'* at *G*. By parallels, *A'B'* is parallel to *BA* and half of it. But the triangles *AGB* and *A'GB'* are similar and so $A'G = \frac{1}{2}GA$ and $B'G = \frac{1}{2}GB$. So *BB'* meets *AA'* one-third of the way up. Similarly *CC'* meets *AA'* one-third of the way up.

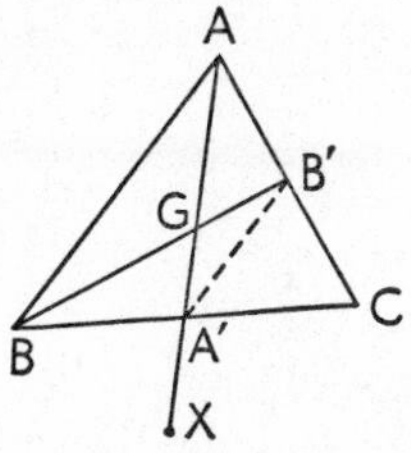

Therefore the medians of a triangle are concurrent and meet at the centre of gravity. This is the statical centre of gravity of a uniform lamina in the shape of the triangle and is often called *the centroid*. If *GA'* is produced to *X* where *GA' = A'X*, *BGCX* is a parallelogram (the diagonals bisect each other).

FIG. 37

Therefore *BX* and *XC* are two-thirds of the medians to which they are parallel. The point *X* is often useful in dealing with problems and constructions on the centroid.

The Centre of Similitude

Consider two circles centres *A* and *B*, radii *r* and *R*.

Draw two parallel lines in the same direction, *AP* and *BQ*. Let *QP* and *BA* produced meet at *T*.

Then by parallels, $AT/BT = r/R$ and so T divides AB externally in the fixed ratio of the radii. The joins of the ends of all such parallel radii will therefore pass through T, as will also the external common tangents since the lines joining their points of contact to the centres are parallel.

Conversely, if any line is drawn through T, the meet of the external common tangents, to meet the circles at P,P' and Q,Q' then AP and

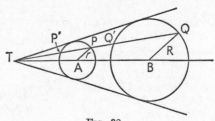

FIG. 38.

BQ are parallel as are also AP' and BQ'. T is called the external *centre of similitude* of the two cirlces. The following important result follows :

If T is any fixed point and P lies on a fixed circle, then if a point Q is taken on TP or TP produced so that TQ/TP equals a fixed ratio k, the locus of Q is a circle with its radius k times that of the given circle and its centre k times as far from T as the centre of the given circle.

If the radii AP and BQ are drawn parallel but in opposite directions, and if PQ meets AB at S, then S is called the internal centre of similitude of the two circles.

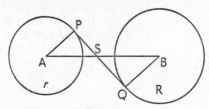

FIG. 39.

As before, $AS/BS = r/R$ and S divides the distance between the centres internally in the ratio of the radii.

The centres of similitude of two circles divide the join of the centres internally and externally in the ratio of the radii.

The same principle can be applied to similar polygons. Polygons are similar if they have corresponding angles equal and corresponding sides proportional.

(*N.B.*—Both these conditions are needed for the general polygon although for the triangle these conditions are equivalent.)

They are similar and similarly placed if, in addition, corresponding sides are parallel (or homothetic). The theorem corresponding to the centre of similitude for polygons is :

The lines joining corresponding vertices of two similar, similarly situated polygons are concurrent.

This is often used in constructions as in the following example.

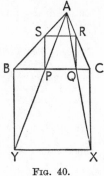

Example. Given a triangle *ABC*, construct a square *PQRS* so that *P* and *Q* lie on *BC*, *R* on *CA* and *S* on *AB*.

On the side of *BC* remote from *A*, draw the square *BCXY*. Join *AX* and *AY* to meet *BC* at *Q* and *P*. Erect perpendiculars at *Q* and *P* and we have then constructed the required square.

Fig. 40.

AB, *AY*, *AX* and *AC* are four concurrent lines with *BCXY* a square. Since *PQ* is parallel to *XY*, the figure got by drawing parallels to the corresponding sides through *P* and *Q* will also be a square.

Apollonius' Circle

The locus of a point P which moves in a plane so that the ratio of its distances from two fixed points in that plane is constant, is a circle.

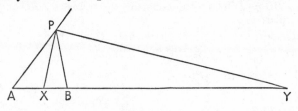

Fig 41.

Let *P* be any one position such that $AP/PB =$ the given constant, *k*. Bisect $A\widehat{P}B$ internally and externally to meet *AB*, produced as necessary, at *X* and *Y*.

Then

$AX/XB = AP/PB = k$ and
$$AY/YB = AP/PB = k \text{ (angle bisectors)}.$$

Therefore *X* and *Y* are the points which divide *AB* internally and externally in the given ratio. Therefore X and Y are fixed points. But $X\widehat{P}Y$, being the angle between the internal and external bisectors of the angle P, is a right angle. So P lies on the circle which has XY as diameter.

Example. To find the radius of the circle P describes if $AB = a$, $AP/PB = k$.

$$AX/XB = k/1. \qquad \therefore \ \frac{AX}{AX + XB} = \frac{k}{1 + k}.$$

But $\quad AX + XB = a \quad$ and so $\quad AX = ka/1 + k$.

$$AY/YB = k/1. \qquad \therefore \ \frac{AY}{AY - YB} = \frac{k}{k - 1}.$$

But $\quad AY - YB = a \quad$ and so $\quad AY = ak/k - 1$.

But $$XY = AY - AX = \frac{ak}{k - 1} - \frac{ak}{k + 1} = \frac{2ak}{k^2 - 1}$$

and therefore the radius is $\dfrac{ak}{k^2 - 1}$.

Ptolemy's Theorem

In a cyclic quadrilateral, the product of the diagonals is equal to the sum of the products of opposite sides.

Let $ABCD$ be the quadrilateral and suppose the diagonals meet at O. Construct a point X on AC so that $X\widehat{D}C = A\widehat{D}B$. Then since $A\widehat{B}D = X\widehat{C}D$ (on the same arc) the triangles ABD and XCD are similar.

Therefore $\qquad\qquad AB/XC = BD/CD$

and so $\qquad\qquad AB.CD = BD.XC.$

Adding $O\widehat{D}X$ to $A\widehat{D}B$ and $X\widehat{D}C$, we see that

$$A\widehat{D}X = C\widehat{D}O.$$

But $\ D\widehat{A}C = D\widehat{B}C\ $ (on same arc) and so triangles DAX and DBC are similar.

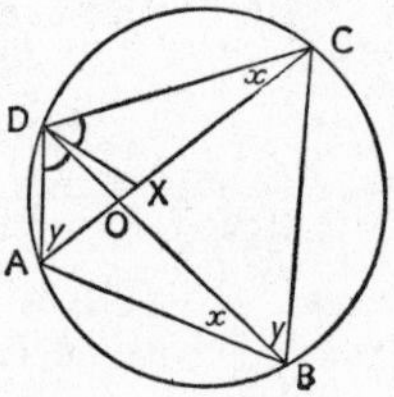

Therefore $\qquad\quad DA/DB = AX/BC$

and so $\qquad\qquad DA.BC = DB.AX$

Adding $\ AB.CD + BC.DA = BD(XC + AX)$

$$= BD.AC.$$

Fig. 42.

Example. If ABC is an equilateral triangle inscribed in a circle, and P is any point on the minor arc AB, prove that $PC = PA + PB$.

In the cyclic quadrilateral $APBC$ by Ptolemy,

$$PA.BC + PB.CA = PC.AB.$$

But

$$BC = CA = AB$$

and so

$$PA + PB = PC.$$

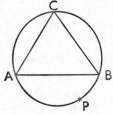

Fig. 43.

The Euler Line

The circumcentre, centre of gravity and the orthocentre of any triangle are collinear. The line on which they lie is called the Euler Line.

Produce OG to X so that $GX = 2OG$. We know $AG = 2GA'$ (property of C.G.) and so the triangles AGX, $A'GO$ are similar since the vertically opposite angles are equal.

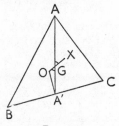

Fig. 44.

Therefore AX is parallel to OA' and consequently AX is perpendicular to BC. Similarly it may be proved that BX is perpendicular to AC and so X must be the orthocentre of the triangle, H.

It is worth noting that from the similarity of the triangles, we get

$$AH = 2OA'.$$

The Nine-point Circle

If X, Y, Z are the mid points of AH, BH and CH respectively, then the nine points A', B', C', D, E, F, X, Y, Z lie on a circle, called the nine-point circle of the triangle ABC.

XC' is parallel to HB (join of mid points);

$C'A'$ is parallel to AC (join of mid points).

But HB is perpendicular to AC and so XC' is perpendicular to $C'A'$, i.e. $XC'A' = 90°$.

Similarly XB' is parallel to HC and $B'A'$ is parallel to AB. Therefore $XB'A' = 90°$. But also $XDA' = 90°$ and so the circle on XA as diameter passes through B', C' and D.

The five points $A'B'C'XD$ therefore lie on a circle;

similarly $A'B'C'YE$ lie on a circle;

and $A'B'C'ZF$ lie on a circle.

But three points determine a circle uniquely and the points $A'B'C'$ are common. So all nine points must lie on the same circle, called the nine-point circle of the triangle ABC.

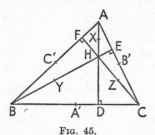

Fig. 45.

Its radius. $A'B'C'$ is similar to ABC and so its circum-radius is half that of ABC. The radius of the nine-point circle is therefore $\frac{1}{2}R$.

Its centre. $A'D$ is a chord of the nine-point circle. Therefore N, the nine-point centre, must lie on the perpendicular bisector of $A'D$. Similarly it lies on the perpendicular bisector of $B'E$. But the perpendiculars to the sides at A' and B' meet at O; the perpendiculars to the sides at E and D meet at H; so N must be the mid point of OH. Therefore N also lies on the Euler Line. The order of the points is $OGNH$ and $OG : ON : OH = 2 : 3 : 6$.

An alternative proof. It is useful to note that as ABC lie on the circumcircle of the triangle and as $HX = \frac{1}{2}HA$, $HY = \frac{1}{2}HB$ and $HZ = \frac{1}{2}HC$ then XYZ must lie on a circle so that H is the external centre of similitude of it and the circumcircle. The centre N will be the mid point of HO and the radius will be half that of the circumcircle (see centre of similitude). The ratio OH/HN also equals 2, the ratio of the radii, and so the internal centre of similitude will divide ON in the ratio $2 : 1$ and since $OG/GN = 2$, that point is G.

So the centres of similitude of the circumcircle and the nine-point circle are G and H. If any line is drawn through H, the distance along this line to the circumcircle will be double the distance from H to the nine-point circle in the same direction.

For example, if AD produced meets the circumcircle at Q, then $HD = DQ$.

If any line is drawn through G, the distance from G to the circumcircle is double the distance along the line from G to the nine-point circle in *the opposite direction*.

Ceva's Theorem

If AX, BY, CZ are three lines concurrent at O then

$$\frac{BX}{XC} \cdot \frac{CY}{YA} \cdot \frac{AZ}{ZB} = +1.$$

(Here of course a line has sign as well as magnitude. As BX and XC

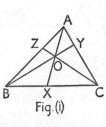

Fig. (i)

FIG. 46.

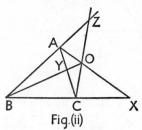

Fig.(ii)

FIG. 47.

are in the same sense in figure (i), BX/XC is positive; in figure (ii) as BX and XC are in opposite directions, BX/XC is negative. By considering the two figures, we see in each case the continued product must be positive.)

$$\frac{BX}{XC} = \frac{\triangle BAX}{\triangle CAX} = \frac{\triangle BOX}{\triangle COX} \quad \text{(Triangles with equal heights.)}$$

$$= \frac{\triangle BAX - \triangle BOX}{\triangle CAX - \triangle COX}$$

$$= \frac{\triangle BOA}{\triangle COA}.$$

Therefore

$$\frac{BX}{XC} \cdot \frac{CY}{YA} \cdot \frac{AZ}{ZB} = \frac{\triangle BOA}{\triangle COA} \cdot \frac{\triangle COB}{\triangle AOB} \cdot \frac{\triangle AOC}{\triangle BOC} = 1.$$

Menelaus' Theorem

If a transversal cuts the sides of a triangle in P, Q and R then

$$\frac{AR}{RB} \cdot \frac{BP}{PC} \cdot \frac{CQ}{QA} = -1.$$

By considering the figures, we see that in each case the continued product must be negative.

Let p_1, p_2, p_3 be the lengths of the perpendiculars from ABC to the transversal. Then, by parallels, *numerically*

$$AR/RB = p_1/p_2; \quad BP/PC = p_2/p_3; \quad CQ/QA = p_3/p_1.$$

So the numerical value of $\dfrac{AR}{RB}\cdot\dfrac{BP}{PC}\cdot\dfrac{CQ}{QA}$ is $\dfrac{p_1}{p_2}\cdot\dfrac{p_2}{p_3}\cdot\dfrac{p_3}{p_1}=1,$

and so $\qquad \dfrac{AR}{RB}\cdot\dfrac{BP}{PC}\cdot\dfrac{CQ}{QA}=-1.$

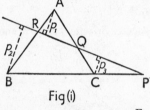

Fig (i)   Fig (ii)

FIG. 48.

Converses. The converses of these last two theorems are easily deduced from the theorems themselves and are very useful for proving concurrency and collinearity.

(1) If three points X, Y and Z are taken on the sides of a triangle ABC such that $\dfrac{BX}{XC}\cdot\dfrac{CY}{YA}\cdot\dfrac{AZ}{ZB}=+1,$ then AX, BY, CZ are concurrent; but if (2) the continued product

$$\frac{BX}{XC}\cdot\frac{CY}{YA}\cdot\frac{AZ}{ZB}=-1,$$

then X, Y, Z are collinear.

The Simson or Pedal Line

If P is any point on the circumcircle of the triangle ABC, then L, M, N the feet of the perpendiculars from P to the sides of the triangle ABC are collinear.

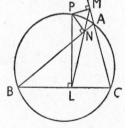

Join MN and NL.

Since $PNAM$ is cyclic,

$$P\widehat{N}M = P\widehat{A}M$$
$$= P\widehat{B}C \ (PABC \text{ cyclic}).$$

But

$$P\widehat{B}C = 180° - P\widehat{N}L \ (PNLB \text{ cyclic})$$

and therefore $\ P\widehat{N}M + P\widehat{N}L = 180°$

FIG. 49.

and so MNL is a straight line.

The converse. If a transversal cuts the sides of a triangle at L, M and N and if the perpendiculars at these points to the respec tive sides are concurrent, then the point of concurrence must be on the circumcircle of the triangle.

This may easily be proved by reversing the steps of the previous argument and is left as an exercise for the reader.

The pedal line of a point P is perpendicular to AQ where Q is the point on the circle such that PQ is parallel to BC

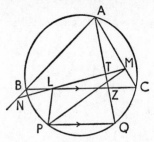

FIG. 50.

Suppose AQ meets BC at Z and the pedal line at T. Then

$$T\widehat{Z}L = A\widehat{Q}P \text{ (corresponding)}$$
$$= N\widehat{B}P \text{ (QPBA cyclic)}$$
$$= N\widehat{L}P \text{ (NBLP cyclic)}$$
$$= 90° - B\widehat{L}N$$
$$= 90° - T\widehat{L}Z.$$

Therefore $T\widehat{Z}L + T\widehat{L}Z = 90°$, and so $L\widehat{T}Z = 90°$.

The angle between the pedal lines of two points is equal to the angle subtended by the two points at the circumference of the circle

If P, P' are two given points and we construct points Q, Q' on

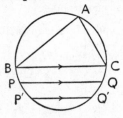

FIG. 51.

the circle so that PQ and $P'Q'$ are parallel to BC, by the last theorem, the pedal line of P is perpendicular to AQ and the pedal line of P' is perpendicular to AQ'. Therefore the angle between the two pedal lines is equal to QAQ'. But, by parallels, arc QQ' is equal to arc PP' and so $QAQ' = PAP'$. Hence the angle between the pedal lines is equal to the angle subtended by PP' at the circumference of the circle.

The pedal line of a point bisects the line joining the point to the orthocentre of the triangle

Let AH produced meet the circumcircle at Q and suppose PQ meets BC at X.

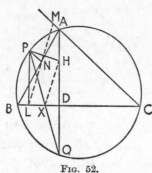

FIG. 52.

Since $HD = DQ$, $\ \widehat{XHD} = \widehat{XQD}$.

But $\qquad\qquad\qquad \widehat{XQD} = \widehat{QPL} \ $ (HQ parallel to PL)

and $\qquad\qquad\qquad \widehat{PQA} = \widehat{PBA} \ $ (cyclic property)

$\qquad\qquad\qquad\qquad\quad = \widehat{PLN} \ $ ($PBLN$ cyclic).

Therefore $\quad \widehat{XQH} = \widehat{XHQ} = \widehat{PBN} = \widehat{PLN} = \widehat{LPQ}$.

(*N.B.*—Look for five equal angles.)

Since $\widehat{PLN} = \widehat{XHQ}$ and PL is parallel to HQ; LN, the pedal line, must be parallel to XH.

But in the right-angled triangle PLX, if the pedal line meets PX at Z, we have proved

$$Z\widehat{P}L = Z\widehat{L}P.$$

As the complements of these angles must be equal,

$$Z\widehat{L}X = Z\widehat{X}L$$

and so $\qquad PZ = ZL = ZX.$

FIG 53.

Therefore Z is the mid point of PX. But the pedal line is parallel to XH, so if it bisects PX, it must also bisect PH.

The Radical Axis and Coaxal Circles

(1) NON-INTERSECTING CIRCLES

Definition. The radical axis of two circles is the locus of points from which tangents drawn to the two circles are equal.

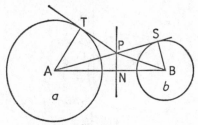

Fig. 54.

Consider two circles, centres A and B, radii a and b. Let P be any point such that the tangents from P to the two circles are equal. If PT, PS are the tangents and PN the perpendicular to AB,

$$PT^2 = PA^2 - a^2 = PN^2 + AN^2 - a^2$$

and $$PS^2 = PB^2 - b^2 = PN^2 + NB^2 - b.$$

Therefore $$PN^2 + AN^2 - a^2 = PN^2 + NB^2 - b^2$$

or $$AN^2 - NB^2 = a^2 - b^2$$

or $$(AN + NB)(AN - NB) = a^2 - b^2.$$

But $AN + NB = AB$ is constant and so $AN - NB$ must be constant for all possible positions of P. This means that N is a fixed point and the locus of P is therefore a straight line perpendicular to the line of centres.

Coaxal circles. Let us now choose any other point C on AB or AB produced and take c so that

$$AN^2 - a^2 = NB^2 - b^2 \text{ (as above)}$$
$$= NC^2 - c^2.$$

If we now draw a circle centre C radius c, any two of the three circles will have the same radical axis PN. We can in this way draw an infinite number of such circles and these are said to form a non-intersecting coaxal system. If $AN^2 - a^2 = k^2$, and we choose a point L so that $NL^2 = k^2$, the corresponding radius for the circle centre L will be zero. We thus get two point circles of the system L and L', equidistant from N, and no real circle of the system may have its centre between L and L'.

(2) Intersecting Circles

If P is any point on the common chord CD produced of two intersecting circles and PT, PS are the tangents to the circles,

$$PT^2 = PD.PC$$

and
$$PS^2 = PD.PC.$$

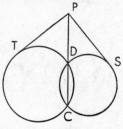

Fig. 55.

Therefore the common chord is the radical axis and the coaxal system is the system of circles passing through C and D.

The orthogonal system

If P is any point on the radical axis of a coaxal system, the

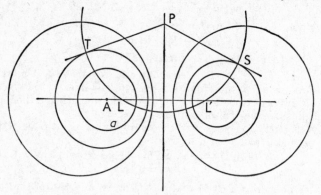

Fig. 56.

tangents from P to the circles are all equal in length and are also equal to PL or PL' (tangents to point circles). Therefore we can draw a circle, centre P, to pass through all the points of contact and L and L'. This circle, having each of its radii as a tangent to the corresponding circle of the coaxal system, must be orthogonal to every circle of the coaxal system. We may draw, by varying P, an infinite number of these circles and so a non-intersecting system of coaxal circles has associated with it an intersecting system of coaxal circles so that every circle of one system is orthogonal to every circle of the other system.

It follows immediately from this that $AL.AL' = a^2$.

Example 1. The common tangent to two circles of a coaxal system subtends a right angle at a limiting point.

If the common tangent XY meets the radical axis at Z, then $ZX = ZY = ZL$. So we may draw a circle centre Z to pass through X, Y and L. XY will be a diameter of this circle and so $X\widehat{L}Y$ is a right angle.

Example 2. The radical axes of three circles taken in pairs are concurrent.

Suppose two of the radical axes meet at O and let OP, OQ and OR be tangents from O to the three circles.

Then $OP = OQ$ (O being on the radical axis of these two circles) ;

$OP = OR$ (O being on the radical axis of these two circles).

Therefore $OQ = OR$ and so O is on the radical axis of the third pair.

If with centre O and radius OP we draw a circle, the circle will be orthogonal to each of the three given circles. So there is a unique circle orthogonal to each of three given circles, provided that their centres are not in the same straight line.

EXERCISES XXVIII

1. Show how to construct a triangle given the lengths of two sides and the included median.

2. Given a triangle ABC, show how to construct a rectangle $PQRS$ so that P lies on AB, Q on AC, R and S on CB and so that $PQ = 2QR$.

3. If A and B are fixed points 5 cm apart and P moves so that $AP/PB = 3/2$, prove the locus of P is a circle and find its radius.

4. If $ABCD$ is a square inscribed in a circle and P is any point on the minor arc AB, prove that $\dfrac{PC}{PD} = \dfrac{PB + PD}{PA + PC}$.

5. Given that AB is a fixed chord of a circle centre O, and that P is a variable point on the major arc AB, prove that (i) the centroid of APB lies on a fixed circle, (ii) the orthocentre of APB lies on another fixed circle.

6. Prove that $A'X$, $B'Y$, $C'Z$ are concurrent.

7. Prove that angle $FNE = 360° - 4B\hat{A}C$.

8. If HA' produced meets the circumcircle of ABC at Z, prove that $HA' = A'Z$.

9. If the internal bisectors of the angles B and C of the triangle ABC meet the opposite sides in Q and R and QR produced meets BC produced at Z, prove that AZ is the external bisector of the angle A.

10. If X, Y, Z are points on the sides of the triangle ABC so that $BX = BC/3$, $CY = CA/3$, $AZ = AB/3$ and AX, BY, CZ form a triangle of area S, prove that S is $1/7$ of the area of ABC.

11. Given a triangle ABC, show how to find a point P on its circumcircle, so that the pedal line of P is parallel to a given line.

12. If YZ is a diameter of the circumcircle of ABC, show that the pedal lines of Y and Z are perpendicular.

13. If ABC is an equilateral triangle and O is the centre of its circumcircle, prove that the pedal line of P, any point on this circumcircle, bisects PO.

14. Prove that the mid points of the four common tangents to two circles are collinear.

15. Given the two limiting points of a system of coaxal circles, show how to construct the circle of the system passing through a given point P.

SOLID GEOMETRY

The plane

A plane is a surface such that the straight line joining any two points of the surface lies entirely on the surface.

A plane is defined by any one of the following:
1. Three points (not in the same straight line).
2. Two parallel straight lines.
3. A straight line and a point not on the line.
4. Two intersecting straight lines.

Any two planes which are not parallel intersect in a straight line and any three planes, no two of which are parallel, have a common point.

Skew lines

Lines which are not parallel and do not intersect are called "skew lines". No one plane contains two given skew lines.

Generators

A generator of a surface is a straight line lying entirely in the surface. As examples, the generators of a cylinder are parallel to the axis and the generators of a cone are lines through the apex.

Angle between a line and a plane

The angle between a line and a plane is the angle between the line and its projection on the plane.

A line perpendicular to a plane is perpendicular to every line in that plane.

Angle between two planes

The angle between two planes is the angle between two lines, one in each plane, each perpendicular to the line of intersection of the planes.

Example. Given two skew lines and a point P, lying on neither line, show there is a unique line through P to intersect the given skew lines.

Suppose the lines are l and L. P and l define a plane; P and L define another plane. These two planes have a common line of intersection which must meet both l and L as it is coplanar with either of them. So there is one line to satisfy the conditions and one only.

If a line is perpendicular to each of two intersecting lines, it is perpendicular to their plane and consequently to any other line in that plane

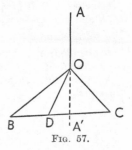

FIG. 57.

Suppose AO is perpendicular to OB and to OC. (We are not taking a special case by considering the lines to be concurrent at O; AO will also be perpendicular to any line parallel to OB or to OC.)

Suppose any other line through O in the plane BOC meets BC at D. Produce AO to A' so that $AO = OA'$. Since BO is a perpendicular bisector of AA', $BA = BA'$. Since CO is a perpendicular bisector of AA', $CA = CA'$.

Therefore the triangles BAC and $BA'C$ are congruent (SSS).

In particular,

$$A\widehat{B}D = A'\widehat{B}D.$$

So the triangles ABD, $A'BD$ are also congruent (SAS), and in particular

$$DA = DA'.$$

Therefore D lies on a perpendicular bisector of AA' and so DO is perpendicular to AO.

The following examples will show how concisely this theorem may be used and how useful it is.

Example 1. OA, OB, OC are three mutually perpendicular lines and H is the foot of the perpendicular from O to the plane ABC. Show that H is the orthocentre of the triangle ABC.

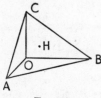

FIG. 58.

OH is perpendicular to the plane ABC and is therefore perpendicular to AB;

OC is perpendicular to OA and to OB; therefore it is perpendicular to any line in their plane and in particular to AB;

AB, being perpendicular to both OC and OH, is perpendicular to any line in their plane; in particular to CH.

Similarly AC is perpendicular to BH and therefore H is the orthocentre of the triangle ABC.

Example 2. A, B, C and D are any four points in space such that DB is perpendicular to AC. If N is the foot of the perpendicular from D to the plane ABC, prove that BN is perpendicular to AC.

DN is perpendicular to the plane ABC and therefore is perpendicular to AC;

DB is given perpendicular to the line AC.

Therefore AC is perpendicular to the plane DBN and in particular is perpendicular to BN.

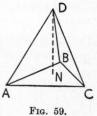

FIG. 59.

The tetrahedron

A tetrahedron is the figure obtained by joining four points in space provided, of course, that they are not all in one plane.

A regular tetrahedron is a tetrahedron in which all the six edges are equal.

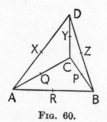

FIG. 60.

The lines joining the mid points of opposite edges of a tetrahedron intersect and bisect each other.

If P, Q, R, X, Y, Z are the mid points as shown in the diagram, then XY and RP are each parallel to and one half of AC (join of mid points).

Therefore $XRPY$ is a parallelogram and so XP and RY intersect and bisect each other.

Similarly XP and QZ intersect and bisect each other. So all joins of the mid points of opposite edges meet and bisect each other.

The lines joining the vertices of a tetrahedron to the centroids of the opposite faces intersect and divide each other in the ratio 1 : 3

Let G_1 be the centroid of the triangle ABC ;
   let G_2 be the centroid of the triangle DCB ;
   let G_3 be the centroid of the triangle DCA ;
   let G_4 be the centroid of the triangle ABD.

DG_2 and AG_1 will both intersect CB at X, its mid point (property of C.G.).

Therefore DG_2G_1A all lie in the same plane and so AG_2 meets DG_1 at G, say.

Now

$$XG_2 = \tfrac{1}{3}XD \quad \text{and} \quad XG_1 = \tfrac{1}{3}XA \text{ (property of C.G.)}$$

and therefore G_1G_2 is parallel to AD and one third of it.

So the triangles G_1GG_2 and DGA are similar and the ratio of corresponding sides is $1 : 3$.

Therefore AG_2 meets DG_1 at G where $G_1G : GD = 1 : 3$, i.e. it meets DG_1 three-quarters of the way down.

Similarly the other corresponding lines meet DG_1 at the same point and so all four lines intersect at the same point, and divide each other in the ratio $1 : 3$.

G is the centre of gravity of the solid tetrahedron and is three-quarters of the way down any one of the lines joining a vertex to the centroid of the opposite face.

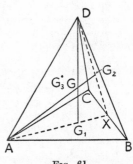

Fig. 61.

The circumscribing parallelepiped

Given two skew lines l and L, l and a parallel to L through any point of l will define a plane ; similarly L and a parallel to l through any point of L will define another plane. These planes are obviously parallel to each other, so it is possible, given any two skew lines, to draw a plane through each parallel to the other.

If we draw these planes for the three pairs of opposite edges of a tetrahedron, we shall get six planes, parallel in pairs. These planes form a parallelepiped and the tetrahedron $ABCD$ will be inscribed in the parallelepiped as shown in the figure.

(*N.B.*—Draw the parallelepiped first, *not* the tetrahedron.)

If the tetrahedron is regular, the circumscribing parallelepiped is a cube.

The opposite edges of the tetrahedron are different diagonals of the opposite faces of the parallelepiped and the mid point of any

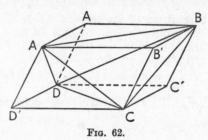

FIG. 62.

edge of the tetrahedron is the centroid of the parallelogram of which it is a diagonal.

Therefore, by symmetry, the lines joining the mid points of opposite edges of the tetrahedron will be parallel to four edges of the parallelepiped and will also pass through the centre of the parallelepiped. So these lines meet and bisect each other (alternative proof).

If two pairs of opposite edges of a tetrahedron are perpendicular, the third pair must be also

Suppose that AD is perpendicular to BC and that AB is perpendicular to CD.

As AD is perpendicular to CB, the diagonals of the parallelogram $AA'DD'$ are perpendicular. This face is therefore a rhombus and $AA' = A'D$.

Similarly $AA'BB'$ is a rhombus and $AA' = A'B$.

Therefore the parallelepiped is a rhomboid and, in particular, the face $AB'CD'$ is a rhombus; so AC and BD must be perpendicular to each other.

N.B.—If the three pairs of opposite edges of a tetrahedron are equal (i.e. $AB = CD$, $AC = BD$ and $AD = BC$) the circumscribing parallelepiped is rectangular, commonly called a cuboid or box; but if two pairs of opposite edges are equal, it does not follow that the third pair must be also.

Any tetrahedron has a unique circumscribing sphere

To prove this we shall need to know that any point P on the perpendicular to the plane of a triangle XYZ through its circumcentre is equidistant from the vertices of the triangle.

For $\quad PX^2 = PO^2 + OX^2,$
$\qquad\quad PY^2 = PO^2 + OY^2,$
$\qquad\quad PZ^2 = PO^2 + OZ^2;$

and as $\quad OX = OY = OZ \quad$ then $\quad PX = PY = PZ.$

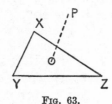

FIG. 63.

Now let S be the circumcentre of the triangle ABC and S' the circumcentre of the triangle BCD. Draw perpendiculars to their respective planes through S and S'. Let A' be the mid point of BC and call the perpendiculars p and p'. Then SA' is perpendicular to

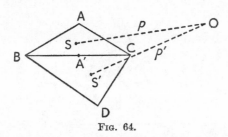

FIG. 64.

BC; but p being perpendicular to the plane ABC is also perpendicular to BC. Therefore p lies in the plane which bisects BC at right angles.

Similarly p' lies in the plane which bisects BC at right angles. So p and p' must meet, say at O. By our preliminary proof, $OA = OB = OC$ and $OB = OC = OD$.

Therefore a sphere may be drawn with centre O to pass through A, B, C and D.

Example. *If the sides of a tetrahedron are a, a, a, b, b, b, find the radius of the circumscribing sphere.*

Letter the tetrahedron as in the figure, and let DN be the perpendicular from D to the face ABC. By symmetry, N is the centre of the equilateral triangle ABC and the circumcentre O of the sphere is on DN. The perpendicular OX from O to DC must bisect DC since DC is a chord of the sphere.

From the triangle DOX,

$$\cos CDO = \tfrac{1}{2}b/R$$

where R is the radius of the sphere; from triangle DCN,

$$\cos CDO = DN/b.$$

Therefore

$$b/2R = DN/b$$

and so

$$R = b^2/2DN.$$

But

$$AN = \tfrac{1}{2}a \sec 30°$$

$$= \tfrac{1}{2}a\frac{2}{\sqrt{3}} = \frac{a}{\sqrt{3}}.$$

$$\therefore DN^2 = b^2 - a^2/3$$

and so

$$R = \frac{b^2}{2\sqrt{b^2 - a^2/3}}.$$

$N.B.$—If the tetrahedron is regular of side a,

$$R = \frac{a^2}{2\sqrt{\tfrac{2}{3}a^2}} = \sqrt{\tfrac{3}{8}}a.$$

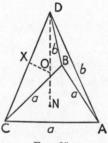

Fig. 65.

In this case, the circumcentre, the incentre and the centre of gravity of the tetrahedron all coincide.

OD is the radius of the circumscribing sphere, ON is the radius of the inscribed sphere and, since O is also the centre of gravity, O is one quarter the way up ND. Therefore the radius of the inscribed sphere is one third that of the circumsphere and equals

$$\tfrac{1}{3}\sqrt{\tfrac{3}{8}}a = \frac{a}{\sqrt{24}}.$$

Any two skew lines have a common perpendicular which is also the shortest distance between the two lines

Construction. Suppose l and L are the two skew lines. Through any point P of L, draw a line l' parallel to l, to make with L a plane π.

From any point Q of l draw a perpendicular QN to the plane π and in this plane draw NY parallel to l' to meet L at Y.

Since l and NY are parallel, the line l, QN and NY must all be in the same plane and so a line through Y parallel to NQ will meet l. Draw this line and suppose it meets l at X. Then XY is the common perpendicular and the shortest distance between points of the two lines.

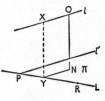

FIG. 66.

Proof. QN is perpendicular to the plane π. It is therefore perpendicular to both L and l'. But l' is parallel to l and so QN must be perpendicular to l and to L. But XY is parallel to QN and so XY is perpendicular to both l and L.

Q is *any* point of l. Take R, *any* point on L. Since QN is perpendicular to π, $Q\widehat{N}R = 90°$ and so $QN < QR$.

But $QNYX$ is a rectangle and therefore $XY < QR$.

So XY is the shortest possible distance between points of the two lines.

THE SPHERE

The intersection of any plane with a sphere is a circle

Let P be any point of intersection of the plane and the sphere, and let CN be the perpendicular from C, the centre of the sphere to the plane.

Then
$$NP^2 = CP^2 - CN^2.$$

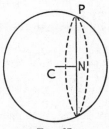

FIG. 67.

But CP is constant for all positions of P as it is the radius of the sphere and CN is also independent of P. Therefore NP is constant. But N is a fixed point and P lies in a fixed plane and so the locus of P is a circle, centre N.

Example. Show that a sphere can always be drawn to contain a given circle and a point P, not in the plane of the circle.

Consider *any* triangle ABC inscribed in the circle. One and only one sphere can be drawn through the four points $ABCP$ (previous

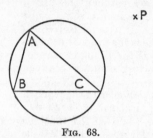

FIG. 68.

theorem) and the plane ABC will cut this sphere in the circle ABC. Therefore this sphere will contain the circle and the point P.

Any two spheres intersect in a circle

Suppose the centres of the spheres are A and B and that P_1 and P_2 are *any* two points of intersection of the spheres.

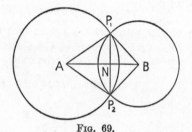

FIG. 69.

Since $AP_1 = AP_2$ and $BP_1 = BP_2$ (radii), the triangles AP_1B and AP_2B are congruent (SSS). So if we draw perpendiculars from P_1 and P_2 to the base AB, these perpendiculars will hit AB at the same point, N, say, and moreover the altitudes of the two triangles must be equal in length, i.e. $NP_1 = NP_2$. But N is a fixed point, NP_1 is constant for all positions of the point of intersection and P_1 lies in the fixed plane through N, perpendicular to AB. Therefore the locus of all such points is a circle centre N.

EXERCISES XXIX

1. If $ABCD$ is a tetrahedron whose opposite edges are perpendicular, and N is the foot of the perpendicular from A to the triangle BCD, prove that N is the orthocentre of the triangle BCD.

2. If P, Q are two variable points, one on each of two given skew lines, prove that the locus of the mid point of PQ is a plane.

3. In a regular tetrahedron, prove that the line joining the mid points of two opposite edges is perpendicular to these edges.

4. Find the radius of the circumsphere of a regular tetrahedron of side $2a$.

5. If two spheres, radii R and r, have their centres a distance d apart $(d < R + r)$, find the radius of their circle of intersection.

6. Find the perpendicular distance between opposite edges of a regular tetrahedron, side $2a$.

7. Find the locus of points from which tangents drawn to three given spheres are equal.

8. If two spheres, radii R and r, cut orthogonally find the radius of their circle of intersection.

ORTHOGONAL PROJECTION

Throughout this section, we shall be considering two planes, one horizontal π' and the other π inclined at an angle θ to the horizontal. The two planes are supposed to meet in the horizontal line XY.

If P is any point in π and P' is the foot of the perpendicular from P to π', then P' is said to be the orthogonal projection of the point P.

If P describes some curve S in π, then P' will describe some other curve S' in π'. S' is said to be the orthogonal projection of S.

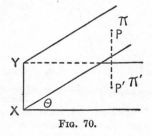

Fig. 70.

Lines

If P describes a straight line in π, then all the perpendiculars from points of this line to π' will be in a plane perpendicular to π' and so the orthogonal projection of a line is another line. Obviously parallel lines in π, since they do not intersect, will remain parallel on projection but not of course parallel to their original direction.

A line of length l along the greatest slope of π will become a line of length $l \cos \theta$ but a line perpendicular to the greatest slope will be unaltered in length. Other lines in π will have their lengths altered in the ratio $\cos \beta$, where β is the angle *the line to be projected* makes with the horizontal.

If three points P, Q, R on a straight line become on projection P', Q' and R', we see from the figure by parallels that

$$PQ/QR = P'Q'/Q'R'.$$

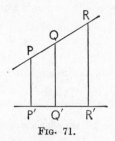

Fig. 71.

So ratios of lengths along the same line (or along parallel lines) will remain unaltered on projection. In particular, the mid point of a line remains as the mid point of the projected line.

Centre of gravity

Consider a triangle ABC with D the mid point of BC and with G as its centroid. On projection, we shall get another triangle $A'B'C'$

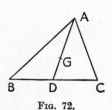

Fig. 72.

with D' as the mid point of $B'C'$ and G' as the point dividing $A'D'$ in the ratio $2:1$. So the centre of gravity of a triangle projects into the centre of gravity of the new triangle.

Since the centre of gravity of any uniform lamina is ultimately a matter of ratios, the centre of gravity of any figure will become the centre of gravity of the projected figure.

N.B.—In general the angle between two lines will not retain any simple property on projection. A right angle will not generally project into a right angle except in the case when one of the arms is a line of greatest slope.

Areas

Consider the area of any closed figure in π and take an element perpendicular to the greatest slope of breadth l and thickness δx. The breadth of this element will be unaltered but its thickness will become $\delta x \cos \theta$. If A and A' are the areas of the two figures

Fig. 73.

$$A = \Sigma \, l . \delta x \quad \text{and} \quad A' = \Sigma \, l . \delta x \cos \theta.$$

Therefore $A' = A \cos \theta$

and so the area of any figure is decreased on projection in the ratio $\cos \theta$.

The circle

Consider an ellipse axes $2a$ and $2b$ in π with its major axis along a line of greatest slope. Take the x-axis to be along a line of greatest slope and the coordinates of any point P on the ellipse may be expressed as $(a \cos \alpha, b \sin \alpha)$.

The centre of the ellipse, having the property that all chords through it are bisected at the centre, will project into the centre of the new figure and the axes will project into two perpendicular lines through the new centre. The x coordinate of P being along a line of greatest slope will be shortened in the ratio $\cos \theta$ on projection

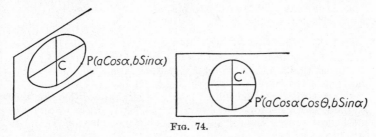

FIG. 74.

while the y coordinate will be unchanged. The coordinates of P' will then be $(a \cos \alpha \cos \theta, b \sin \alpha)$. This point, as α varies, will always lie on the ellipse

$$\frac{x^2}{a^2 \cos^2 \theta} + \frac{y^2}{b^2} = 1.$$

An ellipse of semi-axes a and b projects therefore into another ellipse of semi-axes $a \cos \theta$ and b. If the original ellipse were situated so that its minor axis lay along the line of greatest slope, the semi-axes of the projected ellipse would be $b \cos \theta$ and a. If the ellipse has its major axis along a line of greatest slope, by choosing the angle of projection so that $\cos \theta = b/a$, we shall get on projection an ellipse of semi-axes b and b, i.e. *a circle*. Conversely, we can always project a circle of radius a into an ellipse of semi-axes a and b by choosing the angle of projection so that $\cos \theta = b/a$. Note that in this case the major axis of the ellipse will be parallel to XY.

The main properties

These are the main properties of projection and they may be used to deduce properties of one figure from those of another ; they are especially useful in deducing properties of the ellipse from those of the circle.

Before illustrating the method, we give a list of the most important properties of projection.

1. A line projects into a line.
2. Parallel lines project into parallel lines.
3. The ratio of distances along the same line or along parallel lines is unaltered.
4. The mid point of a line remains the mid point.
5. The centre of gravity of an area remains the centre of gravity.
6. An area is reduced in the ratio $\cos \theta$.
7. An ellipse projects into another ellipse.
8. An ellipse may always be projected into a circle.
9. A circle may always be projected into an ellipse of given eccentricity (i.e. a given ratio for the axes).

Geometrical properties of the ellipse

Since a tangent to the curve is a line joining two coincident points on the curve, it will remain a tangent to the projected curve ; pole and polar, therefore, will remain pole and polar.

Many properties of the ellipse may be easily proved by using this method and the properties listed in the last paragraph and the methods of projection used are illustrated in the following examples.

Example 1.   Prove that the area of an ellipse is πab.

The area of a circle of radius a is πa^2. If the circle is projected through an angle θ where $\cos \theta = b/a$, we shall get an ellipse of semi-axes a and b whose area must be $\pi a^2 \cos \theta$ or πab.

Example 2.   Prove that the locus of the mid points of parallel chords of an ellipse is a diameter.

The locus of the mid points of parallel chords of a circle is the perpendicular diameter. Parallel chords remain parallel chords, the mid points remain mid points and the diameter remains a diameter but *not* the perpendicular diameter. So the locus of the mid points of parallel chords of an ellipse is a diameter.

Diameters of the ellipse such that each bisects all chords parallel to the other are called conjugate diameters and we see that perpendicular diameters of the circle project into conjugate diameters of the ellipse.

Example 3.   Prove that the eccentric angles at the ends of conjugate diameters differ by 90°.

If the y-axis of a circle is taken along a line of greatest slope, the point $(a \cos \alpha, \ a \sin \alpha)$ projects into the point $(a \cos \alpha, \ b \sin \alpha)$ on the ellipse. The angle α is therefore the eccentric angle of the point on the ellipse and its geometrical interpretation is the angle the radius makes with the x-axis *in the circle*. For perpendicular diameters, these angles differ by 90°; so the eccentric angles at the ends of conjugate diameters differ by 90°.

Example 4. Prove the triangle of greatest area which can be inscribed in a circle is equilateral. Deduce a property of the ellipse.

Suppose ABC is the triangle of greatest area inscribable in the circle ABC. Then it is certainly the greatest triangle on AB as base and so C will be at its greatest possible distance from AB. The diameter through C must therefore be perpendicular to AB and so $CA = CB$. Similarly $CA = AB$ and so the triangle must be equilateral. Its area is $3\left(\tfrac{1}{2}a^2 \sin 120°\right)$ or $3\sqrt{3}a^2/4$.

Fɪɢ. 75.

The equilateral triangle will not remain equilateral on projection but the property that the tangent at each vertex is parallel to the opposite side will remain on projection: so the triangle of greatest area inscribable in an ellipse is such that the tangent at any vertex is parallel to the opposite side. Its area is $\dfrac{3\sqrt{3}a^2 \cos\theta}{4}$ or $3\sqrt{3}ab/4$.

This alternative proof is worthy of note. If in *any closed figure* APB is a triangle of maximum area, then APB must be the greatest triangle on AB as base and so the area of the triangle must have a stationary value for the point P. This means that if we take an adjacent point P' on the curve, the area APB must equal the area $AP'B$. So PP' is parallel to AB and, in the limit, the tangent at P must be parallel to AB.

Example 5. Prove the quadrilateral of greatest area inscribable in a circle is a square. Deduce a property of the ellipse.

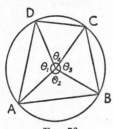

Fɪɢ. 76.

If O is the centre of the circle, the area of triangle AOB in the figure is $\tfrac{1}{2}a^2 \sin\theta_2$. This has its greatest possible value when $\theta_2 = 90°$.

The area of the quadrilateral $ABCD$ is

$$\tfrac{1}{2}a^2(\sin\theta_1 + \sin\theta_2 + \sin\theta_3 + \sin\theta_4)$$

and each term of this sum attains its maximum value at the same time, i.e. when

$$\theta_1 = \theta_2 = \theta_3 = \theta_4 = 90°.$$

So the greatest quadrilateral is a square and its area is $2a^2$. Since the diagonals of a square are perpendicular, the square will project into a parallelogram joining the ends of conjugate diameters. This is the quadrilateral of greatest possible area in the ellipse and its area is $2a^2 \cos\theta$ or $2ab$.

Example 6. Project the theorem that the angle in a semi-circle is a right angle.

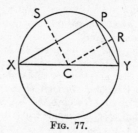

Fig. 77.

In the circle, $X\hat{P}Y = 90°$. XY will project into a diameter $X'Y'$, P will project into P' on the ellipse but the right angle will not project into a right angle. To overcome the difficulty of projecting the right

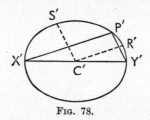

Fig. 78.

angle, we use Pythagoras' theorem and project the property

$$XY^2 = XP^2 + PY^2.$$

At first sight, this seems to be equally difficult to project, as the lengths will all be altered in different ratios on projection.

There is a very useful trick to circumvent this. Dividing each side of the equation by a^2, we have

$$XY^2/a^2 = XP^2/a^2 + PY^2/a^2$$

and we now choose each fraction so that the radius in the denominator is parallel to the line in the numerator. The equation becomes

$$XY^2/XC^2 = XP^2/CR^2 + PY^2/CS^2$$

where CR and CS are radii parallel to XP and YP respectively. This reduces to

$$XP^2/CR^2 + PY^2/CS^2 = 4.$$

Since each of the fractions is now the ratio of lengths along parallel lines and such a ratio is unaltered on projection, we get for the ellipse,

$$X'P'^2/C'R'^2 + P'Y'^2/C'S'^2 = 4$$

where $C'R'$ and $C'S'$ are radii parallel to $X'P'$ and $Y'P'$ respectively.

This is the theorem in the ellipse corresponding to the angle in a semi-circle theorem.

EXERCISES XXX

1. Prove that the centre of an ellipse is the centre of gravity of a triangle of maximum area inscribed in it.

2. If T is any point on a radius CA produced of an ellipse and the polar of T meets CA in N, prove $CN.CT = CA^2$.

3. Prove that the quadrilateral obtained by joining the ends of conjugate diameters of an ellipse is a parallelogram of constant area and find that area.

4. If the tangents at P and Q to an ellipse meet at T, prove that the triangles CPT and CTQ are equal in area.

5. If P is the mid point of a chord HK of an ellipse and CP meets the ellipse at R, prove that triangles RPH and RPK are equal in area.

6. If TP, TQ are tangents from T to an ellipse, prove that CT bisects PQ.

7. Show how to construct a triangle of maximum area in an ellipse, having a given point P on the ellipse as one vertex.

8. Project orthogonally the theorem that the tangent to a circle is perpendicular to the radius at its point of contact.

REVISION PAPER VII

1. A variable point X, on the side BC of a fixed triangle ABC, forms with A and another point Y a triangle AXY similar to, and described in the same sense as, the triangle ABC. Prove that the locus of Y is a straight line. (L)

2. In a tetrahedron $ABCD$ it is given that $AB = CD$, $BC = AD$, $CA = BD$. If X, Y are the mid points of AB, CD respectively, show that (i) $YA = YB$, (ii) XY is perpendicular to AB and CD.

Determine the shortest distance between two opposite edges of a regular tetrahedron of edge a. (NU)

3. Prove that, if L is the reflection of the vertex B in the altitude AD of the triangle ABC (so that BL is bisected at right angles by AD), then the reflection of L in the side AC lies on the circumcircle of the triangle. (L)

4. Prove that if a transversal meets the sides BC, CA, AB of a triangle at X, Y, Z respectively then

$$\frac{BX}{XC} \cdot \frac{CY}{YA} \cdot \frac{AZ}{ZB} = -1.$$

The mid points of the sides BC, CA, AB of a triangle ABC are L, M, N respectively. Concurrent lines through the vertices A, B, C meet the opposite sides respectively at P, Q, R. The sides BC, CA, AB meet RM, PN, QL respectively at X, Y, Z. Prove that X, Y, Z are collinear. (NU)

5. Prove that the feet of the perpendiculars to the sides of a triangle ABC from any point P on its circumcircle lie on a straight line (the Simson line of the point).

A circle, centre O, circumscribes a triangle ABC, right angled at C. The Simson line of a point P on the circle meets PC at K. Prove that the locus of K, for varying positions of P, is the circle on OC as diameter. (NU)

6. Prove that an ellipse of semi-axes a, b $(a > b)$ can be projected orthogonally so that every point of the projected figure lies on a circle.

The circle is itself projected orthogonally into an ellipse similar to the given ellipse ; find the lengths of the semi-axes. $(O \& C)$

7. Prove that if two straight lines are parallel and one of them is perpendicular to a plane, then the other one is also perpendicular to that plane.

The tetrahedron $OABC$ is such that the angles AOB, BOC, COA are right angles. The perpendicular from O to BC cuts it at N. The edges AB, AC are bisected at L and M. Prove that LM is perpendicular to the plane AON. (NU)

8. ABC is a triangle and the altitudes through A, B, C meet the opposite sides at D, E, F respectively. Prove that AD, BE, CF meet at a common point, the orthocentre of the triangle.

Prove that the circumcentre, the median point and the orthocentre are collinear. $(O \& C)$

9. If I is the incentre of a triangle ABC and if the perpendicular bisectors of BI, CI meet at P, prove that the angles ABP, ACP are supplementary and deduce that PI passes through A. (L)

10. If B', C', are points on the sides AB, AC of a triangle ABC such that $B'C'$ is parallel to BC, prove that $AB/AB' = AC/AC'$.

From a point O in the plane of a parallelogram $AXBY$ the line OX is drawn meeting the sides AY, BY at X_1, X_2 and the line OY meeting AX, BX at Y_1, Y_2. Prove that X_1Y_1 is parallel to X_2Y_2. (L)

TRIGONOMETRY

ABBREVIATIONS USED

The following abbreviations have been used throughout this section:

O stands for the circumcentre of the triangle ABC.
I stands for the incentre of the triangle ABC.
I_1, I_2, I_3 stand for the ex-centres of the triangle ABC.
H stands for the orthocentre of the triangle ABC.
D, E, F stand for the feet of the altitudes of the triangle ABC.
A', B', C' stand for the mid points of the sides of the triangle ABC.
R stands for the circum-radius of the triangle ABC.
r stands for the in-radius of the triangle ABC.
r_1, r_2, r_3 stand for the ex-radii of the triangle ABC.
s stands for the semi-perimeter of the triangle ABC.
Δ stands for the area of the triangle ABC.

FORMULAE

A list of the formulae which is important to know follows. These formulae are numbered and are referred to in the text by the numbers assigned to them. Other formulae have been proved but, if not numbered, are not considered sufficiently important to be learnt by heart.

(1) $\cos^2 \theta + \sin^2 \theta = 1$.

(2) $\sec^2 \theta = 1 + \tan^2 \theta$.

(3) $\operatorname{cosec}^2 \theta = 1 + \cot^2 \theta$.

(4) $\cos (90° - \theta) = \sin \theta$.

(5) $\sin (90° - \theta) = \cos \theta$.

(6) $\tan (90° - \theta) = \cot \theta$.

(7) $c^2 = a^2 + b^2 - 2ab \cos C$.

(8) $a/\sin A = b/\sin B = c/\sin C = 2R$.

(9) $\cos (A - B) = \cos A \cos B + \sin A \sin B$.

(10) $\sin (A - B) = \sin A \cos B - \cos A \sin B$.

(11) $\cos (A + B) = \cos A \cos B - \sin A \sin B$.

(12) $\sin (A + B) = \sin A \cos B + \cos A \sin B$.

(13) $\cos 2A = \cos^2 A - \sin^2 A$.

(14) $\cos 2A = 2 \cos^2 A - 1$.

(15) $\cos 2A = 1 - 2 \sin^2 A$.

(16) $\sin 2A = 2 \sin A \cos A$.

(17) $\tan (A + B) = (\tan A + \tan B)/(1 - \tan A \tan B)$.

(18) $\tan (A - B) = (\tan A - \tan B)/(1 + \tan A \tan B)$.

(19) $\tan 2A = 2 \tan A/(1 - \tan^2 A)$.

(20) $\tan (A + B + C) = (\tan A + \tan B + \tan C - \tan A \tan B \tan C)/(1 - \tan B \tan C - \tan C \tan A - \tan A \tan B)$.

(21) $\tan(A+B+C+\ldots) = (s_1-s_3+s_5\ldots)/(1-s_2+s_4-\ldots)$.

(22) If $A + B + C = 180°$,

$$\tan A + \tan B + \tan C = \tan A.\tan B.\tan C.$$

(23) If $A + B + C = 180°$,

$$\cot \tfrac{1}{2}A + \cot \tfrac{1}{2}B + \cot \tfrac{1}{2}C = \cot \tfrac{1}{2}A.\cot \tfrac{1}{2}B.\cot \tfrac{1}{2}C.$$

(24) $1 + \cos A = 2\cos^2 \tfrac{1}{2}A$.

(25) $1 - \cos A = 2\sin^2 \tfrac{1}{2}A$.

(26) $\sin 2A = 2\tan A/(1 + \tan^2 A)$.

(27) $\cos 2A = (1 - \tan^2 A)/(1 + \tan^2 A)$.

(28) $\sin X + \sin Y = 2\sin \tfrac{1}{2}(X + Y).\cos \tfrac{1}{2}(X - Y)$.

(29) $\sin X - \sin Y = 2\cos \tfrac{1}{2}(X + Y).\sin \tfrac{1}{2}(X - Y)$.

(30) $\cos X + \cos Y = 2\cos \tfrac{1}{2}(X + Y).\cos \tfrac{1}{2}(X - Y)$.

(31) $\cos X - \cos Y = 2\sin \tfrac{1}{2}(X + Y).\sin \tfrac{1}{2}(Y - X)$.

(32) If $A + B + C = 180°$,

$$\sin A + \sin B + \sin C = 4\cos \tfrac{1}{2}A.\cos \tfrac{1}{2}B.\cos \tfrac{1}{2}C.$$

(33) If $A + B + C = 180°$,

$$\cos A + \cos B + \cos C - 1 = 4\sin \tfrac{1}{2}A.\sin \tfrac{1}{2}B.\sin \tfrac{1}{2}C.$$

(34) Solution of $\sin x = \sin \alpha$ is $x = n\pi + (-1)^n\alpha$.

(35) Solution of $\cos x = \cos \alpha$ is $x = 2n\pi \pm \alpha$.

(36) Solution of $\tan x = \tan \alpha$ is $x = n\pi + \alpha$.

(37) $\dfrac{a - b}{a + b} \cot \dfrac{C}{2} = \tan \tfrac{1}{2}(A - B)$.

(38) $c = a\cos B + b\cos A$.

(39) $\tan^{-1} x + \tan^{-1} y = \tan^{-1}(x + y)/(1 - xy)$.

(40) $\tan^{-1} x - \tan^{-1} y = \tan^{-1}(x - y)/(1 + xy)$.

(41) $\cos \tfrac{1}{2}C = \sqrt{\dfrac{s(s - c)}{ab}}$.

(42) $\sin \tfrac{1}{2}C = \sqrt{\dfrac{(s - a)(s - b)}{ab}}$.

(43) $\tan \tfrac{1}{2}C = \sqrt{\dfrac{(s - a)(s - b)}{s(s - c)}}$.

(44) $\Delta = \tfrac{1}{2}ab \sin C$.

(45) $\Delta = \sqrt{s(s - a)(s - b)(s - c)}$.

(46) $AH = 2R \cos A$.

(47) $HD = 2R \cos B \cos C$.

(48) If A is acute, the angles of the pedal triangle are $180° - 2A$, $180° - 2B$, $180° - 2C$.

(49) If A is acute, the sides of the pedal triangle are $a\cos A$, $b\cos B$, $c\cos C$.

(50) If A is obtuse, the angles of the pedal triangle are $2A - 180°$, $2B$, $2C$.

(51) If A is obtuse, the sides of the pedal triangle are $-a \cos A$, $b \cos B$, $c \cos C$.

(52) $R = abc/4\Delta$.

(53) $r = \Delta/s$.

(54) $r = 4R \sin \frac{1}{2}A \sin \frac{1}{2}B \sin \frac{1}{2}C$.

(55) $r_1 = \Delta/(s - a)$.

(56) $r_1 = 4R \sin \frac{1}{2}A \cos \frac{1}{2}B \cos \frac{1}{2}C$.

(57) $I_2 I_3 = 4R \cos \frac{1}{2}A$.

(58) $II_1 = 4R \sin \frac{1}{2}A$.

Definitions of the ratios

Consider two perpendicular Cartesian axes, Ox and Oy, together with a radius OP of unit length; if the angle xOP (measured counterclockwise from Ox) is θ, then the coordinates of P are defined as $\cos \theta$ and $\sin \theta$ whatever the position of P.

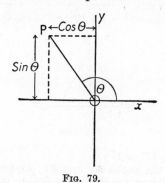

FIG. 79.

Signs are defined as in ordinary Algebraic graphs. From $\cos \theta$ and $\sin \theta$, the other ratios are defined as follows:

$$\tan \theta = \sin \theta / \cos \theta; \quad \operatorname{cosec} \theta = 1/\sin \theta;$$

$$\sec \theta = 1/\cos \theta; \quad \cot \theta = 1/\tan \theta.$$

These definitions are easily seen to fit in with the right-angle definitions usually given for the ratios and it follows immediately from the figure that

$$\cos^2 \theta + \sin^2 \theta = 1 \qquad . \qquad . \qquad . \qquad (1)$$

Dividing by $\cos^2 \theta$

$$1 + \tan^2 \theta = \sec^2 \theta \qquad . \qquad . \qquad . \qquad (2)$$

Dividing (1) by $\sin^2 \theta$,

$$1 + \cot^2 \theta = \operatorname{cosec}^2 \theta \qquad . \qquad . \qquad (3)$$

Special angles

From the definitions follow immediately the ratios of 0°, 90°, 180° and 270° as shown in the table.

	sin	cos	tan
0°	0	1	0
90°	1	0	∞
180°	0	− 1	0
270°	− 1	0	∞

We also see that cos 45° = sin 45° and as the sum of their squares

Fig. 80.

is 1, cos 45° = sin 45° = $1/\sqrt{2}$.

In dealing with the angles 30° and 60°, we are able to construct equilateral triangles as shown which enable us to calculate the coordinates of P.

From these diagrams, we see

$$\cos 60° = \tfrac{1}{2}; \qquad \sin 60° = \sqrt{3}/2.$$
$$\cos 30° = \sqrt{3}/2; \quad \sin 30° = \tfrac{1}{2}.$$

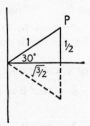

Fig. 81.

Complementary angles

If $x\widehat{O}P$ and $x\widehat{O}Q$ are complementary, then $x\widehat{O}P = Q\widehat{O}y$ and so the projection of OP on the x-axis is equal to the projection of OQ on the y-axis.

Therefore

$$\cos (90° - \theta) = \sin \theta \quad . \quad . \quad (4)$$

and similarly

$$\sin (90° - \theta) = \cos \theta \quad . \quad . \quad (5)$$

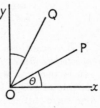

FIG. 82.

N.B.—The prefix co- in the ratios stands for complementary and means that the ratio of any angle is equal to the co-ratio of the complementary angle; e.g.

$$\tan (90° - \theta) = \cot \theta \quad . \quad . \quad . \quad (6)$$

Angles larger than 90°

From the definitions, we see at once that

in the first quadrant, sin is +ve, cos is +ve, tan is +ve;
in the second quadrant, sin is +ve, cos is −ve, tan is −ve;
in the third quadrant, sin is −ve, cos is −ve, tan is +ve;
in the fourth quadrant, sin is −ve, cos is +ve, tan is −ve.

FIG. 83.

These signs can be remembered by the word CAST, written as shown in the diagram.

C stands for cos +ve; sin and tan −ve;
A stands for all +ve;
S stands for sin +ve; cos and tan −ve;
T stands for tan +ve; cos and sin −ve.

Since the magnitude of the projections of the unit radius on the axes depends solely on the *acute* angle the radius makes with the x-axis, *any ratio of any angle is equal numerically to the same ratio of the acute angle the radius makes with the x-axis.* The sign must *first* be found from the diagram above.

Example. Find the value of sin 240°.

As 240° is in the third quadrant, its sine is −ve and the acute angle the radius makes with the x-axis is 60°.

Therefore $\quad \sin 240° = - \sin 60° = - \sqrt{3}/2.$

To simplify expressions such as $\tan (270° - \theta)$, follow the same argument but, for simplicity, imagine θ to be acute. *Your formula will apply for all values of θ but the argument is simplified by supposing it to be acute.*

Examples. $\sin (180° - θ) = + \sin θ$;
$\cos (180° + θ) = - \cos θ$;
$\tan (270° - θ) = + \tan (90° - θ) = \cot θ$;
$\sec (360° - 3θ) = + \sec 3θ$;
$\cot (- 2θ) = - \cot 2θ$.

N.B.—cosec, sec and cot follow the same rules as sin, cos and tan respectively since they are their reciprocals.

It is perhaps worth noting in the examples above that if the multiple of 90° is *even* (e.g. 0°, 180°, 360°), the answer contains *the same ratio* ; if it is *odd* (e.g. 90° or 270°), the answer contains *the co-ratio.*

EXERCISES XXXI

Prove the following identities :

1. $\dfrac{1}{1 - \cos θ} + \dfrac{1}{1 + \cos θ} = 2 \operatorname{cosec}^2 θ$;

2. $(1 + \cot θ)(1 + \tan θ) = 2 + \operatorname{cosec} θ \sec θ$;

3. $\dfrac{\cos θ}{\cos (90° - θ)} + \dfrac{\sin θ}{\sin (90° - θ)} = \operatorname{cosec} θ \sec θ$;

4. $\cos^4 θ + \sin^4 θ = 1 - 2 \cos^2 θ \sin^2 θ$;

5. $\cos^3 θ + \sin^3 θ = (\cos θ + \sin θ)(1 - \cos θ \sin θ)$.

Simplify the following :

6. $\tan (90° + θ)$;   7. $\sec (90° - 3θ)$;   8. $\operatorname{cosec} (4θ - 180°)$;

9. $\cos (θ - 180°)$;   10. $\sin (2θ - 90°)$.

The cos formula and the sine formula

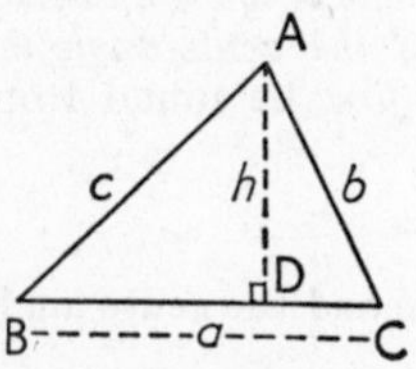

FIG. 84.

If AD, the height of an acute-angled triangle, is h, then

$$CD = b \cos C$$

and so $BD = a - b \cos C.$

By Pythagoras,

$$h^2 = b^2 - (b \cos C)^2.$$

and $$h^2 = c^2 - (a - b \cos C)^2.$$

Therefore $b^2 - b^2 \cos^2 C = c^2 - a^2 - b^2 \cos^2 C + 2ab \cos C.$

or $$c^2 = a^2 + b^2 - 2ab \cos C.$$

If C is obtuse,

$$CD = b \cos (180° - C)$$

and $\qquad BD = a + b \cos (180° - C).$

Therefore $\qquad h^2 = b^2 - b^2 \cos^2 (180° - C)$

and $\qquad h^2 = c^2 - (a + b \cos \overline{180° - C})^2.$

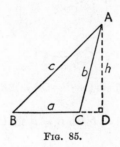

FIG. 85.

Therefore

$$b^2 - b^2 \cos^2 (180° - C)$$
$$= c^2 - a^2 - b^2 \cos^2 (180° - C) - 2ab \cos (180° - C)$$

or $\qquad c^2 = a^2 + b^2 + 2ab \cos (180° - C)$

$$= a^2 + b^2 - 2ab \cos C \qquad . \qquad . \qquad . \qquad . \qquad (7)$$

Notice that the same formula holds in both cases.

The sine formula

Consider a triangle ABC with its circumcircle. Draw the diameter BX through B. Then since $\widehat{BAX} = 90°$, and $\widehat{AXB} = C$

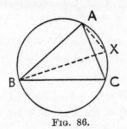

FIG. 86.

$$c = 2R \sin C.$$

Therefore, by symmetry,

$$a/\sin A = b/\sin B = c/\sin C = 2R.$$

Obtuse case

If A is obtuse, since $B\widehat{X}C = 180° - A$,

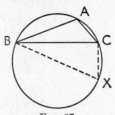

Fig. 87.

$$a = 2R \sin(180° - A) = 2R \sin A.$$

Therefore, as before,

$$a/\sin A = b/\sin B = c/\sin C = 2R \quad . \quad . \quad (8)$$

The addition formulae

If two unit radii OP, OQ are taken such that $x\widehat{O}P$ and $x\widehat{O}Q$ are

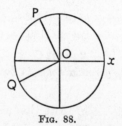

Fig. 88.

B and A respectively, then the coordinates of P and Q are $P = (\cos B, \sin B)$ and $Q = (\cos A, \sin A)$ whatever the magnitudes of A and B.

Therefore $PQ^2 = (\cos B - \cos A)^2 + (\sin B - \sin A)^2$

$$= 2 - 2\cos A \cos B - 2\sin A \sin B, \quad \text{using (1)}.$$

But by (7), since $\widehat{POQ} = A - B$,

$$PQ^2 = 1 + 1 - 2\cos(A - B).$$

Therefore $\cos(A - B) = \cos A \cos B + \sin A \sin B \quad . \quad . \quad (9)$

for all values of A and B.

Write $(90° + A)$ for A and then

$$\cos(90° + A - B) = \cos(90° + A)\cos B + \sin(90° + A)\sin B$$

or $\quad \sin(A - B) = \sin A \cos B - \cos A \sin B \quad . \quad . \quad (10)$

If, in (9) and (10), we replace B by $-B$, remembering that $\cos B = \cos(-B)$ and $-\sin B = \sin(-B)$, we get

$$\cos(A+B) = \cos A \cos B - \sin A \sin B \qquad . \quad (11)$$

$$\sin(A+B) = \cos A \sin B + \sin A \cos B \qquad . \quad (12)$$

Putting $B = A$ in (11) we get

$$\cos 2A = \cos^2 A - \sin^2 A \qquad . \qquad . \qquad . \quad (13)$$

and using (1), the alternative forms

$$\cos 2A = 2\cos^2 A - 1 \qquad . \qquad . \qquad . \quad (14)$$

and

$$\cos 2A = 1 - 2\sin^2 A \qquad . \qquad . \qquad . \quad (15)$$

Treating (12) in the same way,

$$\sin 2A = 2\sin A \cos A \qquad . \qquad . \qquad . \quad (16)$$

Tangents of sum and difference

$$\tan(A+B) = \frac{\sin(A+B)}{\cos(A+B)} = \frac{\sin A \cos B + \cos A \sin B}{\cos A \cos B - \sin A \sin B}$$

$$= \frac{\tan A + \tan B}{1 - \tan A \tan B} \cdot \qquad . \quad (17)$$

Writing $-B$ for B,

$$\tan(A-B) = \frac{\tan A - \tan B}{1 + \tan A \tan B} \cdot \qquad . \quad (18)$$

From (17), putting $B = A$,

$$\tan 2A = \frac{2\tan A}{1 - \tan^2 A} \cdot \qquad . \qquad . \quad (19)$$

It is worth noting here that

$$\tan(A+B+C) = \frac{\tan A + \tan(B+C)}{1 - \tan A \tan(B+C)}$$

$$= \frac{\tan A + \tan B + \tan C - \tan A \tan B \tan C}{1 - \tan B \tan C - \tan C \tan A - \tan A \tan B} \quad (20)$$

This is a particular case of the more general formula,

$$\tan(A+B+C+\ldots) = \frac{s_1 - s_3 + s_5 - \ldots}{1 - s_2 + s_4 - \ldots} \quad . \quad (21)$$

where s_n stands for the sum of all the possible products of $\tan A$, $\tan B$, etc., taken n at a time.

It follows from (20), since $\tan 180° = 0$, that if A, B, C are the angles of a triangle,

$$\tan A + \tan B + \tan C = \tan A \cdot \tan B \cdot \tan C \qquad . \quad (22)$$

Also, by expanding $\tan(\tfrac{1}{2}A + \tfrac{1}{2}B + \tfrac{1}{2}C)$, which is ∞ if A, B, C

F*

are the angles of a triangle

$$\tan \tfrac{1}{2}A \cdot \tan \tfrac{1}{2}B + \tan \tfrac{1}{2}C \cdot \tan \tfrac{1}{2}B + \tan \tfrac{1}{2}C \cdot \tan \tfrac{1}{2}A = 1$$

or $$\cot \tfrac{1}{2}A + \cot \tfrac{1}{2}B + \cot \tfrac{1}{2}C = \cot \tfrac{1}{2}A \cdot \cot \tfrac{1}{2}B \cdot \cot \tfrac{1}{2}C \quad . \quad (23)$$

So, in any triangle, *the sum of the tangents of the angles equals their product* and *the sum of the cotangents of the half angles equals their product*.

From the formulae for $\cos 2A$, we get

$$1 + \cos A = 2 \cos^2 \tfrac{1}{2}A \quad . \quad . \quad . \quad (24)$$

and $$1 - \cos A = 2 \sin^2 \tfrac{1}{2}A \quad . \quad . \quad . \quad (25)$$

These are worth remembering and using whenever you meet the expressions $(1 - \cos A)$ and $(1 + \cos A)$.

Two more useful formulae

$$\sin 2A = 2 \sin A \cdot \cos A = \frac{2 \tan A}{\sec^2 A} = \frac{2 \tan A}{1 + \tan^2 A} \quad . \quad . \quad (26)$$

$$\cos 2A = \cos^2 A - \sin^2 A = \frac{\cos^2 A - \sin^2 A}{\cos^2 A + \sin^2 A} = \frac{1 - \tan^2 A}{1 + \tan^2 A} \quad (27)$$

It is quite easy to expand further multiples as shown in the following two examples :

$$\begin{aligned}
\sin 3A &= \sin (2A + A) = \sin 2A \cdot \cos A + \cos 2A \cdot \sin A \\
&= 2 \sin A \cdot \cos^2 A + (1 - 2 \sin^2 A) \sin A \\
&= 3 \sin A - 4 \sin^3 A.
\end{aligned}$$

$$\begin{aligned}
\cos 3A &= \cos (2A + A) = \cos 2A \cdot \cos A - \sin 2A \cdot \sin A \\
&= (2 \cos^2 A - 1) \cos A - 2 \sin^2 A \cdot \cos A \\
&= 4 \cos^3 A - 3 \cos A.
\end{aligned}$$

The product formulae

Since $$\sin (A + B) = \sin A \cdot \cos B + \cos A \cdot \sin B$$

and $$\sin (A - B) = \sin A \cdot \cos B - \cos A \cdot \sin B,$$

by addition,

$$\sin (A + B) + \sin (A - B) = 2 \sin A \cdot \cos B$$

and by subtraction,

$$\sin (A + B) - \sin (A - B) = 2 \cos A \cdot \sin B.$$

Putting $(A + B) = X$ and $(A - B) = Y$ so that

$$A = \tfrac{1}{2}(X + Y) \quad \text{and} \quad B = \tfrac{1}{2}(X - Y)$$

$$\sin X + \sin Y = 2 \sin \tfrac{1}{2}(X + Y) \cdot \cos \tfrac{1}{2}(X - Y) \quad . \quad (28)$$

and $$\sin X - \sin Y = 2 \cos \tfrac{1}{2}(X + Y) \cdot \sin \tfrac{1}{2}(X - Y) \quad . \quad (29)$$

Proceeding in a similar way with $\cos (A + B)$ and $\cos (A - B)$ we get

$$\cos X + \cos Y = 2 \cos \tfrac{1}{2}(X + Y) . \cos \tfrac{1}{2}(X - Y) \qquad . \quad (30)$$

and $\quad \cos X - \cos Y = - 2 \sin \tfrac{1}{2}(X + Y) . \sin \tfrac{1}{2}(X - Y)$

$$= 2 \sin \tfrac{1}{2}(X + Y) . \sin \tfrac{1}{2}(Y - X) \qquad . \quad (31)$$

Notice the change of sign in $\cos X - \cos Y$.

Factorization of sums of sines and cosines

Example 1. If A, B, C are the angles of a triangle, factorize
$$\sin A + \sin B + \sin C.$$

$\sin A + \sin B + \sin C$

$\qquad = \sin A + 2 \sin \tfrac{1}{2}(B + C) . \cos \tfrac{1}{2}(B - C),$ using (28),

$\qquad = 2 \sin \tfrac{1}{2}A . \cos \tfrac{1}{2}A + 2 \sin \tfrac{1}{2}(B + C) . \cos \tfrac{1}{2}(B - C)$

$\qquad = 2 \sin \tfrac{1}{2}A . \cos \tfrac{1}{2}A + 2 \cos \tfrac{1}{2}A . \cos \tfrac{1}{2}(B - C)$

(since $\tfrac{1}{2}(B + C)$ is the complement of $\tfrac{1}{2}A$)

$\qquad = 2 \cos \tfrac{1}{2}A[\sin \tfrac{1}{2}A + \cos \tfrac{1}{2}(B - C)]$

$\qquad = 2 \cos \tfrac{1}{2}A . 2 \cos \tfrac{1}{2}B . \cos \tfrac{1}{2}C,$ using (30).

Therefore $\quad \sin A + \sin B + \sin C$

$$= 4 \cos \tfrac{1}{2}A . \cos \tfrac{1}{2}B . \cos \tfrac{1}{2}C \qquad . \quad . \quad . \quad . \quad (32)$$

Example 2. If A, B, C are the angles of a triangle, factorize
$$\cos A + \cos B + \cos C - 1.$$

$\cos A + \cos B + \cos C - 1$

$\quad = 2 \cos \tfrac{1}{2}(A + B) . \cos \tfrac{1}{2}(A - B) - 2 \sin^2 \tfrac{1}{2}C,$ using (30) and (25),

$\quad = 2 \sin \tfrac{1}{2}C . \cos \tfrac{1}{2}(A - B) - 2 \sin^2 \tfrac{1}{2}C$

since $\tfrac{1}{2}(A + B)$ is complement of $\tfrac{1}{2}C$.

$\quad = 2 \sin \tfrac{1}{2}C(\cos \tfrac{1}{2}(A - B) - \sin \tfrac{1}{2}C)$

$\quad = 2 \sin \tfrac{1}{2}C(\cos \tfrac{1}{2}(A - B) - \cos \tfrac{1}{2}(A + B))$

since $\tfrac{1}{2}C$ is complement of $\tfrac{1}{2}(A + B)$.

$\quad = 2 \sin \tfrac{1}{2}C . 2 \sin \tfrac{1}{2}A \sin \tfrac{1}{2}B$

therefore

$$\cos A + \cos B + \cos C - 1 = 4 \sin \tfrac{1}{2}A \sin \tfrac{1}{2}B \sin \tfrac{1}{2}C \quad . \quad (33)$$

EXERCISES XXXII

Express as products :

1. $\sin 40° + \sin 60°$; **2.** $\cos 20° - \cos 50°$; **3.** $\cos 30° + \cos 70°$;

4. $\sin 60° - \sin 40°$; **5.** $\sin 2A + \sin 6A$; **6.** $\cos 2A - \cos 4A$.

Express as a sum or difference :

7. $2 \sin 10° \sin 30°$; **8.** $2 \cos 20° \cos 50°$; **9.** $2 \cos 30° \sin 20°$;

10. $2 \sin 30° \cos 10°$; **11.** $2 \sin 3A \sin 5A$; **12.** $2 \cos 2A \sin 4A$.

Prove the following identities :

13. $\dfrac{a - b}{a + b} = \tan\dfrac{A - B}{2}\tan\dfrac{C}{2}$;

14. $a + b + c = 8R\cos\dfrac{A}{2}\cos\dfrac{B}{2}\cos\dfrac{C}{2}$;

15. $\cos 2A + \cos 2B - \cos 2C = 1 - 4\sin A\sin B\cos C$;

16. $\cos 4A = 8\cos^4 A - 8\cos^2 A + 1.$

If $A + B + C = 180°$, factorize the following :

17. $\cos 2A + \cos 2B + \cos 2C + 1$;

18. $\sin 2A + \sin 2B + \sin 2C$;

19. $\sin 2A - \sin 2B - \sin 2C$;

20. $\cos 4A + \cos 4B + \cos 4C + 1.$

The auxiliary angle

An expression such as $a\cos x + b\sin x$ can be expressed in the form $R\cos(x + \alpha)$ or $R\sin(x + \alpha)$.

Example. $3\cos x - 2\sin x.$

Draw a right-angled triangle with sides 2 and 3 as shown in the diagram.

Fig. 89.

Then $3 = \sqrt{13}\cos\alpha$

and $2 = \sqrt{13}\sin\alpha,$

therefore

$$3\cos x - 2\sin x = \sqrt{13}\,(\cos\alpha.\cos x - \sin\alpha.\sin x)$$

$$= \sqrt{13}\cos(x + \alpha)$$

where $\tan\alpha = 2/3$.

This is often easier to deal with than $3\cos x - 2\sin x$; for example, if we are asked to find the greatest possible value of $3\cos x - 2\sin x$, from its new form, we see that the greatest value occurs when

$$(x + \alpha) = 0°$$

and is $\sqrt{13}$.

Solution of equations

This form is useful too in solving equations of the type

$$a \cos x + b \sin x = c.$$

Example. Find all the solutions between 0° and 360° of the equation

$$3 \cos x - 2 \sin x = 1.$$

Using the auxiliary angle,

$$\sqrt{13} \cos (x + \alpha) = 1.$$

Therefore

$$\cos (x + \alpha) = 1/\sqrt{13}$$

so

$$x + \alpha = \cos^{-1} \cdot 2773 = 73° \ 54' \text{ or } 286° \ 6'.$$

But $\qquad \alpha = \tan^{-1} 2/3 = 33° \ 42'.$

(*N.B.*—One value for α is sufficient.)

By subtraction $\qquad x = 40° \ 12' \text{ or } 252° \ 24'.$

General solution of $\sin x = \sin \alpha$

Since $\sin (\pi - x) = \sin x$, the solutions here are

$$x = 2n\pi + \alpha$$

or

$$x = (2n + 1)\pi - \alpha.$$

These may be combined into the single solution

$$x = n\pi + (- 1)^n \alpha \qquad . \qquad . \qquad . \quad (34)$$

General solution of $\cos x = \cos \alpha$

Since $\cos (2\pi - x) = \cos x$, the general solution is

$$x = 2n\pi \pm \alpha \quad . \qquad . \qquad . \qquad . \quad (35)$$

General solution of $\tan x = \tan \alpha$

Since $\tan (\pi + x) = \tan x$, the solution is

$$x = n\pi + \alpha \quad . \qquad . \qquad . \qquad . \quad (36)$$

Now follow a few examples illustrating the different methods of solution.

Example 1. Find the general solution of $\cos 2x = \sin 3x$.

$$\cos 2x = \sin 3x = \cos \left(\frac{\pi}{2} - 3x \right).$$

From (35) $\qquad 2x = 2n\pi \pm \left(\frac{\pi}{2} - 3x \right).$

Therefore either

$$2x = 2n\pi + \frac{\pi}{2} - 3x \quad \text{or} \quad 2x = 2n\pi - \frac{\pi}{2} + 3x$$

$$5x = (4n + 1)\frac{\pi}{2} \quad \text{,,} \quad -x = (4n - 1)\frac{\pi}{2}$$

$$x = (4n + 1)\frac{\pi}{10} \quad \text{,,} \quad x = (1 - 4n)\frac{\pi}{2}.$$

Since we may take any integral value of x, positive or negative, the sign of n may be changed in the second solution without loss of generality and this may be more conveniently written

$$x = (4n + 1)\frac{\pi}{2},$$

which solutions are actually included in

$$x = (4n + 1)\frac{\pi}{10}.$$

Example 2. Find the general solution of $2 \sec^2 x = 5 \tan x$.

Here we form a quadratic in $\tan x$.

$$2(1 + \tan^2 x) = 5 \tan x.$$

Therefore
$$2 \tan^2 x - 5 \tan x + 2 = 0$$
$$(2 \tan x - 1)(\tan x - 2) = 0$$
$$\tan x = \tfrac{1}{2} \text{ or } 2.$$

Therefore
$$x = n\pi + \tan^{-1} \tfrac{1}{2}$$
or
$$n\pi + \tan^{-1} 2.$$

Example 3. Find the general solution of $\sin 3x + \sin 5x = \sin 4x$.

Using (28),
$$2 \sin 4x \cdot \cos x = \sin 4x.$$
Therefore either

$$\sin 4x = 0 \quad \text{or} \quad \cos x = \tfrac{1}{2} = \cos \frac{\pi}{3}.$$

So either
$$4x = n\pi \quad \text{or} \quad x = 2n\pi \pm \frac{\pi}{3}.$$

Solution of triangles

The cos formula and the sine formula together are sufficient to solve any triangle but the cos formula is unwieldy in use and is often replaced by the following formula which is adapted for logarithmic calculation.

$$\frac{a-b}{a+b} = \frac{2R\sin A - 2R\sin B}{2R\sin A + 2R\sin B}, \text{ using (8),}$$

$$= \frac{2\cos\frac{1}{2}(A+B).\sin\frac{1}{2}(A-B)}{2\sin\frac{1}{2}(A+B).\cos\frac{1}{2}(A-B)}, \text{ using (28) and (29),}$$

$$= \frac{\tan\frac{1}{2}(A-B)}{\tan\frac{1}{2}(A+B)}$$

$$= \frac{\tan\frac{1}{2}(A-B)}{\cot\frac{1}{2}C}$$

as $\frac{1}{2}C$ and $\frac{1}{2}(A+B)$ are complements.

Therefore $\qquad \dfrac{a-b}{a+b}\cot\dfrac{C}{2} = \tan\dfrac{A-B}{2}$ . . . (37)

This is the quickest way of solving a triangle given two sides and the included angle.

Example. If $a = 18\cdot4$ cm, $b = 12\cdot2$ cm, and $C = 42°$, find the other side and angles of the triangle.

$$\tan\tfrac{1}{2}(A-B) = \frac{18\cdot4 - 12\cdot2}{18\cdot4 + 12\cdot2}\cot 21°$$

$$= \frac{6\cdot2}{30\cdot6}\cot 21°.$$

Therefore

$$\tfrac{1}{2}(A-B) = 27°\ 50'$$

and so $\qquad\qquad A - B = 55°\ 40'.$

But $\qquad\qquad A + B = 138°$

(the angles of a triangle add up to 180°).

By adding and subtracting,

$$A = 96'\ 50'\ ;\ B = 41°\ 10'.$$

Also $\qquad\qquad c/\sin C = b/\sin B.$

There $\qquad\qquad c = 12\cdot2\sin 42°/\sin 41°\ 10'$

$$= 12\cdot4 \text{ cm.}$$

Another triangle formula which is sometimes useful is

$$c = a\cos B + b\cos A \qquad . \quad (38)$$

This is proved by drawing the perpendicular CN from C to AB and then using the fact

$$c = AN + NB.$$

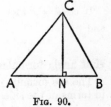

Fig. 90.

EXERCISES XXXIII

Find the solutions between $0°$ and $360°$ of the following equations :

1. $\tan^2 x - 3 \tan x + 2 = 0$;　　**2.** $3 \sin x + 4 \cos x = 2$;

3. $3 \sin x = 4 \cos x$;　　**4.** $\sin x + \cos x = \frac{1}{2}$;

5. $\sin 2x = \cos 3x$.

Find the general solutions of the following equations :

6. $\sin x + \sin 2x = \cos \dfrac{x}{2}$;　　**7.** $\sin x + \sin 2x + \sin 3x = 0$;

8. $\sin x = \cos 5x$;　　**9.** $\cos (90° - 3x) = \sin x$;

10. $2 \tan x = \sqrt{3}(1 - \tan^2 x)$.

Inverse ratios

If $\tan^{-1} x = \theta$ and $\tan^{-1} y = \phi$, then $\tan \theta = x$ and $\tan \phi = y$.

Therefore
$$\tan (\theta + \phi) = \frac{\tan \theta + \tan \phi}{1 - \tan \theta \tan \phi}$$

$$= \frac{x + y}{1 - xy}$$

so
$$\theta + \phi = \tan^{-1}\left(\frac{x + y}{1 - xy}\right)$$

or
$$\tan^{-1} x + \tan^{-1} y = \tan^{-1}\left(\frac{x + y}{1 - xy}\right) \quad . \quad . \quad (39)$$

Similarly
$$\tan^{-1} x - \tan^{-1} y = \tan^{-1}\left(\frac{x - y}{1 + xy}\right) \quad . \quad . \quad (40)$$

These are the only formulae of any importance used for the inverse ratios. The corresponding formulae for cos and sin are too awkward to be worth remembering and any example is best considered from first principles.

Example. Simplify $\sin (2 \cos^{-1} x)$.

Let $\cos^{-1} x = \theta$ so that $\cos \theta = x$ and we need to find the value of $\sin 2\theta$ given that $\cos \theta = x$.

If $\cos \theta = x$ then 　　$\sin \theta = \sqrt{1 - x^2}$

and 　　$\sin 2\theta = 2 \sin \theta . \cos \theta$

$$= 2x \sqrt{1 - x^2}.$$

Half angle formulae

The cos formula can be used to find the ratios of the half angles in terms of the sides of the triangle and these are often used for the solution of triangles, being easier to handle than the cos formula when all three sides are given.

From (7),

$$\cos C = \frac{a^2 + b^2 - c^2}{2ab}.$$

Therefore $\quad 2 \cos^2 \tfrac{1}{2}C - 1 = \dfrac{a^2 + b^2 - c^2}{2ab}$

or $\quad\quad 2 \cos^2 \tfrac{1}{2}C = \dfrac{a^2 + b^2 - c^2}{2ab} + 1$

$$= \frac{(a^2 + 2ab + b^2) - c^2}{2ab}$$

$$= \frac{(a + b + c)(a + b - c)}{2ab}$$

$$= \frac{2s \cdot 2(s - c)}{2ab}.$$

Therefore $\quad\quad \cos \tfrac{1}{2}C = \sqrt{\dfrac{s(s - c)}{ab}}$ . . . . (41

Similarly,

$$1 - 2 \sin^2 \tfrac{1}{2}C = \frac{a^2 + b^2 - c^2}{2ab}.$$

Therefore $\quad\quad 2 \sin^2 \tfrac{1}{2}C = 1 - \dfrac{a^2 + b^2 - c^2}{2ab}$

$$= \frac{c^2 - (a^2 - 2ab + b^2)}{2ab}$$

$$= \frac{(c + a - b)(c - a + b)}{2ab}$$

$$= \frac{2(s - b) \cdot 2(s - a)}{2ab}$$

and so $\quad\quad \sin \tfrac{1}{2}C = \sqrt{\dfrac{(s - a)(s - b)}{ab}}$ . . . (42)

By division, $\quad\quad \tan \tfrac{1}{2}C = \sqrt{\dfrac{(s - a)(s - b)}{s(s - c)}}$ . . . (43)

Area of the triangle

From first principles,

$$\Delta = \tfrac{1}{2}AD \cdot BC.$$

But $\quad\quad AD = b \sin C.$

Therefore $\quad \Delta = \tfrac{1}{2}ab \sin C$

$$= \tfrac{1}{2}bc \sin A = \tfrac{1}{2} \cdot ac \sin B \quad\quad (44)$$

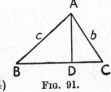

Fig. 91.

Since $$\Delta = \tfrac{1}{2}ab \sin C$$

$$\Delta = \tfrac{1}{2}ab \cdot 2 \sin \tfrac{1}{2}C \cdot \cos \tfrac{1}{2}C, \quad \text{using (16),}$$

$$= ab \cdot \sqrt{\frac{(s-a)(s-b)}{ab}} \sqrt{\frac{s(s-c)}{ab}}, \quad \text{using (41) and (42),}$$

$$= \sqrt{s(s-a)(s-b)(s-c)} \qquad . \qquad . \qquad . \qquad . \qquad (45)$$

This is Heron's formula for the area of a triangle.

EXERCISES XXXIV

Solve the following triangles :

1. $a = 10\cdot1$, $b = 8\cdot2$, $c = 7\cdot3$;   **2.** $a = 10\cdot1$, $b = 8\cdot2$, $C = 40°$;

3. $a = 10\cdot1$, $B = 50°$, $C = 60°$.

4. Find the areas of the triangles given in questions 1, 2 and 3.

Simplify the following :

5. $\tan(\cos^{-1} x)$;   **6.** $\sec(\cos^{-1} 2x)$;

7. $\tan 2(\sin^{-1} x)$;   **8.** $2\tan\left(\tan^{-1}\dfrac{x}{2}\right)$.

9. Solve the equation $\tan(\sec^{-1} x) = 2$.

10. Solve the equation $\sin(\tan^{-1} x) = \tfrac{1}{2}$.

The median and centre of gravity

By Apollonius,

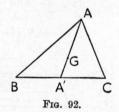

Fig. 92.

$$AB^2 + AC^2 = 2AA'^2 + 2BA'^2$$
$$\therefore \; b^2 + c^2 = 2AA'^2 + 2(\tfrac{1}{4}a^2)$$
$$\therefore \; 4AA'^2 = 2b^2 + 2c^2 - a^2$$
$$\therefore \; AA' = \tfrac{1}{2}\sqrt{2b^2 + 2c^2 - a^2}.$$

Also $$AG = \frac{2}{3} AA' = \frac{\sqrt{2b^2 + 2c^2 - a^2}}{3}.$$

The orthocentre

Using the sine formula for the triangle AHB,

$$\frac{AH}{\sin ABH} = \frac{c}{\sin AHB}.$$

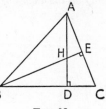

But $A\widehat{B}H = 90° - A$, $A\widehat{H}B = 180° - C$.

Therefore
$$\frac{AH}{\cos A} = \frac{c}{\sin C}$$
$$= 2R, \text{ using (8).}$$

Fig. 93.

Therefore
$$AH = 2R.\cos A \quad . \quad . \quad . \quad . \quad (46)$$

Also
$$HD/HB = \sin H\widehat{B}D.$$

But
$$H\widehat{B}D = 90° - C$$

and
$$BH = 2R \cos B, \text{ using (46).}$$

Therefore
$$HD = 2R \cos B \cos C \quad . \quad . \quad . \quad (47)$$

The angle bisector

If AX bisects $B\widehat{A}C$ internally,
$$BX/XC = c/b$$

and as $BX + XC = a$,
$$BX = ca/(b + c).$$

Applying the sine formula to AXB,

$$\frac{AX}{\sin B} = \frac{BX}{\sin \frac{1}{2}A}$$

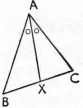

Fig. 94.

$$= \frac{ac}{(b + c) \sin \frac{1}{2}A}.$$

Therefore
$$AX = \frac{ac \sin B}{(b + c) \sin \frac{1}{2}A}$$

$$= \frac{cb \sin A}{(b + c) \sin \frac{1}{2}A}, \text{ using (8),}$$

$$= \frac{2cb \cos \frac{1}{2}A}{b + c}, \text{ using (16).}$$

The pedal triangle

The pedal triangle of ABC is the triangle formed by joining the feet of the altitudes of the triangle ABC.

(*i*) *If all the angles of the triangle are acute*

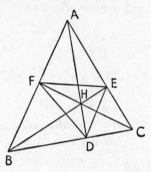

Fig. 95.

Since $FHDB$ is cyclic,
$$H\widehat{D}F = H\widehat{B}F = 90° - A.$$
Since $DHEC$ is cyclic,
$$H\widehat{D}E = H\widehat{C}E = 90° - A.$$
By addition,
$$F\widehat{D}E = 180° - 2A.$$

The angles of the pedal triangle are $180° - 2A$, $180° - 2B$, $180° - 2C$ **and** H **is the incentre of the pedal triangle** . (48)

Using the sine formula for triangle AFE,
$$\frac{EF}{\sin A} = \frac{AE}{\sin AFE}$$
$$= \frac{c \cdot \cos A}{\sin C}$$
$$= 2R \cdot \cos A.$$
Therefore
$$EF = 2R \cos A \cdot \sin A$$
$$= a \cos A \quad \text{or} \quad R \sin 2A.$$

The sides of the pedal triangle are $a \cos A$, $b \cos B$, $c \cos C$ (49)

(*ii*) *If A is obtuse*

Since $DBEA$ is cyclic,
$$A\widehat{E}D = A\widehat{B}D = B.$$
Since $BEFC$ is cyclic,
$$F\widehat{E}A = F\widehat{B}C = B.$$

Therefore $D\widehat{E}F = 2B.$

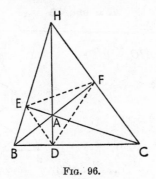

Similarly $E\widehat{F}D = 2C.$

By subtraction, $E\widehat{D}F = 180° - 2B - 2C$
$$= 180° - 2(180° - A)$$
$$= 2A - 180°.$$

The angles of the pedal triangle are $2A - 180°$, $2B$, $2C$ and A is the incentre of the pedal triangle   .   .   .   (50)

Using the sine formula for the triangle AFE,

$$\frac{EF}{\sin EAF} = \frac{AF}{\sin AEF}.$$

Therefore $\dfrac{EF}{\sin A} = \dfrac{b \cos (180 - A)}{\sin B}$

and so $EF = -2R \cos A \sin A$
$$= -a \cos A \quad \text{or} \quad -R \sin 2A.$$

The sides of the pedal triangle are $-a \cos A$, $b \cos B$, $c \cos C$ (51)

It is worth noting that in either case the four points A, B, C and H comprise the three ex-centres and the incentre of the pedal triangle.

The circumcircle

We have so far one formula only for the circum-radius.

$$a/\sin A = b/\sin B = c/\sin C = 2R.$$

From this $\dfrac{abc}{bc \sin A} = 2R.$

Therefore
$$\frac{abc}{2\Delta} = 2R, \quad \text{using (44)},$$

and so
$$R = abc/4\Delta \qquad . \qquad . \qquad . \qquad . \quad (52)$$

The incircle
$$\Delta = AIB + AIC + BIC.$$
But
$$AIB = \tfrac{1}{2}c.r, \text{ etc.}$$
Therefore
$$\Delta = r.\tfrac{1}{2}(a + b + c)$$
$$= r.s$$
and so
$$r = \Delta/s \qquad . \qquad . \qquad . \quad (53)$$

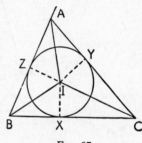

Fig. 97.

If X, Y, Z are the points of contact,
$$BX = BZ; \quad CX = CY; \quad AY = AZ.$$

Therefore
$$BX + XC + AY = s.$$
So
$$a + AY = s$$
and
$$AY = s - a, \text{ etc.}$$

From triangle AZI,
$$r = AI \sin \tfrac{1}{2}A.$$

Using the sine formula for AIB,
$$\frac{AI}{\sin \tfrac{1}{2}B} = \frac{c}{\sin AIB}$$
$$= \frac{c}{\sin\left(180 - \dfrac{A + B}{2}\right)}$$
$$= \frac{c}{\sin \tfrac{1}{2}(A + B)}$$
$$= \frac{c}{\cos \tfrac{1}{2}C}$$
$$= \frac{2R \sin C}{\cos \tfrac{1}{2}C}$$
$$= 4R \sin \tfrac{1}{2}C.$$

Therefore
$$AI = 4R \sin \tfrac{1}{2}B.\sin \tfrac{1}{2}C$$
and so
$$r = 4R \sin \tfrac{1}{2}A.\sin \tfrac{1}{2}B.\sin \tfrac{1}{2}C \qquad . \qquad . \quad (54)$$

The ex-circles

We shall consider the ex-circle opposite A. Similar formulae will of course hold for the ex-circles opposite B and C. Let P, Q and R

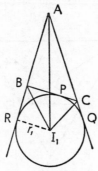

FIG. 98.

be the points of contact with the sides of the triangle ABC.

$$\Delta = AI_1B + AI_1C - BI_1C.$$

But $\qquad AI_1B = \tfrac{1}{2}c.r_1,$ etc.

Therefore $\qquad \Delta = \tfrac{1}{2}r_1(c + b - a)$

$$= r_1(s - a)$$

and so $\qquad r_1 = \Delta/(s - a)$ . . . . . (55)

$$AR = AQ; \quad BR = BP; \quad CQ = CP.$$

Therefore $\quad AB + BP = AC + CP = \tfrac{1}{2}$ perimeter $= s$

and so $\qquad BP = s - c; \quad PC = s - b.$

From AI_1R, $\qquad r_1 = AI_1 \sin \tfrac{1}{2}A.$

Using the sine formula in triangle ABI_1,

$$\frac{AI_1}{\sin ABI_1} = \frac{c}{\sin AI_1B}.$$

Therefore $\quad \dfrac{AI_1}{\sin (90° + \tfrac{1}{2}B)} = \dfrac{c}{\sin (90° - \tfrac{1}{2}B - \tfrac{1}{2}A)}$

or $\qquad \dfrac{AI_1}{\cos \tfrac{1}{2}B} = \dfrac{c}{\sin \tfrac{1}{2}C}$

$$= \frac{2R \sin C}{\sin \tfrac{1}{2}C}$$

$$= 4R.\cos \tfrac{1}{2}C.$$

So $AI_1 = 4R \cos \frac{1}{2}B \cos \frac{1}{2}C$

and $r_1 = 4R \sin \frac{1}{2}A \cdot \cos \frac{1}{2}B \cdot \cos \frac{1}{2}C$. (56)

It should be noted that this formula can be deduced from (54) by writing $(180° - B)$ for B and $(180° - C)$ for C.

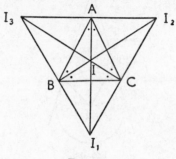

FIG. 99.

It is worth considering the triangle formed by the three ex-centres. Since AI_2, AI_3 are the external bisectors of the angle A, $I_2 A I_3$ is a straight line as is also $A I I_1$ (the internal bisector).

As the internal and external bisectors of an angle are perpendicular, AI_1 is at right angles to $I_2 I_3$.

Therefore the triangle ABC is the pedal triangle of $I_1 I_2 I_3$ and I is the orthocentre of $I_1 I_2 I_3$.

Since $I_1 BC = 90° - \frac{1}{2}B$ and $I_1 CB = 90° - \frac{1}{2}C$,

           $BI_1 C = \frac{1}{2}(B + C) = 90° - \frac{1}{2}A$.

Therefore $BC = I_2 I_3 \cos (90° - \frac{1}{2}A)$,   using (49),

and so $I_2 I_3 = a/\sin \frac{1}{2}A$

                    $= 2R \sin A/\sin \frac{1}{2}A$

                    $= 4R \cos \frac{1}{2}A$.   .   .   .   .   . (57)

The nine-point circle of $I_1 I_2 I_3$ will pass through the feet of its altitudes ABC. The radius of its nine-point circle is therefore R. But since the radius of a nine-point circle is half that of the circumcircle, the radius of the circumcircle of $I_1 I_2 I_3$ is $2R$.

Therefore $I I_1 = 2(2R) \cos (90° - \frac{1}{2}A)$,   using (46),

                    $= 4R \sin \frac{1}{2}A$.   .   .   .   .   . (58)

EXERCISES XXXV

1. Prove that $AG^2 + BG^2 + CG^2 = \frac{1}{3}(a^2 + b^2 + c^2)$.

2. Prove that

$$AH \cdot HD = BH \cdot HE = CH \cdot HF = -R^2(1 + \cos 2A + \cos 2B + \cos 2C).$$

3. If AX is the internal bisector of BAC and X is on BC, prove that

$$AX \sin \frac{A}{2}(b + c) = 2\Delta.$$

4. Find the circumradius of the pedal triangle.

5. Find the inradius of the pedal triangle.

6. Prove $s\Delta = abc \cos \dfrac{A}{2} \cos \dfrac{B}{2} \cos \dfrac{C}{2}$.

7. Prove $\dfrac{s - a}{s - b} = \dfrac{\tan B/2}{\tan A/2}$.

8. Prove $\dfrac{1}{r_1} + \dfrac{1}{r_2} + \dfrac{1}{r_3} = \dfrac{1}{r}$.

9. Prove $r_1 + r_2 = c \cot \frac{1}{2}C$.

10. Prove $(r_1 - r)(r_2 - r)(r_3 - r) = 4r^2R$.

11. Prove $I_2I_3{}^2 + II_1{}^2 = 16R^2$.

12. Find the circumradius of the triangle II_2I_3.

13. Find the circumradius of the triangle $I_1I_2I_3$.

14. Prove $a^2 + AH^2 = 4R^2$.

15. Prove that the perimeter of the pedal triangle is

$$4R \sin A \sin B \sin C.$$

16. Find the area of the pedal triangle.

17. Find the radius of the circumcircle of the triangle BHC.

18. Find the area of the triangle $I_1I_2I_3$.

REVISION PAPER VIII

1. From a mountain peak P, 1000 m above sea level, observations are taken of two further peaks, A and B. The horizontal distance of A from P is 3 km, its angle of elevation from P is 10°, and its bearing from P is N. 20° E. The horizontal distance of B from P is 1 km, its angle of depression from P is $15°$, and its bearing from P is N. $80°$ E. Find (i) the horizontal distance of A from B, (ii) the heights of A and B above sea level, (iii) the angle of elevation of A from B. (*NU*)

2. (i) By considering the roots of the equation $\sin 2\theta = \cos 3\theta$, prove that $\sin 18° = (\sqrt{5} - 1)/4$ and deduce the value of $\cos 36°$.

(ii) Prove that

$$\cos^2\left(\frac{\pi}{8} - \alpha\right) - \cos^2\left(\frac{\pi}{8} + \alpha\right) = \frac{1}{\sqrt{2}} \sin 2\alpha. \qquad (L)$$

3. Prove that $\tan(A + B) = \dfrac{\tan A + \tan B}{1 - \tan A \tan B}.$

If $\tan \alpha = \frac{1}{5}$ and $4\alpha - \beta = \dfrac{\pi}{4}$, find the exact value of $\tan \beta$ without tables. (*C*)

4. If Δ is the area of the triangle ABC, r the radius of the inscribed circle, and $2s = a + b + c$, show that $r = \dfrac{\Delta}{s}$.

In the triangle ABC, $a = 9$, $b = 16$, $c = 15$. The internal bisector of angle B meets AC at D. Calculate BD and the radius of the inscribed circle of the triangle ABD. (*NU*)

5. Define the angle between two planes.

$ABCD$ is a tetrahedron in which $BC = 5a$, $BD = CA = 4a$ $DA = DC = AB = 3a$. Find the angle between the planes ABC DBC. (*O & C*)

6. (i) Find the solutions of the equation

$$\cos(40° + x) = 3 \sin(50° + x)$$

between $0°$ and $360°$.

(ii) Prove that

$$\tan \tfrac{1}{2}(A + B) + \tan \tfrac{1}{2}(A - B) = \frac{2 \sin A}{\cos A + \cos B}. \qquad (L)$$

7. (i) Assuming the appropriate formulae for $\cos 2\theta$, prove that

$$\cos 4A = 1 - 8 \sin^2 A + 8 \sin^4 A.$$

Simplify $(\sin 5A - \sin A)/\sin A$, and hence or otherwise show that

$$\sin 5A = 5 \sin A - 20 \sin^3 A + 16 \sin^5 A.$$

(ii) Express $2 \cos \theta + 3 \sin \theta$ in the form $r \cos(\theta - \alpha)$, where r is positive, stating the values of r and α. What is the maximum value of $2 \cos \theta + 3 \sin \theta$? (*NU*)

8. A quadrilateral $ABCD$ is inscribed in a circle of diameter d. If $AB = AD$, $CB = CD$ and if BD passes through a point of trisection

of AC, prove that the area of the quadrilateral is $\frac{1}{3}d^2\sqrt{2}$ and deduce that the radius of the inscribed circle is $(2 - \sqrt{2})d/\sqrt{3}$.   (L)

9. Show that if $a^2 + b^2 > c^2$ there are in general two solutions of $a\cos\theta + b\sin\theta = c$ within the range of $0 < \theta < 360°$.

Solve $8\cos\theta - \sin\theta = 4$, and if α and β are the values of θ within the above range, find the quadratic equation whose roots are $\sin\alpha$ and $\sin\beta$.

10. Express $\sin 4\theta$ in terms of $\tan\theta$.

Hence find the roots of the equation $t^4 + 8t^3 + 2t^2 - 8t + 1 = 0$ correct to two places of decimals.   (O & C)

REVISION PAPER IX

1. Show that the radius of the incircle of a triangle equals Δ/s.

A ball rests on a horizontal wire triangle of sides 13 cm, 37 cm and 40 cm. If the distances of the lowest and highest points of the ball from the plane of the triangle are in the ratio $1:4$, prove that the centre of the ball is 4 cm from the plane.   (L)

2. (i) Find all the angles between $-180°$ and $+180°$ which satisfy the following equations:

      (a) $\tan(2\theta + 30°) = \tan 60°$;
      (b) $\cos 4\theta + \cos 2\theta = \cos\theta$.

(ii) Show that when written in terms of t, where $t = \tan\frac{1}{2}\theta$, the expression $2(1 + \cos\theta)(5\sin\theta + 12\cos\theta + 13)$ is a perfect square.   (NU)

3. Prove that in the triangle ABC, in which the angle A may be assumed to be acute, $a^2 = b^2 + c^2 - 2bc\cos A$.

A quadrilateral $ABCD$ is such that $AB = 3$ cm, $BC = CD = 5$ cm, $DA = 6$ cm and the diagonal $AC = 7$ cm. Find, as accurately as the tables allow, the angle BCD and the length of BD.   (C)

4. The altitudes from the vertices A, B, C of a triangle are of lengths h_1, h_2, h_3 and the radius of the circumcircle is R. Prove that

      (i) $h_1\sin A = h_2\sin B = h_3\sin C$;
      (ii) $h_1\cos A + h_2\cos B + h_3\cos C = (a^2 + b^2 + c^2)/4R$.   (L)

5. (a) Solve completely the equation $\sin 3x = \cos 2x$, where x is in radians.

(b) A vertical flagstaff, AB, stands with its foot, A, on the top of a tower. From a point X due South of the flagstaff the elevation of A is $44°$: from a point Y due East of the flagstaff and in the same horizontal plane as X the elevations of A and B are $31°$ and $38°$ respectively. If XY is 40 m, calculate the length of AB.   (NU)

6. (i) Prove that, when A, B, C are the angles of a triangle,

$$\cos^2 A + \cos^2 B + \cos^2 C = 1 - 2 \cos A \cos B \cos C.$$

(ii) Express $\sin 2\theta$ and $\cos 2\theta$ in terms of $\tan \theta$, and prove that

$$\cos 4\theta = \frac{1 - 6 \tan^2 \theta + \tan^4 \theta}{1 + 2 \tan^2 \theta + \tan^4 \theta}.$$

Hence or otherwise, prove that

$$\tan^2 \frac{\pi}{8} + \tan^2 \frac{3\pi}{8} + \tan^2 \frac{5\pi}{8} + \tan^2 \frac{7\pi}{8} = 12. \qquad (O \ \& \ C)$$

7. Prove that the area Δ of the triangle ABC is equal to $\tfrac{1}{2}ab \sin C$. The internal bisectors of the angles A, B, C meet the opposite sides at X, Y, Z. Prove that

$$AX = \frac{2\Delta}{b + c} \operatorname{cosec} \frac{A}{2} = \frac{2bc}{b + c} \cos \tfrac{1}{2}A.$$

Prove also that

$$\frac{1}{AX} \operatorname{cosec} \tfrac{1}{2}A + \frac{1}{BY} \operatorname{cosec} \tfrac{1}{2}B + \frac{1}{CZ} \operatorname{cosec} \tfrac{1}{2}C = \frac{2}{r}. \qquad (L)$$

8. Calculate the area of the smaller of the two triangles ABC having $A = 40°$, $a = 4.65$, $b = 6.28$. $\qquad (C)$

9. A vertical tower of height h metres stands at the top of a slope of inclination α to the horizontal. A man at the foot of the slope finds the angle of elevation of the top of the tower to be β. He walks a distance of d m. up a line of greatest slope, towards the foot of the tower, and finds the angle of elevation of the top of the tower to be γ. If he is then a distance of x metres away from the foot of the tower, prove that

$$\text{(i)} \quad h = \frac{d \sin (\beta - \alpha) \sin (\gamma - \alpha)}{\sin (\gamma - \beta) \cos \alpha},$$

$$\text{(ii)} \quad x = \frac{d \sin (\beta - \alpha) \cos \gamma}{\sin (\gamma - \beta) \cos \alpha}. \qquad (NU)$$

10. Prove that $\cos (A + B) = \cos A \cos B - \sin A \sin B$. You may assume that A, B, $A + B$ are all acute.

A, B, C are three positive acute angles such that

$$\cos^2 A + \cos^2 B + \cos^2 C = 1 - 2 \cos A \cos B \cos C.$$

By considering this relation as a quadratic equation in $\cos A$, or otherwise, prove that $A + B + C = \pi$. $\qquad (O \ \& \ C)$

APPENDIX

COMPLEX NUMBERS

Definition

ANY number of the form $a + b\sqrt{(-1)}$, where a and b are real numbers, is called a complex number. It is conventional to use the symbol i to represent $\sqrt{(-1)}$ and so any complex number may be written as $(a + ib)$. A complex number is therefore the sum of two parts ; a, called the real part, and ib, called the imaginary part.

If $b = 0$, the number is wholly real.

If $a = 0$, the number is wholly imaginary.

Example 1. Find the roots of the equation $x^2 - 8x + 25 = 0$.

Using $x = \dfrac{-b \pm \sqrt{(b^2 - 4ac)}}{2a}$, we have $x = \dfrac{8 \pm \sqrt{(64 - 100)}}{2}$.

$$\therefore x = \frac{8 \pm \sqrt{(-36)}}{2} = 4 \pm \sqrt{-9} = 4 \pm 3i.$$

The roots are $4 \pm 3i$.

Complex numbers of the form $a \pm ib$ are called conjugate. The complex roots of a quadratic equation with real coefficients must always be conjugate.

If $z = a + ib$, it is convenient to express the conjugate as $\bar{z}$; i.e. $\bar{z} = a - ib$.

So $z + \bar{z} = 2a$ and $z\bar{z} = a^2 + b^2$ (see example 2).

Example 2. Factorise $a^2 + b^2$.

$$a^2 + b^2 = a^2 - (-b^2) = a^2 - i^2b^2 = (a + ib)(a - ib).$$

The sum of two complex numbers

The sum of $(x_1 + iy_1)$ and $(x_2 + iy_2)$ is defined as

$$(x_1 + x_2) + i(y_1 + y_2).$$

So in addition the quantity i is treated as an ordinary algebraic symbol.

Compare $(x_1 + ay_1) + (x_2 + ay_2) = (x_1 + x_2) + a(y_1 + y_2)$.

The difference between two complex numbers

As an extension of addition, it follows that

$$(x_1 + iy_1) - (x_2 + iy_2) = (x_1 - x_2) + i(y_1 - y_2).$$

The product of two complex numbers

The product of $(x_1 + iy_1)$ and $(x_2 + iy_2)$ is defined to be

$$(x_1x_2 - y_1y_2) + i(x_1y_2 + x_2y_1).$$

173

As in addition, the ordinary processes of algebra apply.

$$(x_1 + ay_1)(x_2 + ay_2) = (x_1x_2 + a^2y_1y_2) + a(x_1y_2 + x_2y_1).$$

Putting $a = i$ and $a^2 = -1$, we have

$$(x_1 + iy_1)(x_2 + iy_2) = (x_1x_2 - y_1y_2) + i(x_1y_2 + x_2y_1).$$

The equality of two complex numbers

Two complex numbers $(x_1 + iy_1)$ and $(x_2 + iy_2)$ are equal if and only if $x_1 = x_2$ and $y_1 = y_2$.

For suppose that $\qquad x_1 + iy_1 = x_2 + iy_2.$

Then $\qquad\qquad\qquad\qquad x_1 - x_2 = i(y_2 - y_1).$

Squaring both sides, $\qquad (x_1 - x_2)^2 = -(y_2 - y_1)^2$

or $\qquad (x_1 - x_2)^2 + (y_1 - y_2)^2 = 0.$

Since the square of a real number cannot be negative, it follows that $x_1 = x_2$ and $y_1 = y_2$.

Example. Given that $A + iB = (3 - 2i)(4 + 3i)$, find A and B.

$$(3 - 2i)(4 + 3i) = 12 + 9i - 8i - 6i^2$$
$$= 18 + i.$$
$$\therefore \ A + iB = 18 + i$$

from which it follows that $A = 18$ and $B = 1$.

This process is called "equating real and imaginary parts".

To express a fraction in its real and imaginary parts

To express $\dfrac{1}{3 - 2i}$ in its real and imaginary parts, multiply both numerator and denominator by the expression obtained by changing the sign of i in the denominator.

$$\frac{1}{3 - 2i} = \frac{3 + 2i}{(3 - 2i)(3 + 2i)} = \frac{3 + 2i}{9 - 4i^2} = \frac{3}{13} + \frac{2}{13}i.$$

More generally,

$$\frac{1}{x + iy} = \frac{x - iy}{(x + iy)(x - iy)} = \frac{x - iy}{x^2 + y^2}.$$

More generally still,

$$\frac{a + ib}{x + iy} = \frac{(a + ib)(x - iy)}{(x + iy)(x - iy)} = \frac{(ax + by) + i(bx - ay)}{x^2 + y^2}.$$

Example 1. Find the real and imaginary parts of $\dfrac{3 - 2i}{4 + 3i}$.

$$\frac{3 - 2i}{4 + 3i} = \frac{(3 - 2i)(4 - 3i)}{(4 + 3i)(4 - 3i)} = \frac{12 - 9i - 8i + 6i^2}{16 - 9i^2}$$

$$= \frac{6 - 17i}{25}.$$

Example 2. Find the real and imaginary parts of

$$\frac{(1 + 2i)(2 - 3i)}{3 + 4i}$$

$$\frac{(1 + 2i)(2 - 3i)}{3 + 4i} = \frac{(2 - 6i^2) + i(4 - 3)}{3 + 4i} = \frac{8 + i}{3 + 4i}$$

$$= \frac{(8 + i)(3 - 4i)}{(3 + 4i)(3 - 4i)} = \frac{(24 - 4i^2) + i(3 - 32)}{9 - 16i^2}$$

$$= \frac{28 - 29i}{25}.$$

EXERCISES XXXVI

1. Solve the equation $x^2 - 6x + 10 = 0$.

2. Factorise $x^3 + 27$ and hence solve the equation $x^3 + 27 = 0$.

3. Find the real and imaginary parts of

(i) $i(3 + i)$; (ii) $(2 - i)(3 + i)$; (iii) $(3 + i)^2$; (iv) $\dfrac{2 - i}{2 + i}$;

(v) $\dfrac{(1 + i)(2 + i)}{1 - i}$.

4. If $z = 2 + 3i$, evaluate $z\bar{z}$ and express $\dfrac{z}{\bar{z}}$ in the form $a + ib$.

5. If $z = \cos\theta + i\sin\theta$, find the value of $z\bar{z}$.

6. If $z = \dfrac{1}{2 + 3i}$, find the value of $z\bar{z}$.

7. If $x + iy = \dfrac{3 + i}{2 - i}$, find the values of x and y.

8. If $z = \cos\theta + i\sin\theta$, find the value of $z + \dfrac{1}{z}$.

9. Find the three cube roots of unity.

10. If $a + ib = \dfrac{1}{x + iy}$, show that $(a^2 + b^2)(x^2 + y^2) = 1$.

The Argand Diagram

A complex number, $x + iy$, requires two quantities to fix it, namely x and y. It is therefore a vector quantity. The complex number $x + iy$ can be represented graphically by a point P with coordinates (x, y) and one can think of the complex number as represented by the point $P(x, y)$ or by the vector OP, where O is the origin.

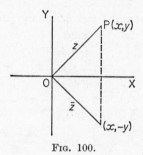

Fig. 100.

It is convenient to let $z = x + iy$ and Fig. 100 shows a representation of the complex numbers z and $\bar{z}$.

Such a diagram is called an Argand diagram. A real number is represented by a point on the x-axis ; a wholly imaginary number by a point on the y-axis.

Modulus and amplitude

If P represents $(x + iy)$ in the Argand diagram, the length of OP, always taken to be positive, is called the modulus of $(x + iy)$ and is written $|x + iy|$ or $|z|$.

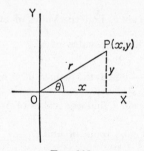

Fig. 101.

From Fig. 101, $|x + iy| = \sqrt{(x^2 + y^2)}$.

The angle turned through anticlockwise from OX to OP is called the amplitude of P and is written amp $(x + iy)$ or amp z. It is convenient to choose the amplitude so that it always lies between

$\pm \pi$ (or $\pm 180°$). For example, the amplitude of a point in the second quadrant lies between $\frac{\pi}{2}$ and π; in the third quadrant between $-\frac{\pi}{2}$ and $-\pi$; in the fourth quadrant between 0 and $-\frac{\pi}{2}$.

From Fig. 101, it is easily seen that
$$x = r \cos \theta \quad \text{and} \quad y = r \sin \theta.$$
The value of z is given by $(x + iy)$ or $r(\cos \theta + i \sin \theta)$.

This is called the modulus-amplitude form of the complex number and is specially useful in dealing with products and quotients as will be seen later.

Notice that $\tan \theta = \frac{y}{x}$.

Example 1. Find the modulus and amplitude of $1 + i$.
From Fig. 102,
$$OP^2 = 1 + 1 = 2.$$
$$\therefore |1 + i| = \sqrt{2}.$$
$$\text{amp} (1 + i) = 45°.$$

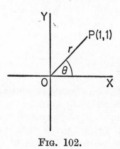

FIG. 102.

Example 2. Find the modulus and amplitude of $-3 - 4i$.
From Fig. 103,
$$OP^2 = 3^2 + 4^2.$$
$$\therefore OP = 5 \text{ and } |z| = 5.$$
$$\tan \alpha = \frac{4}{3} \therefore \alpha = 53° 8'.$$

The amplitude is $-(180° - 53° 8')$ or $-126° 52'$.

G

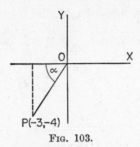

FIG. 103.

Addition of complex quantities

If $z_1 = x_1 + iy_1$ and $z_2 = x_2 + iy_2$ are represented in the Argand diagram as shown in Fig. 104, their sum may be found by the parallelogram law for the addition of vectors.

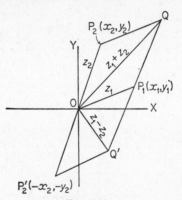

FIG. 104.

The vector OQ represents their sum and the coordinates of Q can be seen to be $(x_1 + x_2, y_1 + y_2)$ by projection on the two axes. The reflection of P_2 in the origin gives the point $(-x_2, -y_2)$ and $z_1 - z_2$ is found by the vector addition of OP_1 and OP_2'. If the difference is represented by OQ', the coordinates of Q' are $(x_1 - x_2, y_1 - y_2)$.

Example. Show that $|z_1 + z_2| \leqslant |z_1| + |z_2|$.

In Fig. 104, $OQ = |z_1 + z_2|$; $OP_1 = |z_1|$ and $|z_2| = OP_2 = P_1Q$. Since $OQ \leqslant OP_1 + P_1Q$,

$$|z_1 + z_2| \leqslant |z_1| + |z_2|.$$

Equality occurs only when O, P_1 and P_2 are collinear, i.e. when amp z_1 = amp z_2.

EXERCISES XXXVII

1. Represent on the Argand diagram the points (i) $1 - 2i$; (ii) $3 + 4i$; (iii) $-5 - 2i$.

2. Find the moduli of (i) $1\frac{1}{2} - 2i$; (ii) $12 + 5i$; (iii) $15 - 8i$.

3. Find the amplitudes of (i) $1 - i$; (ii) $-\sqrt{3} - i$; (iii) $-2 - 3i$.

4. Find $\left| \dfrac{3 + 4i}{5 + 12i} \right|$.

5. Find amp $\left(\dfrac{1 + \sqrt{3}i}{1 + i} \right)$.

6. Show that $|z_1 - z_2| \geqslant |z_1| - |z_2|$.

7. Write down the modulus and amplitude of $3\left(\sin \dfrac{\pi}{3} + i \cos \dfrac{\pi}{3} \right)$.

8. If $z = 3\left(\cos \dfrac{\pi}{4} + i \sin \dfrac{\pi}{4} \right)$, find the amplitude of iz.

9. Write down the amplitude of $z - \bar{z}$.

10. If $z = r(\cos \theta + i \sin \theta)$, show that $z\bar{z} = r^2$.

The product of two complex numbers

Suppose that

$$z_1 = r_1(\cos \theta_1 + i \sin \theta_1) \text{ and } z_2 = r_2(\cos \theta_2 + i \sin \theta_2).$$

Then

$$\begin{aligned} z_1 z_2 &= r_1 r_2 (\cos \theta_1 + i \sin \theta_1)(\cos \theta_2 + i \sin \theta_2) \\ &= r_1 r_2 \{ (\cos \theta_1 \cos \theta_2 + i^2 \sin \theta_1 \sin \theta_2) \\ &\qquad\qquad + i(\cos \theta_1 \sin \theta_2 + \sin \theta_1 \cos \theta_2) \} \\ &= r_1 r_2 \{ (\cos \theta_1 \cos \theta_2 - \sin \theta_1 \sin \theta_2) + i \sin (\theta_1 + \theta_2) \} \\ &= r_1 r_2 \{ \cos (\theta_1 + \theta_2) + i \sin (\theta_1 + \theta_2) \}. \end{aligned}$$

So $|z_1 z_2| = r_1 r_2$ and amp $z_1 z_2 = \theta_1 + \theta_2$.

The modulus of the product is therefore the product of the separate moduli; the amplitude of the product is the sum of the separate amplitudes.

If $z_3 = r_3(\cos \theta_3 + i \sin \theta_3)$,

$$\begin{aligned} z_1 z_2 z_3 &= r_1 r_2 r_3 \{ \cos (\theta_1 + \theta_2) + i \sin (\theta_1 + \theta_2) \}(\cos \theta_3 + i \sin \theta_3) \\ &= r_1 r_2 r_3 \{ \cos (\theta_1 + \theta_2 + \theta_3) + i \sin (\theta_1 + \theta_2 + \theta_3) \}. \end{aligned}$$

de Moivre's theorem

Since $z_1 z_2 z_3 = r_1 r_2 r_3 \{ \cos (\theta_1 + \theta_2 + \theta_3) + i \sin (\theta_1 + \theta_2 + \theta_3) \}$, it follows that

$$\begin{aligned} (\cos \theta_1 + i \sin \theta_1)&(\cos \theta_2 + i \sin \theta_2)(\cos \theta_3 + i \sin \theta_3) \\ &= \cos (\theta_1 + \theta_2 + \theta_3) + i \sin (\theta_1 + \theta_2 + \theta_3). \end{aligned}$$

If this is extended to n variables $\theta_1, \theta_2, \theta_3 \ldots$ and each is put equal to θ, we get

$$(\cos \theta + i \sin \theta)^n = \cos n\theta + i \sin n\theta.$$

This is a very important theorem, called de Moivre's theorem and is true for all values of n, positive, negative and fractional. The scope of this book is restricted to the proof already given for a positive integer.

The quotient of two complex numbers

Since by the product rule,

$$r_1(\cos \theta_1 + i \sin \theta_1) . \, r_2\{\cos (\theta_2 - \theta_1) + i \sin (\theta_2 - \theta_1)\}$$
$$= r_1 r_2(\cos \theta_2 + i \sin \theta_2),$$

it follows that

$$\frac{r_1 r_2(\cos \theta_2 + i \sin \theta_2)}{r_1(\cos \theta_1 + i \sin \theta_1)} = r_2\{\cos (\theta_2 - \theta_1) + i \sin (\theta_2 - \theta_1)\}.$$

The modulus of the quotient of two complex numbers is therefore the quotient of the separate moduli ; the amplitude of the quotient is the difference of the separate amplitudes.

Example 1. Use de Moivre's theorem to expand $\cos 3\theta$ and $\sin 3\theta$.

$$\cos 3\theta + i \sin 3\theta = (\cos \theta + i \sin \theta)^3$$
$$= \cos^3 \theta + 3 \cos^2 \theta(i \sin \theta) + 3 \cos \theta(i \sin \theta)^2$$
$$+ (i \sin \theta)^3.$$

Equating real and imaginary parts,

$$\cos 3\theta = \cos^3 \theta - 3 \cos \theta \sin^2 \theta \,;$$
$$\sin 3\theta = 3 \cos^2 \theta \sin \theta - \sin^3 \theta.$$

This method may be used to expand cos and sin of any multiple angle.

Example 2. Evaluate $\left| \dfrac{3i + 4}{8i - 15} \right|.$

$$\left| \frac{3i + 4}{8i - 15} \right| = \frac{|3i + 4|}{|8i + 15|} = \frac{\sqrt{(3^2 + 4^2)}}{\sqrt{(8^2 + 15^2)}} = \frac{5}{17}.$$

Example 3. Express in modulus-amplitude form $3 - 3\sqrt{3}i$ and hence find amp $(3 - 3\sqrt{3}i)$.

Draw a right-angled triangle whose right angle includes sides of 3 and $3\sqrt{3}$ as shown in Fig. 105.

The hypotenuse $= \sqrt{(9 + 27)} = 6.$
Also $\tan \alpha = \sqrt{3} \therefore \alpha = 60°.$

$$3 - 3\sqrt{3}i = 6(\cos \alpha - i \sin \alpha)$$
$$= 6(\cos 60° - i \sin 60°)$$
$$= 6\{\cos (-60°) + i \sin (-60°)\}.$$

The modulus is therefore 6 and the amplitude $-60°$.

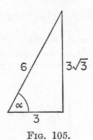

F<small>IG</small>. 105.

EXERCISES XXXVIII

1. Evaluate $\left| \dfrac{7-i}{1+i} \right|$.

2. Find amp $\{(2+i)(3+i)\}$.

3. Expand $\cos 4\theta$ and $\sin 4\theta$.

4. Simplify $\left(\cos \dfrac{\pi}{3} + i \sin \dfrac{\pi}{3} \right)\left(\cos \dfrac{\pi}{6} + i \sin \dfrac{\pi}{6} \right)$.

5. Simplify $\left(\cos \dfrac{\pi}{5} + i \sin \dfrac{\pi}{5} \right)\left(\cos \dfrac{2\pi}{5} + i \sin \dfrac{2\pi}{5} \right)^2$.

6. Simplify $\left(\cos \dfrac{\pi}{6} + i \sin \dfrac{\pi}{6} \right)^3$.

7. Simplify $\dfrac{\cos 2\theta + i \sin 2\theta}{\cos \theta + i \sin \theta}$.

8. Simplify $\dfrac{\cos 3\theta + i \sin 3\theta}{\cos 2\theta + i \sin 2\theta}$.

9. Evaluate $\left(\dfrac{-1+i\sqrt{3}}{2} \right)^3$.

10. Evaluate $|(6-3i)(2+i)|$.

Loci

In Fig. 106, let P_1 represent z_1 and P_2 represent z_2.

$(z_1 - z_2)$ is represented by the vector addition of z_1 and $-z_2$ and is shown by the vector OQ in Fig. 106.

$P_1Q = OR = OP_2$ ∴ QOP_2P_1 is a parallelogram and OQ is parallel to P_2P_1.

∴ $(z_1 - z_2)$ is represented by the vector P_2P_1.

So $|z_1 - z_2| = P_2P_1$ and amp $(z_1 - z_2) =$ angle between OX and P_2P_1.

The equation $|z - a| = r$, where r is a real quantity and a complex, tells us that the distance between z and the fixed point a is constant. The locus of z is therefore a circle, centre a and radius r.

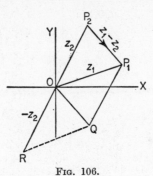

Fig. 106.

Example 1. Describe the locus of z given that $|z - 2 + 3i| = 4$.
$$|z - (2 - 3i)| = 4.$$
The distance between z and the point $(2 - 3i)$ is constant and equal to 4. The locus is a circle, centre $(2 - 3i)$ or $(2, -3)$, radius 4.

Example 2. Describe the locus of z given that
$$\left|\frac{z - 1 - i}{z - 1 + i}\right| = 2.$$
$$\left|\frac{z - 1 - i}{z - 1 + i}\right| = \frac{|z - (1 + i)|}{|z - (1 - i)|}.$$

The numerator is the distance between the point z and the point $(1 + i)$ or $(1, 1)$; the denominator is the distance between the point z and the point $(1, -1)$.

The distance of z from $(1, 1)$ is therefore twice the distance of z from the point $(1, -1)$. The locus is a circle of Apollonius with its centre lying on the join of $(1, 1)$ and $(1, -1)$.

EXERCISES XXXIX

1. Plot a point P to represent z and on the same diagram plot points to represent the numbers (i) $\bar{z}$; (ii) $\dfrac{1}{z}$; (iii) $z - 1$; (iv) $z + i$; (v) $z - 1 - i$.

2. If $|z - 1| = |z + 1|$, describe the locus of z.

3. Show that the points z_1, z_2 and z_3 are collinear if, and only if, amp $\left(\dfrac{z_1 - z_3}{z_1 - z_2}\right)$ is zero.

4. If $\left|\dfrac{z - 1}{z + 2}\right| = 2$, describe the locus of z.

5. If $\left|\dfrac{z - i}{z + i}\right| = 2$, describe the locus of z.

6. Find the angles of the triangle formed by the points $1 + i$, $3 + 4i$ and $4 + 3i$.

7. Find the centre and radius of the circle $|z - 1 - 2i| = 3$.

8. Given that $|z - a| + |z - b| = k$, show that the locus of z is an ellipse. (Use the focal distance property.)

9. Show that the lines joining the points z_1 and z_2 to the origin are perpendicular if amp $\left(\dfrac{z_1}{z_2}\right) = \dfrac{\pi}{2}$.

10. If $|z_1 - z_2| = |z_1 + z_2|$, show that the amplitudes of z_1 and z_2 differ by $\dfrac{\pi}{2}$.

RECURRING SERIES

The sequence $1, 1, 2, 3, 5, 8, 13, \ldots$ is known as Fibonacci's series. In this sequence each term is equal to the sum of the two preceding terms, i.e.

$$u_n = u_{n-1} + u_{n-2},$$

where u_n is the general term, for all values of n.

In general, a relation of the form $u_n + au_{n-1} + bu_{n-2} = 0$, where a and b are constants, is called a recurrence relation of the second order. A relation connecting four consecutive terms is said to be of the third order and so on.

Fibonacci's series cannot be completed from the relationship $u_n = u_{n-1} + u_{n-2}$ alone. It is also necessary to be given the first two terms and this applies to any recurrence relation of the second order. Given the first two terms and the recurrence relation of the second order, the series may be built up term by term.

For example if the series is $u_0 + u_1 + u_2 + \ldots$ and it is given that $u_0 = 2$, $u_1 = 5$ and that $u_n = u_{n-1} + u_{n-2}$, $u_2 = 7$, $u_3 = 12$ and so on.

The series $2 + 5 + 7 + 12 \ldots$ is called a recurring series and $u_n = u_{n-1} + u_{n-2}$ is called its scale of relation.

Given a scale of relation of the second order, the rth term of a recurring series will depend on the values u_0 and u_1 of the first two terms. So the general term of a recurring series with a scale of relation of the second order would be expected to contain two arbitrary constants.

If $u_r = v_r$ and $u_r = w_r$ both satisfy the equation

$$u_r + au_{r-1} + bu_{r-2} = 0,$$

it is easily seen that $Av_r + Bw_r$, where A and B are arbitrary constants, will also satisfy the equation.

Since v_r satisfies, $v_r + av_{r-1} + bv_{r-2} = 0 \ldots$ (i)

Since w_r satisfies, $w_r + aw_{r-1} + bw_{r-2} = 0 \ldots$ (ii)

Multiply (i) by A, (ii) by B and add:

$$(Av_r + Bw_r) + a(Av_{r-1} + Bw_{r-1}) + b(Av_{r-2} + Bw_{r-2}) = 0.$$

This shows that $u_r = Av_r + Bw_r$ is also a solution and since it contains two arbitrary constants, it is the general solution. The general solution can therefore be found from two particular solutions. Particular solutions can be found by writing $u_r = x^r$ and solving the resulting quadratic equation for x.

Finding the general term

Suppose that $u_r - 3u_{r-1} + 2u_{r-2} = 0$ and that $u_0 = 1, u_1 = 3$. How do we find the rth term?

Let $u_r = x^r$, then $x^r - 3x^{r-1} + 2x^{r-2} = 0$

and so $x^2 - 3x + 2 = 0$ or $(x - 1)(x - 2) = 0$.

The possible values for x are 1 and 2.

Two particular solutions for u_r are $(1)^r$ and $(2)^r$ and the general solution is $A(1)^r + B(2)^r$.

We need to choose A and B so that $u_0 = 1$ and $u_1 = 3$.

Put $r = 0$; $A + B = 1.$

Put $r = 1$; $A + 2B = 3.$

$$\therefore \ A = -1 \text{ and } B = 2.$$

The value of u_r is $-1 + 2^{r+1}$.

Notice that the rth term is u_{r-1} and so the rth term is $2^r - 1$.

Building up the series term by term gives:

$$u_2 = 3u_1 - 2u_0 = 9 - 2 = 7 ;$$

$$u_3 = 3u_2 - 2_{n1} = 21 - 6 = 15,$$

and we see that each term is 1 less than a multiple of 2.

To find the scale of relation

There are two unknowns in the scale of relation

$$u_r + au_{r-1} + bu_{r-2} = 0$$

and so we need two equations to find them.

Three terms of the sequence will be needed for one equation, four terms for two equations. So if we know that a scale of relation of the second order holds, the first four terms of the sequence must be given before the scale of relation can be found ; if the scale of relation is of the third order, then six terms of the sequence are necessary.

Example. Find the scale of relation of the second order determined by the four terms 2, 3, 7, 18.

Suppose that $u_r + au_{r-1} + bu_{r-2} = 0$.

Then $7 + 3a + 2b = 0$ and $18 + 7a + 3b = 0$.

The solution of these equations is $a = -3, b = 1$.

The scale of relation is $u_r - 3u_{r-1} + u_{r-2} = 0$.

The next term of the series is $3(18) - 7 = 47$.

Repeated roots

If $u = x^r$ leads to a repeated root for x, the method so far used breaks down. When the roots were x_1 and x_2, the general solution was found to be $Ax_1{}^r + Bx_2{}^r$, which contains two arbitrary constants.

When $x_1 = x_2 = x$, this solution becomes $(A + B)x^r$ or Cx^r and contains one arbitrary constant only.

The general solution is in fact $(A + Br)x^r$ and this may be verified as follows.

Suppose the scale of relation is

$$u_r - 2au_{r-1} + a^2u_{r-2} = 0.$$

Putting $u = x^r$ gives $x^2 - 2ax + a^2 = 0$

and so $x = a$ is a repeated root.

Try $u_r = (A + Br)a^r$.

$u_r - au_{r-1} + a^2u_{r-2}$
$= (A + Br)a^r - 2a\{A + B(r - 1)\}a^{r-1} + a^2\{A + B(r - 2)\}a^{r-2}$
$= Aa^r(1 - 2 + 1) + Ba^r\{r - 2(r - 1) + r - 2\}$
$= 0.$

$\therefore (A + Br)a^r$ is a solution, and since it contains two arbitrary constants, it is the general solution.

Example 1. Find the general term of the series whose scale of relation is $u_r -- 4u_{r-1} + 4u_{r-2} = 0$ and whose first two terms are 1 and 3.

Let $u_r = x^r$ so that $x^r - 4x^{r-1} + 4x^{r-2} = 0$.

$$\therefore x^2 - 4x + 4 = 0 \text{ or } (x - 2)^2 = 0.$$

So $x = 2$ and the general solution is $(A + Br)2^r$.

When $r = 0$, $u_r = 1$. ∴ $A = 1$.

When $r = 1$, $u_r = 3$. ∴ $(A + B)2 = 3$ and $B = \frac{1}{2}$.

The general solution is $u_r = (\frac{1}{2}r + 1)2^r$ or $2^{r-1}(r + 2)$.

Example 2. Find the general term of the Fibonacci series
1, 1, 2, 3, 5, . . .

The scale of relation is $u_r = u_{r-1} + u_{r-2}$.

If $u_r = x^r$, $x^2 - x - 1 = 0$.

$$\therefore x = \frac{1 + \sqrt{5}}{2}.$$

$$\therefore u_r = A\left(\frac{1 + \sqrt{5}}{2}\right)^r + B\left(\frac{1 - \sqrt{5}}{2}\right)^r.$$

When $r = 0$, $u_r = 1$; when $r = 1$, $u_r = 1$.

$$\therefore 1 = A + B,$$

and $1 = A\left(\frac{1 + \sqrt{5}}{2}\right) + B\left(\frac{1 - \sqrt{5}}{2}\right) = \frac{A + B}{2} + \frac{\sqrt{5}}{2}(A - B).$

Substituting $A + B = 1$, we have $1 = \sqrt{5}(A - B)$.

$$\therefore A - B = \frac{1}{\sqrt{5}}.$$

$$A + B = 1.$$

So $2A = 1 + \frac{1}{\sqrt{5}}$ and $A = \frac{\sqrt{5} + 1}{2\sqrt{5}}$,

and $2B = 1 - \frac{1}{\sqrt{5}}$ or $B = \frac{\sqrt{5} - 1}{2\sqrt{5}}$.

$$\therefore u_r = \frac{1}{\sqrt{5}}\left(\frac{1 + \sqrt{5}}{2}\right)^{r+1} - \frac{1}{\sqrt{5}}\left(\frac{1 - \sqrt{5}}{2}\right)^{r+1}.$$

This is the $(r + 1)$th term and so the rth term is

$$\frac{1}{\sqrt{5}}\left(\frac{1 + \sqrt{5}}{2}\right)^r - \frac{1}{\sqrt{5}}\left(\frac{1 - \sqrt{5}}{2}\right)^r.$$

A surprising result for the general term, which proves of course that
$\dfrac{(1 + \sqrt{5})^r - (1 - \sqrt{5})^r}{2^r\sqrt{5}}$ is an integer for all integral values of r.

Example 3. Given the scale of relation $u_r - 2u_{r-1}\cos\theta + u_{r-2} = 0$
and that $u_0 = 1$, $u_1 = \cos\theta$, find the general term of the sequence.

Let $u_r = x^r$. Then $x^r - 2x^{r-1}\cos\theta + x^{r-2} = 0$

and so $x^2 - 2x\cos\theta + 1 = 0$.

$$\therefore x = \cos\theta \pm \sqrt{(\cos^2\theta - 1)} = \cos\theta \pm i\sin\theta.$$
$$\therefore u_r = A(\cos\theta + i\sin\theta)^r + B(\cos\theta - i\sin\theta)^r$$
$$= A(\cos r\theta + i\sin r\theta) + B(\cos r\theta - i\sin r\theta).$$

But $u_0 = 1, u_1 = \cos \theta$.

$$\therefore \ 1 = A + B$$

and
$$\cos \theta = A(\cos \theta + i \sin \theta) + B(\cos \theta - i \sin \theta)$$
$$= (A + B) \cos \theta + (A - B)i \sin \theta.$$
$$\therefore \ \theta = (A - B)i \sin \theta, \text{ since } A + B = 1.$$
$$\therefore \ A = B = \tfrac{1}{2}$$

and
$$u_r = \tfrac{1}{2}(\cos r\theta + i \sin r\theta) + \tfrac{1}{2}(\cos r\theta - i \sin r\theta)$$
$$= \cos r\theta.$$

So the $(r + 1)$th term is $\cos r\theta$.

The following deductions may be made.

(i) $\cos r\theta$ can be expanded as follows.

$$u_0 = 1 \ ; \ \ u_1 = \cos \theta \ ; \ \ u_2 = 2u_1 \cos \theta - u_0 = 2 \cos^2 \theta - 1.$$
$$\therefore \ \cos 2\theta = 2 \cos^2 \theta - 1.$$

$$u_3 = 2u_2 \cos \theta - u_1 = 4 \cos^3 \theta - 2 \cos \theta - \cos \theta = 4 \cos^3 \theta - 3 \cos \theta.$$
$$\therefore \ \cos 3\theta = 4 \cos^3 \theta - 3 \cos \theta \text{ and so on.}$$

(ii) The scale of relation contains the function $\cos \theta$ only.

Since $u_0 = 1$ and $u_1 = \cos \theta$ it follows that u_2 can be expressed as a function of $\cos \theta$ only. Similarly for $\cos 3\theta$ and so on.

$$\therefore \ \cos n\theta \text{ may be expressed in terms of } \cos \theta \text{ only.}$$

(iii) The term containing the highest power of $\cos \theta$ in $\cos 3\theta$ is $4 \cos^3 \theta$ or $2^2 \cos^3 \theta$.

Let us assume that for some value of r, the term containing the highest power of $\cos \theta$ in $\cos (r-1)\theta$ is $2^{r-2} \cos^{r-1} \theta$ and the term containing the highest power of $\cos \theta$ in $\cos (r - 2)\theta$ is $2^{r-3} \cos^{r-2} \theta$.

Since $u_r = 2u_{r-1} \cos \theta - u_{r-2}$, the highest power of $\cos \theta$ in u_r is

$$2 \cos \theta(2^{r-2} \cos^{r-1} \theta) \quad \text{or} \quad 2^{r-1} \cos^r \theta.$$

Since the term containing the highest power follows this rule in the cases $r = 0$ and $r = 1$, it must be generally true.

It follows that $\cos r\theta$ can be expanded as a polynomial in $\cos \theta$ in which the highest power of $\cos \theta$ is $\cos^r \theta$ and the coefficient of this term is 2^{r-1}.

EXERCISES XL

1. Find the scale of relation of the second order determined by the sequence 2, 3, 8, 33.

2. Find the nth term of the sequence defined in question 1.

3. Find the sum of the first n terms of the sequence defined in question 1.

4. If $u_r - u_{r-1} - 6u_{r-2} = 0$ and $u_0 = 1$, $u_1 = 2$, find u_n.

5. If $u_r - 6u_{r-1} + 9u_{r-2} = 0$ and $u_0 = 2$, $u_1 = 3$, find u_n.

6. If $u_r = u_{r-1} - u_{r-2}$ and $u_0 = 1$, $u_1 = 7$, show that u_r can take any one of six possible values.

7. If $u_r - 2au_{r-1} + a^2u_{r-2} = 0$ and $u_0 = 1$, $u_1 = 2a$, find u_n.

8. If $ur - (a + b)u_{r-1} + abu_{r-2} = 0$ and $u_0 = 2$, $u_1 = a + b$, find u_n.

9. Find the nth term and the sum to n terms of the sequence 1, 6, 24, 84, . . ., assuming that it obeys a recurrence relation of the second order.

10. Find the nth term of the sequence 1, 7, 24, 68, . . ., assuming that it obeys a recurrence relation of the second order.

11. If $u_r - 2 \cos \theta \, u_{r-1} + u_{r-2} = 0$ and $u_0 = 0$, $u_1 = \sin \theta$, find u_n.

12. Using the result of question 11, show that $\dfrac{\sin n\theta}{\sin \theta}$ may always be expressed as a polynomial in $\cos \theta$.

ANSWERS

EXERCISES I (p. 4)

1. 7!.   **2.** 20.   **3.** 15.   **4.** 28.   **5.** 42.   **6.** 12.   **7.** 2520.
8. 59.   **9.** 63.   **10.** 729.

EXERCISES III (p. 9)

1. (a) $1 + 3x + 6x^2 + 10x^3$;   (b) $1 - 3x + \frac{15}{2}x^2 - \frac{35}{2}x^3$;
   (c) $1 + x - 2x^2 + 6x^3$;   (d) $1 - 2x - 2x^2 - 4x^3$.

2. $\dfrac{(2n-1)!}{[(n-1)!]^2}$.   **3.** (a) 6·0083, (b) 1·0291, (c) 0·9806, (d) 5·0053.

4. 4th and 5th.   **5.** 352.   **6.** -4.   **7.** $-{}_9C_3 . 3^6 . 4^3$.   **8.** 30.

9. 10.   **10.** ${}_{12}C_5 . (2x)^5 . (3y)^7$.

EXERCISES IV (p. 13)

1. $-\dfrac{1}{x-1} + \dfrac{2}{x-2}$.   **2.** $1 - \dfrac{1}{x-1} + \dfrac{4}{x-2}$.

3. $\dfrac{1}{2(x-1)} - \dfrac{4}{x-2} + \dfrac{9}{2(x-3)}$.   **4.** $-\dfrac{1}{2x} + \dfrac{3}{2(x-2)}$.

5. $\dfrac{1-x}{2(x^2+1)} + \dfrac{1}{2(x-1)}$.   **6.** $\dfrac{1}{4(x-1)} - \dfrac{1}{4(x+1)} + \dfrac{1}{2(x+1)^2}$.

7. $\dfrac{1}{x} - \dfrac{1}{x+1} - \dfrac{1}{(x+1)^2}$.   **8.** $x + \dfrac{1}{2(x-1)} + \dfrac{1}{2(x+1)}$.

EXERCISES V (p. 19)

1. $\dfrac{n(n+1)(n+5)}{3}$.   **2.** $\dfrac{n(n+1)(n+2)(3n+13)}{12}$.

3. $\dfrac{n(4n^2-1)}{3}$.   **4.** $n^2(2n^2-1)$.

5. $\dfrac{1}{4} - \dfrac{1}{2(n+1)} + \dfrac{1}{2(n+2)}$.

6. $\dfrac{x + x^2 - (2n+1)x^{n+1} + (2n-1)x^{n+2}}{(1-x)^2}$.

7. $\dfrac{n(n+1)(6n^3 + 9n^2 + n - 1)}{30}$.   **8.** $1 + (-1)^{n-1}\dfrac{1}{n+1}$.

EXERCISES VI (p. 23)

1. $1 \cdot 099$.

2. $e\left(1 + x + \dfrac{x^2}{2} + \dfrac{x^3}{6}\right)$.

3. $\frac{1}{2}$.

4. $-\frac{1}{8}$.

5. 1.

7. $-1 - \dfrac{1}{x}\log(1 - x)$.

8. $x + \frac{1}{2}x^2 + \frac{5}{6}x^3$.

9. If $n = 0$, $\log 2$ otherwise $-\dfrac{(-2)^{-n}}{n}$

EXERCISES VII (p. 25)

1. ± 2, -3.

2. -1, $\dfrac{-1 \pm \sqrt{5}}{2}$.

3. -1, ± 2.

4. -2, $\dfrac{-1 \pm \sqrt{13}}{2}$.

5. $-(a - b)(b - c)(c - a)$.

6. $-(a - b)(b - c)(c - a)(a^2 + b^2 + c^2 + ab + bc + ca)$.

EXERCISES VIII (p. 33)

1. $(ab - 1)^2 = 4(a - b^2)(b - a^2)$.

2. 6, -3.

3. $y^3 - 6y^2 + 9y - 1 = 0$.

4. $y^3 + 2y^2 + y - 1 = 0$.

5. 3.

6. 240.

7. $-2 \pm 2\sqrt{2}$.

8. $a > 1$.

9 $y^3 - 3y^2 + y(3 + a) + b - a - 1 = 0$.

10. $y^3 + ay - b = 0$.

REVISION PAPER I (p. 33)

1. 6188.

2. $1 + 8x + 28x^2 + 56x^3$; $0 \cdot 01600011$.

3. $n(n + 2)(2n^2 + 4n - 1)$.

4. $\dfrac{2}{x - 2} - \dfrac{1}{x - 1}$; $-\dfrac{3}{x - 1} - \dfrac{1}{(x - 1)^2} + \dfrac{4}{x - 2}$;

$$1 + \frac{3}{x - 1} + \frac{3}{(x - 1)^2} + \frac{1}{(x - 1)^3}$$

5. (a) $\pm \dfrac{\sqrt{29}}{2}$; $\pm \dfrac{\sqrt{59}}{3}$. (b) $a = -\frac{1}{2}$; $-2\frac{1}{2}$.

6. (i) and (ii) x must not lie between 1 and 3.
(iii) $x > 3$ or between 1 and 2.

8. $p = q = \frac{1}{2}$; $a = \frac{1}{48}$.

9. (ii) $y^3 - 2y^2 + 5y - 11 = 0$.

10. $y^2 + 3y + 1 = 0$.

REVISION PAPER II (p. 34)

1. 100; 32.   2. $_{4n}C_n$.

3. $\dfrac{n(n + 1)(2n + 1)}{6}$; $\dfrac{n^2}{2}(n + 1)$.

5. (i) 105, 20. (ii) $1 + \frac{1}{2}x + \frac{3}{8}x^2 + \frac{5}{16}x^3$; $1 \cdot 41421$.

6. $(a^2 + a + 1)$ or $(1 - a)$; $0, -1, \dfrac{-1 \pm \sqrt{5}}{2}$.

8. $x^7 + 2x^6 - 12x^5 - 24x^4 + 48x^3 + 96x^2 - 64x - 128$.

9. $\frac{1}{2}$ or $-\frac{2}{3}$.   10. $135, -329$.

EXERCISES IX (p. 41)

1. $\dfrac{1}{2\sqrt{1 + x}}$.   2. $\dfrac{\cos x}{2\sqrt{\sin x}}$.

3. $12(3x + 1)^3$.   4. $-\dfrac{6}{(2x + 1)^4}$.

5. $\dfrac{2x + 1}{2\sqrt{x^2 + x + 1}}$.   6. $\dfrac{1}{(x + 1)^2}$.

7. $2\cos 2x$.   8. $6\sin^2 2x \cos 2x$.

9. $-a\sin(ax + b)$.   10. $-2a\cos(ax + b)\sin(ax + b)$.

11. $\dfrac{1}{2\sqrt{(1 - x^2)\sin^{-1} x}}$.   12. $-\dfrac{1}{(1 + x^2)(\tan^{-1} x)^2}$.

13. $2axe^{ax^2}$.   14. $\dfrac{3x^2}{1 + x^3}$.

15. $-\cot x$.   16. $\cot x - x\operatorname{cosec}^2 x$.

17. $2x\tan^{-1} x + \dfrac{x^2}{1 + x^2}$.   18. $-\dfrac{1}{\sqrt{(x + 1)(x - 1)^3}}$.

19. $\dfrac{1}{x(x + 1)}$.   20. $a\sec(ax + b)\tan(ax + b)$.

21. $e^x\sin x + xe^x\sin x + xe^x\cos x$.   22. $-\operatorname{cosec}^2 xe^{-x} - \cot xe^{-x}$.

23. $6xe^{3x^2 + 4}$.   24. $(2x + 1)e^{x^2 + x + 1}$.

25. $\dfrac{\cos x + x \sin x}{\cos^2 x}$.

26. $\dfrac{xe^x - e^x}{x^2}$.

27. $\dfrac{x}{\sqrt{x^2 + 1}}$.

28. $\dfrac{2x^2 - 8x + 5}{(x - 2)^2}$.

29. $3(2ax + b)(ax^2 + bx + c)^2$.

30. $\cos x \, a^{\sin x} \log a$.

EXERCISES X (p. 43)

1. $x = 0$, minimum.

2. $x = 1$, inflexion ; $x = -\tfrac{1}{2}$, minimum.

3. $x = 0$, maximum ; $x = \pm 1$, minima.

4. $x = 2n\pi + \dfrac{\pi}{2}$, maxima ; $x = 2n\pi - \dfrac{\pi}{2}$, minima.

5. $x = 0$, inflexion ; $x = \tfrac{2}{3}$, minimum.

EXERCISES XI (p. 45)

1. 36.

2. $\sqrt{2}e^t$, $2e^t$.

3. $\sqrt{2 \sin^2 t + 2t \cos t \sin t + t^2 \cos^2 t}$,
$$\sqrt{5 \cos^2 t - 4t \cos t \sin t + t^2 \sin^2}$$

4. $2y = 3x + 1$.

5. $x + 4y = 5$.

6. $x + y \tan \dfrac{\theta}{2} = a\theta$.

7. $-\dfrac{2 + t^2}{t}$.

8. $y \cos t - x \sin t = a \cos 2t$.

9. $-2t$.

10. $\dfrac{x \cos \theta}{a} + \dfrac{y \sin \theta}{b} = 1$.

EXERCISES XII (p. 48)

1. $\dfrac{(-1)^n 2^n n!}{(2x - 3)^{n+1}}$.

2. $\dfrac{(-1)^n n!}{6} \left\{ \dfrac{1}{(x - 3)^{n+1}} - \dfrac{1}{(x + 3)^{n+1}} \right\}$.

3. $4^n \sin \left(4x + \dfrac{n\pi}{2} \right)$.

4. $-2^{n-1} \cos \left(2x + \dfrac{n\pi}{2} \right)$.

5. $2^{n/2} e^x \cos \left(x + \dfrac{n\pi}{4} \right)$.

6. $y_{n+2} + xy_{n+1} + ny_n$.

7. $(1 - x^2)y_{n+2} - xy_{n+1}(2n + 1) - (n^2 - 1)y_n$.

8. $xe^x + ne^x$.

9. $x^2 \sin\left(x + \dfrac{n\pi}{2}\right) + 2nx \sin\left(x + \dfrac{\overline{n-1}\pi}{2}\right)$

$$+ n(n-1)\sin\left(x + \dfrac{\overline{n-2}\pi}{2}\right).$$

10. $x^2 2^n \cos\left(2x + \dfrac{n\pi}{2}\right) + nx2^n \cos\left(2x + \dfrac{\overline{n-1}\pi}{2}\right)$

$$+ n(n-1)2^{n-2}\cos\left(2x + \dfrac{\overline{n-2}\pi}{2}\right)$$

EXERCISES XIII (p. 51)

1. $x + \dfrac{x^3}{3}$.

2. $1 + x \log a + \dfrac{x^2(\log a)^2}{2!} + \dfrac{x^3(\log a)^3}{3!}$.

3. $x - \dfrac{x^3}{3}$.

4. $1 + x - \dfrac{x^3}{3}$. **5.** $x - \dfrac{x^2}{2} + \dfrac{x^3}{6}$.

EXERCISES XIV (p. 61)

1. $\cos(3 - x)$.

2. $\frac{1}{2}\log \sec 2x$.

3. $2 \log \sin \frac{1}{2}x$.

4. $-e^{1-x}$.

5. $\dfrac{1}{a}\log(ax + b)$.

6. $\frac{2}{3}(x^2 + 3x + 2)^{\frac{3}{2}}$.

7. $-\dfrac{1}{1 + \sin x}$.

8. $-\frac{1}{3}(a^2 - x^2)^{\frac{3}{2}}$.

9. $\dfrac{\cos^3 x}{3} - \cos x$.

10. $\frac{3}{8}x + \frac{1}{4}\sin 2x + \frac{1}{32}\sin 4x$.

11. $\dfrac{\sin^3 x}{3} - \dfrac{\sin^5 x}{5}$.

12. $\sin^{-1}\dfrac{x}{4}$.

13. $\frac{1}{4}\tan^{-1}\dfrac{x}{4}$.

14. $\frac{1}{3}\log(3x + \sqrt{16 + 9x^2})$.

15. $\tan^{-1}(x + 2)$.

16. $\log(x + 2 + \sqrt{x^2 + 4x + 5})$.

17. $\frac{1}{2}\log(x^2 + 4x + 5) - 2\tan^{-1}(x + 2)$.

18. $\sqrt{x^2 + 4x + 5} - 2\log(x + 2 + \sqrt{x^2 + 4x + 5})$.

19. $\sin^{-1}(x - 1)$.

20. $\log(x + 1 + \sqrt{x^2 + 2x})$.

21. $\dfrac{x^2}{2} + x + \log(x - 1)$.

22. $\log(x - 2)(x - 3)$.

23. $x^2 \sin x + 2x \cos x - 2 \sin x$. **24.** $\dfrac{x^3}{3} \tan^{-1} x - \dfrac{1}{2}x + \dfrac{1}{2} \tan^{-1} x$.

25. $\dfrac{x^2}{2}(\log x)^2 - \dfrac{x^2}{2} \log x + \dfrac{x^2}{4}$.

26. $-x^3 e^{-x} - 3x^2 e^{-x} - 6x e^{-x} - 6e^{-x}$.

27. $\dfrac{1}{\sqrt{2}} \log \left\{ \operatorname{cosec} \left(x + \dfrac{\pi}{4} \right) - \cot \left(x + \dfrac{\pi}{4} \right) \right\}$.

28. $\frac{1}{2} \tan^{-1} \left(\frac{1}{2} \tan \dfrac{x}{2} \right)$. **29.** $\dfrac{2}{\sqrt{5}} \tan^{-1} \left(\dfrac{3 \tan \frac{1}{2}x + 2}{\sqrt{5}} \right)$.

30. $\frac{1}{2} \tan^2 x - \log \sec x$.

EXERCISES XV (p. 63)

1. (a) $\frac{8}{3}$, (b) $\frac{16}{3}$, (c) 1, (d) 1, (e) $\log \frac{1}{2}$. **2.** $\frac{1}{8}$.

3. 2. **4.** $2\frac{2}{3}$. **5.** $\frac{4}{5}$. **6.** $\frac{1}{2}\pi^2$.

7. $2\pi^2$. **8.** 6π. **9.** $(1\frac{1}{2}, -\frac{1}{10})$. **10.** $(1\frac{4}{5}, 0)$.

EXERCISES XVI (p. 65)

1. $\dfrac{\pi a}{6}$. **2.** $\frac{26}{27}$. **3.** $\frac{1}{4}\pi a^2$. **4.** $\frac{1}{2}a^2$. **5.** $\dfrac{8\pi}{3}(2\sqrt{2} - 1)$.

EXERCISES XVII (p. 67)

1. $\dfrac{4Ma^2}{3}$. **2.** $\dfrac{5Ma^2}{4}$. **3.** $\frac{7}{5}Ma^2$. **4.** $\dfrac{4Ma^2}{3}$.

5. $\frac{3}{10}Ma^2$. **6.** $\frac{8}{5}M$. **7.** $\dfrac{8M}{3}$.

EXERCISES XVIII (p. 70)

1. $\frac{2}{3}$. **2.** $\dfrac{3\pi}{16}$. **3.** $\dfrac{\pi}{16}$. **4.** 0. **5.** $\dfrac{3\pi}{8}$.

6. $\dfrac{\pi}{8}$. **7.** $\dfrac{15\pi}{32}$. **8.** $\dfrac{3\pi}{4}$. **9.** $\frac{2}{3}$. **10.** $\dfrac{\pi}{2}$.

EXERCISES XIX (p. 71)

1. $2 \sinh 2x$, $2 \sinh x \cosh x$, $\dfrac{\sinh x}{2\sqrt{\cosh x}}$, $-\operatorname{cosech} x \coth x$, $\operatorname{sech}^2 x$.

2. $\cosh^{-1} \dfrac{x}{2}$, $\sinh^{-1} \dfrac{x}{2}$, $\frac{1}{2}\cosh^{-1} \dfrac{2x}{3}$, $\frac{1}{2}\sinh^{-1} \dfrac{2x}{3}$, $\sinh^{-1}(x + 1)$.

EXERCISES XX (p. 73)

1. $y = A(x + 1)$.

2. $y = Ae^{kx}$.

3. $xy = \dfrac{x^2}{2} + C$.

4. $y \sin x = C - \cos x$.

5. $ye^{x^2/2} = x + C$.

6. $y = Ae^x + Be^{4x}$.

7. $y = (A + Bx)e^x$.

8. $y = A e^x + B e^{-x} + C \cos x + D \sin x$.

9. $y = e^x(A \cos x + B \sin x)$. 10. $y = A + B e^x + C e^{-x}$.

REVISION PAPER III (p. 74)

1. (a) $3 \sin\left(\dfrac{\pi}{6} - 3x\right)$, $\dfrac{3x - 4}{x^2 - 2x}$.

2. $(+ 1, \tfrac{1}{2})$ max. ; $(- 1, - \tfrac{1}{2})$ min. ; $(0, 0)$, $\left(\pm \sqrt{3}, \pm \dfrac{\sqrt{3}}{4}\right)$ points of inflexion.

3. $ty - x = t^3$.

4. $xy_{n+2} + (n + 1 - 2x)y_{n+1} + (x - 1 - 2n)y_n + ny_{n-1} = 0$.

5. $\dfrac{x^2}{2} + 2x + \log x$, $\dfrac{1}{\sqrt{3}} \tan^{-1} \dfrac{x + 2}{\sqrt{3}}$, $3 \log 2 - 1$.

6. $2\left(1 - \dfrac{\pi}{4}\right)$.

7. $0, - 3$. $\quad y = 1 + x + \tfrac{1}{2}x^2 - \tfrac{1}{8}x^4$.

8. (i) $\dfrac{x^3}{3} - x^2 + \dfrac{4}{3}$; $\dfrac{4}{3}$; 0. (ii) $\tfrac{1}{16}$, $\tfrac{5}{24}$.

10. $\dfrac{3\pi a^2}{2}$; $(\tfrac{5}{6}a, 0)$.

REVISION PAPER IV (p. 75)

1. $18x^2 \log (x + 1)$, $9x^2 \sin^{-1} x$.

2. (i) $- e^{-x}(\cos 2x + 2 \sin 2x)$, $- \dfrac{1}{2x \sqrt{x - 1}}$.

(ii) $\dfrac{1}{2x - 3} + \dfrac{1}{2x + 3}$, $(- 2)^n n!\left\{\dfrac{1}{(2x - 3)^{n-1}} + \dfrac{1}{(2x + 3)^{n-1}}\right\}$.

4. $\left(\dfrac{at^2}{4}, - \dfrac{at^3}{8}\right)$.

5. (i) $(2, 12)$; $(-1, -6)$; (ii) $\dfrac{3\sqrt{3}}{2}$.

6. (ii) $x(\log x - 1)$; $\dfrac{e^x(\sin 2x - 2\cos 2x)}{5}$; (iii) $\frac{2}{15}$.

7. $\sqrt{2}e^{\frac{\pi}{4}}$, $2e^{\frac{\pi}{4}}$.   8. $\pi(6\pi + 9\sqrt{3})$.

9. (a) $\pi - 2$.   10. α, 0, $\cot \alpha$; $45 \cdot 028°$.

EXERCISES XXI (p. 80)

1. $3y + x = 10$.   2. $y = 2x - 3$.

3. $\dfrac{x}{2} + \dfrac{y}{3} = 1$.   4. $x\sqrt{3} + y = 6$.

5. $y = x - 3$.   6. $y + x = 2$.

7. $3x + 4y = 11$.   8. $5x + 2y = 9$.

9. $2x - y = 7$.   10. $2x - y = 9$.

11. $lx + my = lx' + my'$.   12. $my + x = my' + x'$.

13. 5.   14. 1.

15. $(\frac{9}{5}, \frac{8}{5})$.   16. $(-16, 7)$.

17. $\tan^{-1} 3$.   18. $\tan^{-1} 2$.

19. $\dfrac{4}{\sqrt{13}}$.   20. 1.

EXERCISES XXII (p. 84)

1. $\frac{8}{5}$.   2. $\frac{23}{13}$.

3. $\dfrac{m + c}{\sqrt{1 + m^2}}$.   4. $\dfrac{bx' + ay' - ab}{\sqrt{a^2 + b^2}}$.

5. No.   6. $7x - 4y = 13$; $16x + 28y = 39$.

7. $7x = 8y$.   8. $(1, 1)$.

9. $(2, 3)$.   10. $x^2 + y^2 = l^2$.

EXERCISES XXIII (p. 87)

1. $\tan^{-1} \frac{5}{2}$.   2. $x^2 + 5xy - y^2 = 0$.

3. $10x^2 - 4xy - 5y^2 = 0$.   4. $\tan^{-1} \frac{4}{3}$.

5. $-\frac{15}{4}$.   6. $\dfrac{2\sqrt{2(h^2 - ab)}}{a + b - 2h}$.

7. $\left\{ \dfrac{2}{3} \cdot \dfrac{b - h}{a + b - 2h}, \ \dfrac{2}{3} \cdot \dfrac{a - h}{a + b - 2h} \right\}$.   8. $\left\{ \dfrac{a + b}{a + b - 2h}, \ \dfrac{a + b}{a + b - 2h} \right\}$.

EXERCISES XXIV (p. 91)

1. Centre $(2, -1)$; radius 3. **2.** $y + 6 = 0$.

3. $x + 3y + 1 = 0$. **4.** $x^2 + y^2 = 1$.

5. 1. **6.** $x + 3y = 0$.

7. $4x^2 + 4y^2 - 3x - 9y + 4 = 0$. **8.** $x^2 + y^2 - 3x - y = 0$.

9. $x^2 + y^2 - 4x - 2y + 4 = 0$; $x^2 + y^2 - 2x - y + 1 = 0$.

10. $3x^2 + 3y^2 - 10x - 30y + 3 = 0$.

EXERCISES XXV (p. 96)

1. $x + y = 9$; $(27, -18)$. **3.** $y^2 = 2a(x - a)$.

4. $y^2 = a(x - 3a)$. **5.** $y = 2x$.

6. $(-\frac{1}{2}, -3)$. **7.** $x = -2a$.

8. $m^2 = 2alm^2 + al^3$. **9.** $am^2 = ln$; $\left(\dfrac{n}{l}, -\dfrac{2am}{l}\right)$.

10. $(3, -2)$.

EXERCISES XXVI (p. 103)

1. $(\pm \sqrt{5}, 0)$; $\sqrt{5}/3$. **2.** $(9, 16)$.

3. $a^2l^2 + b^2m^2 = 1$. **4.** $x + 2y = 3$.

5. $25x + 8y = 41$. **6.** $a^2\beta(y - \beta) = b^2\alpha(x - \alpha)$.

7. $3x^2 - 2y^2 = 3x - 4y$. **8.** $a^2p + b^2r = 0$.

10. $4x^2 - 4y^2 = 1$.

EXERCISES XXVII (p. 109)

4. $(-c^2, 3c^2)$. **5.** $x + y = 2$.

6. $x^2 - y^2 - 2x + 2 = 0$. **7.** $y = -1$.

8. $x(k - y) + y(h - x) = 0$. **9.** $c^2(l^2 - m^2)^2 + lm = 0$.

REVISION PAPER V (p. 110)

1. (a) $(-6, -2)$; (b) 40 and 30.

2. $(\frac{5}{3}, 0)$; $\frac{4}{3}$; $3y + 4x = 0$.

4. 3; $(1, 4)$; $\sqrt{0\cdot37}$.

6. $x^2 + y^2 - 5x - y = 0$; $(14 \pm 6\sqrt{5})(x^2 + y^2) - (2x + 2y)(3 \pm \sqrt{5}) + 1 = 0$.

10. $\dfrac{x}{t} + yt = 2c$.

REVISION PAPER VI (p. 112)

1. $(3, 2)$, $(-5, -4)$; $x + 7y = 17$, $x + 7y = -33$, $7x - y = 19$, $7x - y = -31$.

2. $y - x + 1 = 0$, $3y - x + 1 = 0$; $(1, 0)$; 5.

3. $c = \dfrac{a^2}{2a - b}$.

4. $\dfrac{a^2}{b^2}(a^2 \sin^2 \theta + b^2 \cos^2 \theta)$, $\dfrac{a^2 e^2}{b^2}(a^2 \sin^2 \theta + b^2 \cos^2 \theta)$.

6. $2y^2 - 3xy + 9x - 2y - 12 = 0$.

8. $\dfrac{x}{t} + yt = 2c$; $xt - \dfrac{y}{t} = c\left(t^2 - \dfrac{1}{t^2}\right)$.

9. $(x - x_1)(x - x_2) + (y - y_1)(y - y_2) = 0$; $(x - h)^2 = 4ky$.

10. $x + pq\,y = c(p + q)$.

EXERCISES XXVIII (p. 127)

3. 6 cm.

EXERCISES XXIX (p. 136)

4. $\sqrt{\tfrac{3}{2}}a$.　　**5.** $\dfrac{1}{2d}\sqrt{(R + r + d)(R + r - d)(R + d - r)(d + r - R)}$.

6. $\sqrt{2}a$.　　**8.** $\dfrac{Rr}{\sqrt{R^2 + r^2}}$.

EXERCISES XXX (p. 143)

3. $2ab$.

REVISION PAPER VII (p. 143)

2. $\dfrac{a}{\sqrt{2}}$.

EXERCISES XXXI (p. 150)

6. $-\cot \theta$.　　**7.** $\operatorname{cosec} 3\theta$.　　**8.** $-\operatorname{cosec} 4\theta$.

9. $-\cos \theta$.　　**10.** $-\cos 2\theta$.

EXERCISES XXXII (p. 155)

1. $2 \sin 50° \cos 10°$.

2. $2 \sin 35° \sin 15°$.

3. $2 \cos 50° \cos 20°$.

4. $2 \cos 50° \sin 10°$.

5. $2 \sin 4A \cos 2A$.

6. $2 \sin 3A \sin A$.

7. $\cos 20° - \cos 40°$.

8. $\cos 70° + \cos 30°$.

9. $\sin 50° - \sin 10°$.

10. $\sin 40° + \sin 20°$.

11. $\cos 2A - \cos 8A$.

12. $\sin 6A + \sin 2A$.

17. $- 4 \cos A \cos B \cos C$.

18. $4 \sin A \sin B \sin C$.

19. $- 4 \sin A \cos B \cos C$.

20. $4 \cos 2A \cos 2B \cos 2C$.

EXERCISES XXXIII (p. 160)

1. $45°, 225°, 63° 26', 243° 26'$.

2. $103° 20', 330° 30'$.

3. $53° 8', 233° 8'$.

4. $114° 18', 335° 42'$.

5. $18°, 90°, 162°, 234°, 270°, 306°$.

6. $(2n + 1)\pi$; $\frac{2}{3}n\pi + (- 1)^n \frac{\pi}{9}$.

7. $\frac{n\pi}{2}$; $2n\pi \pm \frac{2\pi}{3}$.

8. $\frac{(4n + 1)\pi}{12}$, $\frac{(4n - 1)\pi}{8}$.

9. $n\pi$, $\frac{(2n + 1)\pi}{4}$.

10. $\frac{n\pi}{2} + \frac{\pi}{6}$.

EXERCISES XXXIV (p. 162)

1. $81° 4', 53° 20', 45° 36'$.

2. $A = 85° 55', B = 54° 5', c = 6·51$.

3. $b = 8·23, c = 9·31$.

4. $27·1$; $26·6$; $36·0$.

5. $\frac{\sqrt{1 - x^2}}{x}$.

6. $\frac{1}{2x}$.

7. $\frac{2x \sqrt{1 - x^2}}{1 - 2x^2}$.

8. x.

9. $\sqrt{5}$.

10. $\frac{1}{\sqrt{3}}$.

EXERCISES XXXV (p. 169)

4. $\frac{1}{2}R$.

5. $2R \cos A \cos B \cos C$.

12. $2R$.

13. $2R$.

16. $\frac{1}{2}R^2 \sin 2A \sin 2B \sin 2C$.

17. R.

18. $8R^2 \cos \frac{A}{2} \cos \frac{B}{2} \cos \frac{C}{2}$.

REVISION PAPER VIII (p. 169)

1. (i) $\sqrt{7}$ km; (ii) 1529 m, 732 m; (iii) 16° 46′.

2. (i) $\dfrac{1 + \sqrt{5}}{4}$. **3.** $\frac{1}{239}$.

4. $\sqrt{75}$, 2·46. **5.** $\cos^{-1} \frac{7}{18}$.

6. (i) 149° 12′, 329° 12′. **7.** (ii) $\sqrt{13}$.

9. 53° 8′, 292° 36′; $65x^2 + 8x - 48 = 0$.

10. 0·13, 0·77, $-7\cdot60$, $-1\cdot30$.

REVISION PAPER IX (p. 171)

2. (i) 15°, 105°, $-75°$, $-165°$; $\pm 140°$, $\pm 100°$, $\pm 90°$, $\pm 20°$.

3. 78° 54′, 6·36 cm. **5.** (a) $\dfrac{2n\pi}{5}$; (b) 6·1 m. **8.** 5·05.

EXERCISES XXXVI (p. 175)

1. $3 \pm i$. **2.** $(x + 3)(x^2 - 3x + 9)$; $-3, \frac{1}{2}(3 \pm 3\sqrt{3}i)$.

3. (i) $-1 + 3i$; (ii) $7 - i$; (iii) $8 + 6i$;

(iv) $\dfrac{3}{5} - \dfrac{4}{5}i$; (v) $-1 + 2i$.

4. 13; $-\dfrac{5}{13} + \dfrac{12}{13}i$. **5.** 1. **6.** $\dfrac{1}{13}$.

7. 1; 1. **8.** $2 \cos \theta$. **9.** 1, $\dfrac{1}{2}(-1 \pm \sqrt{3}i)$.

EXERCISES XXXVII (p. 179)

2. (i) $2\frac{1}{2}$; (ii) 13; (iii) 17.

3. (i) $-45°$; (ii) $-150°$; (iii) $-123°$ 41′.

4. $\dfrac{5}{13}$. **5.** 15°. **7.** 3; $\dfrac{\pi}{6}$. **8.** $-\dfrac{3\pi}{4}$. **9.** $\dfrac{\pi}{2}$.

EXERCISES XXXVIII (p. 181)

1. 5. **2.** 45°.

3. $\cos^4 \theta - 6 \cos^2 \theta \sin^2 \theta + \sin^4 \theta$; $4 \cos^3 \theta \sin \theta - 4 \cos \theta \sin^3 \theta$.

4. i. **5.** -1. **6.** i. **7.** $\cos \theta + i \sin \theta$.

8. $\cos \theta + i \sin \theta$. **9.** 1. **10.** 15.

EXERCISES XXXIX (p. 182)

2. Perpendicular bisector of $(1, 0)$ to $(-1, 0)$.   **4.** Circle.

5. Circle centre $(0, -\frac{5}{3})$, radius $\frac{4}{3}$.   **6.** $32°\ 12'$, $73°\ 54'$, $73°\ 54'$.

7. $(1, 2)$; 3.

EXERCISES XL (p. 187)

1. $u_r - 6u_{r-1} + 5u_{r-2} = 0$.   **2.** $\frac{1}{4}(7 + 5^{n-1})$.

3. $\frac{1}{16}(5^n + 28n - 1)$.   **4.** $\frac{1}{5}\{4.3^n + (-2)^n\}$.

5. $(2 - n)3^n$.   **7.** $(n + 1)a^n$.

8. $a^n + b^n$.

9. $4.3^{n-1} - 3.2^{n-1}$; $2.3^n - 3.2^n + 1$.

10. $(5n - 3)2^{n-2}$.   **11.** $\sin n\theta$.